DEPORTED TO PARADISE

EDGAR NKOSI WHITE

DEPORTED TO PARADISE

SELECTED ESSAYS

PEEPAL TREE

First published in Great Britain in 2015
Peepal Tree Press Ltd
17 King's Avenue
Leeds LS6 1QS
England

ISBN13: 97818452322863

Supported using public funding by
ARTS COUNCIL
ENGLAND

CONTENTS

ACKNOWLEDGEMENTS

For Misani, who taught me woman. For Sylvia ("Little Cusha") who found me, washed up by the sea and ran. For Allison(the lioness and wounded healer) who taught me England and believed. For Martha Corprew who always took me in from the rain and chanted over me. (I've known many Marys but only one Martha).For Marina, who busted my heart, thank you. For Peggy who taught me how the White world works. For Suzanne who taught me Israeli Intelligence.

For Nuria Casado I Gual, who was there first, bless you! For Mary by the wall, who photographed me so that I could see. For Dana ("The Madrina") who was always there. For Helen Marie who kept the records.

For Noelle who loved first. For Rosemary who gave me my daughter Nicole. For Dindga who gave me my son Markhus. For my son Markhus who gave me my Grandson Kairo. For Nicole who gave me my granddaughter London-Rose. For Phyllis, my mother when I needed one. And Rita my sister always.

For "Port" and Murphy and Fred White, my spiritual fathers. For Vernon White, an honest man in Montserrat and therefore unique.

For Wali Obara, who taught me family and cries like me. For Sanga of the Valley, who gave me the drum and saved me. For Mama Randolph who took me in and taught me the wisdom of the deep South.

For Dunbar who took the time to care. For Evan who never failed me. For Anthony who went from student to friend. For Basil (Chinaman) Wallace and Lou Furguson the first West-Indians. For the jazz musician Don Small, who believed and remembered me even in death. For those who crossed over: Neville (Bill) Warner, Jackie Fire and Big George Daley (who taught me my father, "Toomer" Dyer). For Basil Chambers and Howard Fergus who made me legit. For John Allen "the Man from Baker Hill" who taught me taxes.

For the women of Montserrat who kept me alive when they didn't have to, (I've travelled the world but only married Montserrat women). And for Montserrat herself who vomited me out into the world and welcomed me back, we the deportees who returned either by will or force.

Live drawing by your friend, Roddy

PROLOGUE

OF ISLANDS AND THEIR SONS

My time is sunrise, dawns and mornings, clean before the wickedness comes in. When I see the Montserrat sunrise, I think of a woman revealing herself – an eye here, a nipple there, then suddenly a mountain. But then, I'm a son of the island so what else would I see?

The late Montserrat poet, Archie (or E. A. Markham, as he liked to be called when feeling famous), used to say to me after the wine and the North London night held him (Pauline Melville was there, and Allison): "You know, my friend, you have a very romantic view of the Caribbean. I hope it doesn't hurt your writing."

Now I can understand what he meant. The eye, that kind organ, has to do with illusion and the entire Caribbean is built on illusion. The illusion for us began the day we landed as slaves after surviving the Middle Passage, when we said to ourselves: *Well maybe there is a God after all, as they say (the ones who took us). Because this land and weather resembles where we've just come from, maybe it won't be so bad after all. Maybe if we just close our eyes we'll wake up back home.* (It turns out that the strange island Olaudah Equiano was talking about in his slave narrative was none other than Montserrat.)

So we kept ourselves in trance with illusion. The rum and sex helped. All the combinations and mixing of genes – like, what happens if you mix African with Chinese? You get Trinidad and Jamaica and Naomi Campbell. The eyes say sunset, but the mind – the mind's not as kind as the eye. So the mind asks the question: how did we get here? The simple answer is that nobody came to the Caribbean for fun. Not even white people who came to rule or make money, and only later for tourist pleasures. We all mostly came to labour.

For instance, there were the Irish, who somehow were never quite white enough. They came to Montserrat, not in leisure but in flight. They came fleeing the madness and zeal for murder which was Oliver Cromwell. The Lord Protector was offering them either the blessing of manacles and the cat-of-nine-tails, or something called being "drawn and quartered" which, as Dr. Johnson said about hanging, "concentrates the mind", and the peculiar habit they had of firing you from a canon if you refused to renounce your faith. (Some of those who did were rewarded well, like the

Guinness family, who were allowed to open a brewery and become wealthy by giving Ireland much good drink with which to kill herself and forget). Everything that was later done to slaves was tried and perfected on the Irish. Cromwell spoke to God and God said, "Break the Irish", and so he did. The wonder is that he never drowned in the rivers of blood he caused; it seems that Cromwell, a God-driven man, could only cleanse himself in the blood of others.

I'd like to say that the Irish, because they experienced cruelty at the hands of the British, were more humane in their colonization, but that's not the way life goes. Just as in America where the Irish became *white* instead of the *despised Irish* by becoming the police, in Montserrat they became, if not Pharaoh, then Pharaoh's army.

Now you would have thought that the Irish, having suffered under the sword of God's appointed, might be a bit more lenient when their turn came to play slave-owner, but such was not the case. They became as barbaric as the British, and at times pushed their slaves even harder because they had no intention of staying in the Caribbean. If you were caught stealing, they nailed your ears to a board. They just wanted to return rich enough to be counted among the landed gentry and, maybe – just maybe – rich enough to be left alone by the British and, if that meant becoming Protestant, fair enough. You could be Protestant by day and Catholic by night. Or as Jews did during the Inquisition, try to blend in. To understand Montserrat history you have to understand Irish history and all the psychic wounds that they passed on to us like a wedding gift at Emancipation.

The Irish also found Black women much to their liking (as we would later find theirs in Liverpool) and gave us such names as Donovan, Fergus, Daley, endless Ryans, Weekes and O'Garros, Lynches and Skerrets, not to mention Dyers and Samuels. So how can you carry the name and not the madness? You find Celtic crosses all over the island, and even our flag has the Irish harp.

So the Irish always leave something behind, be it Sea Island cotton or just a tip for the hangman. Most important, they left behind their Irish love of chat and culture, fun and music. What they didn't realize was that they were taking our Africanness away with them and, as a result, Ireland would never be quite the same. Put it this way: they gave us goats but we gave them goat water (a delicacy). And when the Irish went home to the Emerald Isle (their glorious bog), they also took with them black servants. Nothing was more prestigious for the landed gentry than the presence of a black servant in the household. It was what allowed you to count yourself among the elite. If you look at newspaper articles in the 1770s, you will find in the *Dublin Courier*, for example, the common lament that Irish servants could no longer get jobs in the best houses, because of the use of Caribbean black servants.

There's also quite common mentions of runaway servant-slaves in the Irish newspapers of the time. For example, in the *Belfast Newsletter* of 1776 there is a mention of an escaped slave named John Moore who is described merely as "straight and well-made". A reward of three guineas was offered. You had to be a good strong Montserratian to be worth that.

To reach Montserrat you must first endure Antigua, the larger island. Antigua went mad when it became a US Air Force base. (May the Force never be with you!) As a result, it became all things American, complete with tourism and Kentucky Fried and all the blessings of Disney culture. The island possesses 365 beaches, one for every day of the year, and a thorough casino culture. The relationship of Antigua to Montserrat is one of jailor to prisoner or perhaps jailor to child.

Antiguans regard Montserratians as peculiar children who never quite grew up to become hardened criminals like them. Montserrat, for example, has no real prison. The HMP (Her Majesty's Prison) on the island is a kind of joke stockade that releases its prisoners at Christmas time (especially if the prisoner is known to be a good masquerade jumbie dancer). Antigua, therefore, is where they send the real outlaws because they have a serious prison and still have fond memories of the cat-of-nine-tails. Flogging is a British art form which is part of their history. Montserratians are known as Skerrit people and Antiguans as Garrett people, because of the architecture of their houses. It also has to do with penal institutions (a borstal or skerrit is a home for juvenile offenders). This is how Montserrat is known while Antigua is known as Garrett, which is really from the word garrotte, meaning to choke to death. One famous Governor General was indeed once garrotted by irate slaves there. (Good to know Antigua is famous for something.)

Actually, Antigua produces excellent cricket players (Sir Vivian Richards and Sir Andy Roberts, *et al*) and good cricket. The landscape is flat and boring, like the people themselves, whereas, Montserrat is steep with mountains green and endless as life itself. Sometimes people from Antigua and people from Montserrat marry and create interesting children, but mostly they co-exist.

No, you can never see history. It's too broad and doesn't wear a uniform. At best all you can see is your family and so you use them as history. First you start with yourself. As a child, I believed I was chosen. How could I not be when there was always the house I was born in and the garden that was the largest in Montserrat, my grandmother's garden at Cork Hill, and the soft barefoot tread of servant girls from country always just two steps behind, waiting to pick up after me like gleaners. Yes, there was always someone bending and gleaning. This was called privilege. What I learnt of the world there in Cork Hill, so close to the town of Plymouth, was the difference between a front and back door and who should enter by which. I knew what a closed gate was for: to keep out the people from the North who were poor and inbred, which made them not to be dealt with except at Christmas when everyone was acceptable for masquerade and fête.

I knew that the house was mine – and the garden and the car in the driveway that no one knew how to drive. I was young, young like the servant girls with names like Annie and Sis, who I made so free with. They, too, would be mine when I got old enough to maintain an erection. Until then I would wait and touch and suck on their nipples when they'd let me. They'd say: "Not big enough yet. I'll tell you when it's big enough to do something with," and give it a kindly squeeze of encouragement so as not to shatter my heart forever. Yes, these were servant girls who came from country to town on foot as generations of Irish servant girls had done before them.

Everything I wore was from America, that strange place across the waters where the letters with stamps came from, with money orders and remittances. I could see from the jetty, where the ships came in carrying people with their leather trunks and cars and an occasional white face, that it must have been far. I was named Charles because the Prince was, and at times I confused myself with him. So I lived an illusion, and in the dream that was dreaming me, I was lord of the manor, the young man of great expectations. And if I was confused, my mother was even more so, because she was of the generation before: a different dress for every day of the year and a piano waiting silently in the parlour. She was told who she could speak with and where, and at what hour. There were people from dark parts of the island who were not to be dealt with at all. Places like Kinsale that had a certain reputation for violence and low life. So, of course, who else would she fall in love with but the Kinsale boy who was my father?

Now my father wasn't any good at Shakespeare or writing much past his name, but he could read cards from another table and women from another street. And he was very good at slipping past guardians and bribing servant girls to carry messages.

In Montserrat the art of the passed message is historic and has been responsible for everything from love triangles to betrayed uprisings. Nothing gives a Montserratian more pleasure than being a courier either of disaster or a tryst.

"She say to tell you she can't come today; tomorrow under the cotton tree." Or, "He say he have a lash waiting for you backside and it soon come."

In Montserrat all wounds are fresh and time has no meaning and nothing is sweeter than vengeance. This, too, is a gift of the Irish. One day I saw two men in a nursing home, one on wheels, for he had no legs and the other on foot. The one on foot stops the other and says:

"Aren't you Tyler? We went to school together."

"Yes, I'm Tyler," says the legless one in the cart, looking up longingly at the cigarette in the other's mouth.

"Good, me never did like you." With that he turns the cart over and walks joyously away.

In Montserrat all wounds are fresh.

In Montserrat you never meet all your family. I never met my father until late. You always have a special relationship with the person who introduces you to your father. It's for that reason that Howard Fergus, the Montserrat poet and educator, holds a special place in my life. It was he who one day said:

"If you walk to that bridge at exactly one o clock and wait at that spot, a certain man will come and stop there. That will be your father. You'll know him by his cane."

And so I watched and waited and he came.

Only in Montserrat can that happen with such casualness, be it kindness or cruelty. All my life I'd been looking for my father either beneath the volcano in Montserrat, or else finding him and losing him again and again in my uncles in New York, tailors who bent like Jews over their sewing machines, cheating one more year of use from a trouser. The New York uncles smelled of rum and their wives of Limacol. The men would live for Friday nights when they could watch boxing on television (never having the money to actually go to Madison Square Garden).

I would seek my father in all the bent-back, brooding men in London, old Antiguans who worked for London Transport and cooked and sold black pudding and souse and rum on weekends and sometimes sold their fourteen-year-old daughters in upper rooms in Hackney or Stoke Newington as well. I would search for him among them.

My mother fled the island early. She fled from that place where the main preoccupation was taking other people's business and making it your own. She went to that place from which the envelopes came, America, and what a shock she had when she found where the money came from, the money that bought the house in Montserrat and the car that no one could drive and the servant girls who bent and waited. All came from being a servant in New York.

When they at last sent for me to come, I too would find that out: the nice aunts who worked twenty-hour days as domestics with every other Thursday off. On my first day at school in the South Bronx, to which I'd come with my white, starched shirt and my innocent black episcopalian face and my good behaviour and my expectations from Teacher Biddy's class, I made another discovery. This wasn't Teacher Biddy's. Fists greeted me and feet kicked me on my first day. And as I mention elsewhere, when the girls went to recess they took a girl in the bathroom and stuck her head in the toilet and kept flushing until she drowned; then they smoked cigarettes and left. When they found her, the police shut the school. When I told the nice tanti about this, she didn't believe me because nice tanti lived in kitchens and only knew the lives of white people's children, and evidently did not know the America I was discovering. She didn't want to hear what I had to tell her.

If the Caribbean was built on illusion, America is the dream factory. Here is where the dreams begin. In the Caribbean, small islands dream of becoming bigger ones. They dream of having huge twelve-storey ships in their harbours like Antigua and St. Martin, and tourists who can't remember if they stopped here before, because from a ship all islands look alike. Small islands, small corruption; big ones, big corruptions, bigger slave markets.

So what better way to enter the big people world than through drugs? Indeed, ten years ago, Montserrat was all set to court the big time and go corrupt. She was no longer quite a virgin because she had been fondled already, when the Beatles had built their Air Studios for recording here, and although Kentucky Fried was not quite on the island, it was close by in Antigua, twenty minutes away. There were noises being made about restoring offshore banking following the 1989 banking scandals. For where you have banks, money is sure to follow. Why not make use of the quiet runway to land drugs and become somebody? Then we, too, could have a Montego Bay like Jamaica, and a Baxter Road like Barbados, where former doctors and lawyers wander the roads having lost everything to addiction.

Unfortunately, just when the operation was about to begin, the Soufrière volcano (never quite asleep) decided to erupt and, to quote Archie Markham, "vomit up corruption". Of course, all the wizards were sure it would soon go back to sleep. Four years later, they were not so certain. It was 12:55 when the clock in Plymouth stopped in the square and wept lava. 12:55 beneath the steeple where my father met my mother and her mother had met her father before her. 12:55 when the ash like molten fire took over half the island and then paused like the whip hand of an overseer to study its handiwork. 12:55 when all the jumbies of O'Garro and Weekes and Lynch would rise from their graves and relocate to Antigua and St. Kitts and even England. And so Montserrat lost its big chance at corruption.

Now I wasn't there when the clocks stopped. I was in the city of cities, New York. I was walking the streets of the South Bronx, the highest borough in New York and because of its hills the borough that is closest to God. Here is where I saw my first murder and made love for the first time (both on the same day and so the two acts would remain forever entwined in my mind as a coming of age). The Bronx is the borough that because of its many hills is closest to Montserrat, and where I was when news of the volcano reached me. I immediately came home to die nobly beneath the volcano, but the volcano was not the least bit interested in me or my dying nobly beneath it. The only time it even paid any attention to me was when, as I describe more fully elsewhere, I was foolish enough to try and swim in gale-force winds in order to challenge God, but He won that contest, and when I almost died some mile and a half from shore, my only thought was: well, at least this is better than watching Oprah on television. When I was finally slammed back onto the beach, too weary to even walk, and lay on my back and looked up at the sky, I saw the volcano was laughing at me and belching ash. I would never be so foolish to test God in quite that way again.

But it eased my pain to know that some of that ash would fall in Antigua and maybe go as far as Puerto Rico, more than a hundred and fifty miles away, and make them curse us damn Montserratians and our volcano. The word *schadenfreude* is German, but the delight in taking delight in other people's misery is very Montserratian. When you reach a certain age, you enjoy your friends and your enemies equally, and you take your pleasures where you find them.

Whenever I think of the Caribbean, I think of that painting of the Last Supper by Da Vinci. You see all the disciples seated at the table with Christ in the centre and you know that they are all vying to see who can sit closest to him. That is the situation with the Caribbean, only now it is, of course, America that everyone wants to sit next to. For the right to sit at that table, most islands are willing to sell everything, starting with their sovereignty and ending with their water rights and beaches, and of course, the lives of their children. And what better dumping ground for waste is there than the Caribbean?

When I think of that Last Supper table, I think of Eugenia Charles of Dominica sitting next to President Reagan and selling out Grenada for a chance at a closer seat, thinking that by selling herself she would get a larger aid package, as she'd been promised. Instead, she got her aid grant cut in half because, with Grenada gone, Reagan didn't really need her anymore. She therefore lost both her seat as well her mind.

And what determines where small islands sit at the table? It's who gets paid first in times of crisis that, of course, determines where you sit. In any crisis, the police get paid first and then the soldiers – which means that those islands with strong police forces and soldiers sit first. Then, next to be seated are the blessed, i.e. those rich in resources like oil. The poorest ones, where do they sit? The ones without armies or strong police, when do they get seated? They don't. They sit on the ground like Lazarus and wait for the crumbs to fall from the master's table.

Speaking of Grenada, I had a chance to go there and do a play I had written called *Three Kings Darkly*. It was about their invasion and was directed by a brilliant Barbadian director named Earl Warner (whom God loved and so took early). I remember the beauty of the island, which reminded me of Montserrat, although Grenada (the Spice Island of the Caribbean) has a better breeze from all directions. Then I was reminded of Rome. America insisted that all the wreckage from the invasion remain visible, the downed airplane, for example. So the Grenadian children on their way to school are forced to walk around this monument to their defeat, just as Rome did with the crosses of the crucified left on the hills of every city, as a warning about what happens if you dared to challenge the imperial might of Rome. If you recall, Rome was supposed to last a thousand years. America has another six hundred to go.

So what place at the table do I want for Montserrat?

One thing I know for certain, I don't want to see my island turned into a theme park or a Disney attraction. I don't want them making endless remakes of *The Little Mermaid*. I don't want the sounds of daily gunfire, like Jamaica with its almost military police wars. I also know that anyone in the Caribbean who speaks of genuine change (by which I mean, for example, that the same twelve families who have ruled since Emancipation no longer control the land and the estates) is asking for trouble. Everything must remain exactly the same – with that mulatto elite controlling everything from sugar and rum to newspapers.

I remember when I was in Jamaica doing a play and researching the life of Don Drummond, Jamaica's greatest musician, who died in the madhouse at Bellevue, after killing his beautiful Syrian girlfriend in a jealous rage and then turning himself in (a story of true Caribbean love). I was staying at the Pegasus Hotel and living large because the government was putting me up. There was a man who actually knew and had played with Don Drummond and we would meet every day to drink and talk. One day I couldn't find him, so I found a friend and asked him to show me where the man stayed. His friend, not thinking (and wanting the tip I promised him), took me around in a circle to the back of the hotel, and there, not twenty feet away from the Pegasus, he had built a shanty out of tin and rocks and lived right there in the shadow of the hotel, his one good pants drying in the sun. Imagine his embarrassment and anger at my having found him. Imagine my shame. I hadn't stopped to think how he might feel to be discovered in his nakedness. We looked at each other from eyes of illusion, he jealous of my privilege and I hating it. Now I hated being at the Pegasus and all it stood for.

These days, I can't be comfortable with someone else making my bed. As a child I thought it big fun to throw my clothes around the room just for the simple pleasure of watching the servant girls with their short dresses bending over to collect them. I still like girls in short dresses but I don't like people fetching and carrying for me; it embarrasses me.

Maybe I still carry my mother's guilt. I remember the best conversation my mother and I ever had about Montserrat. She called it living in a bubble – all the things she thought were so important and precious at the time – and it was only when she came to the reality of America that she saw what nonsense the class-conscious world she grew up in really was. My mother, Phyllis White, whom I grew increasingly to love, rejoiced to call me in the kitchen one day to proudly show me her first boiling egg, with her dimpled smile and all the enthusiasm of Christmas. She was aged thirty-five at the time. I don't think I can give a clearer example of the world she came from.

Artists live in a dream world, romantic and removed from reality (which is why I usually avoid fellow artists like the plague), not as removed as, say, preachers and priests, but a good ways away from how people really live and the things that people and islands do for respect and a seat at any table.

As I say, the Caribbean is built on illusion and looking good. Even though the shoes you wear to church are two sizes too small it doesn't matter a damn just as long as you look presentable when you wear them. They're good for you and so you must wear them, especially if they've come all the way from America in a barrel, because America is where God comes from in the first place, and if not in a barrel, then surely on evangelist radio. If you doubt me, listen to the Voice of America broadcasting one radio evangelist after another on those expensive airwaves. Certainly, Pat Robertson and Billy Graham (father and son) know just how important the Caribbean radio market is.

The Caribbean alone, never mind Africa, has been able to keep both James Dobson and Pat Robertson in Arabian racehorses, which they both own aplenty. I sincerely believe that this is why God made us, not only to labour endlessly for others, but then to take our exploited wages and give them away to televangelists from America to keep them in racehorses. You see how slavery has taken a new form? Whereas before the masters had at least to feed and provide clothing for his slaves, now the new slaves feed and clothe the master – and feed him well. We keep them in jet planes and racehorses and they give us the world to come, some distant paradise where we will be rewarded at last and money won't matter. And of course, we'll be asked to serve there too. Yes, Caribbean islands of illusion.

I'll close with something that one of the most vital women to come out of Montserrat once told me. This was Mrs. Ellen Peters, one of the pioneers of the labour movement in Montserrat. It took me some time to see her, because I was shirtless when I met her grandson, owner of a restaurant (The

Harbour Court) in what was then Plymouth and he, Levons, threw me out.
I had forgotten where I was. In episcopalian Montserrat, you do nothing
with your shirt off except swim and go to bed – and then only if alone.
Maybe if you're a worker on a road you might get away with it, but mind
yourself, because someone is looking; someone is always looking in
Montserrat. In polite society, never ever go into town without a shirt,
unless you want to be taken for a Rasta.

But to return to Mrs. Ellen Peters, I had to return to the same premises
with a shirt and my mother's dimpled smile and beg Levons to let me
interview his grandmother. He looked at me as if I had asked to take her on
a first-date. But someone told him I had written a book someplace, and since
Montserratians have a high regard for books and pens and preachers and
lawyers, he allowed me a half hour while he waited just outside the door in
case she screamed rape. Of course, when she started speaking with that sharp
mind of hers that lasted a century, it ended up being two hours. The most
important thing she told me:

"You have to forgive Montserrat, especially the men, they don't like
change, but they like what change brings."

In other words, the fight to start a union was very hard in Montserrat
because we make such good servants. We grumble when they short change
us on our wages or take away our provision lands for taxes, but we take it.
When a man has no money, he looks first at his empty hands and then down
at his feet, because these are all he owns. Then he beats his wife because his
hands are empty and if he doesn't beat her, he beats himself. If it were not
for the women who kept after their men to do something, Montserrat would
still not have a union. It was the women, too, who built the building societies
in America and Canada, the women first and then the men.

Montserrat is still that place where people pass you and give you pieces of
your history, never all of it, for that would be too overwhelming. Even my
sister, Rita, will only give me bits of my father at a time. She knows just how
much I need to have.

For such a tiny island, we have sent pieces of ourselves into every
corner of the world: people like Judge Bruce Wright, whose father came
from Montserrat, and writers and activists like Stokely Carmichael
whose maternal grandfather came from Montserrat (Carmichael visited
Montserrat before he died), actors and poets, preachers and thieves. We,
like the Irish, not only make good servants, we also make revolutions.

May Montserrat never become like Antigua or St. Martin. Fortunately,
our harbours are too small for Leviathan tourist ships. We have no gambling
casinos, no offshore banking, no bauxite, no oil. We have nothing to sell but
ourselves and the faces of our children. In these, I try always to find my own
face and the child I once was before hands I never knew took me for

upliftment to the land of opportunity, that place of Caribbean exiles from every island.

We Monserratians and the Irish have so much in common. We, too, have to believe we came from a land of giants (the mighty Finns of countless Celtic legends) so as to make our present captivity less painful. In Montserrat, every wound is fresh and every pleasure is taken, and even servants have servants and always with a style of our own – whether from Cork Hill and Glenn Mohr or the infamous Kinsale. We have both a sense of illusion and of honour – from my mother I got the sense of privilege, from my father the sense of rage.

MEETING UNCLE SAM

THE GUARD
(for Roy Lee)

When I was eight, they sent me to guard an old woman in a foreign city. Maybe they thought it would be good training for me since West Indians were born to guard things and prevail. I don't know really. But she frightened me, this old woman, because she was mad and smelled of dying.

She was sane by day, mostly. During the day she would watch me, and they paid her. But by night, when her husband went out prowling after women and drink and things they said he shouldn't, she would become someone else. After tying her up securely, he'd go, leaving me with a key to her door, saying: "You don't let her out unless there's a fire. You hear me?"

A key is a mighty thing. It made me older. I didn't understand America yet. I didn't like it.

We were all right together in daytime, the old woman and the boy I was. Auntie, who came to see me on her day off every other week (it was a Thursday always and a sacred day) didn't believe me much. I would tell her things that she didn't want to hear, like how they killed this girl in the toilet in school. How she was screaming and nobody came until they found her and by then she was silent, so they sent us home early. She didn't want to hear *that* on her one day off and you couldn't blame her. It wasn't like the America she wanted to believe in as she ironed the Bancroft's laundry as she watched the soap operas they allowed her to view at work. By the time she came, all she wanted was her cup of Lipton tea, which Mrs. Rhoden, the old lady, would have waiting for her, sweet with condensed milk, just the way she liked it. Then as she sat sipping, she would get the litany of everything wrong I'd done since her last visit, my current abominations. These the old woman and her husband were only too glad to tell her, voices close together as if in a confessional, one whispering in one ear and the second in the other:

"…and he lies."

"Yes."

"And he steals and hides things, even food."

"Yes."

"He comes home late from school and won't say where he's been."

"Yes."

That was enough. There was no need to ask further. One look toward me and I knew. She had a place a few buildings away where she could take me and lock the door. When we were alone together in the hallway, which was painted almshouse green, we climbed the stairs to the second floor and the brown door. I turned and pleaded my case:

"Listen, I already got a beating for taking meat from the stove."

A shake of her head; I was only making it worse.

"He ties her up at night and leaves me to watch her."

"Boy, stop you lying. Come, take off you clothes."

She said it so sweetly you would have thought it was an invitation to the Queen's garden party, but I knew what was coming. My nature was to lie; hers was to cleanse. We both had our work to do and talking only delayed it. Soon leather fell on my back like rain. This was what she came for really, and with each stroke she'd shout a word:

"Too (*lash*) harden (*lash*). Too (*lash*) spiteful (*lash*) and wicked (*lash-lash*)."

Then sometimes a phrase would happen:

"Drive/ Him/ Out/ Of /You

Drive /Him/ Out/ Of/ You

Drive /Him/ Out /Of You"

each with a quick stroke until at last she climaxed, her fury spent and her sweat fell from her body on to me and eased the pain. And Jesus, he watched silent from his cross on the kitchen wall.

Then a fresh week started, as if brand new and waiting to be written. And since I knew that Auntie had only every other week off, I was on parole and could try to breathe. Where there's time there's hope, or at least a maybe.

The old woman played the piano. She didn't even have to look at her hands. She just played and they glided over the keys and danced. She was happy then. Sometimes she would teach, although not many would climb the three flights of stairs there in the Bronx to learn. I'd try but the white keys of the piano would bite my hands and I could never glide like she could.

It had a good smell, the piano, a smell of wood and ivory and churches. When she opened it there was light in the room. So, the piano was a bringer of light but it brought distance too, because it was her piano, not his. He came from a house without a piano, without much of anything except arguments and so he learned to do things with his hands. He was a skilled carpenter and cook and anything else people needed. He took her from her parents' house with promises and hands made for trade. What he wanted to do was make her see the world as he did, but to do that he had to break her, which took him time. Now, when he came home she would shut the piano and the light would leave.

We were all right for some days that week and my parole was going well. I stayed out of the way and resisted temptation, mostly. For example, I didn't go taking food off the stove, which was pretty difficult staying away from since he was a good cook but could tell instantly if anything had been touched (which was how I got busted the first time). Now, I could smell a trap waiting, so there was nothing to report me for. Then one night, after a phone call and a silence, I heard them talking together in the bedroom and then there was crying and then there was none.

He knew that I had been freeing her when she called my name from the other room after he'd left. (He told me not to, but it's hard to ignore when someone is calling your name like a bird.) Sometimes her voice would get inside my head and I would dream her or not sleep at all, so I'd have to let her out. Now, he gagged her mouth as well so she couldn't call me. That was all right because now I could finish my homework.

I didn't owe her anything. After all she betrayed me by reporting me to The Whip (Auntie). Still it was strange not hearing her. Sometimes you just want to know that someone's in the cell next to you, that there's someone there.

She didn't start right away. A slow wailing sound first, almost like keening, then there was the sound of a chair being scraped across the floor. Then it started to build, rocking back and forth, back and forth, as she tried to move the chair to the door. It just kept building like the sound of an animal in a snare. So I got up and went into the living room and turned on the television to try and drown her out. It's funny, one minute you want the sound of a human being and then you don't. But even with the television I could still hear her. It surprised me how strong she was. Suddenly there was a thud and then nothing. I didn't want her dead, not so close to me. Would that be my fault too?

I took the key and opened her door and there she was, the chair turned over. She was still crying, but not loudly. I tried to lift the chair but couldn't while she was still tied. I had no choice. I had to release her. I took her hand and led her into the living room. It amazed me how soft her hands were. We sat in front the television, neither one saying anything. I thought of asking her what was wrong, but I already knew damn well what was wrong. She didn't want to be tied up and gagged there in a locked room, being guarded by an eight-year-old boy from Montserrat. If it was Auntie, she would have offered the old woman cookies. She believed cookies could save the world. That and beatings. So instead of talking we stared at the television but I could see that her eyes weren't watching. She wasn't really there. I wondered where it was that her mind fled to when she wasn't there anymore. Was it someplace where she was once safe? I tried to ease my way to the subject:

"You know... he might come back soon. He won't like it if he finds you out here."

Her eyes got wide with the mention of him. Fear works wonders. She agreed to go back to the bedroom, but not to being tied up. She might need to use the po. Having come to terms, I led her in and locked the door behind her. I lay down before the door in case she called me. She couldn't get out without my knowing and this way at least I could get some sleep without the sounds of screams in my head. Soon the red and random dust was falling and I was somewhere safe with sun, and sleep took me. It wasn't quite death but close enough and so I went with it. Then suddenly I felt something shaking me and slapping me awake. He was standing there over me and my heart starting pounding so loudly in my ears that I couldn't hear what he was saying.

"Wake up! Didn't I tell you not to let her out? She's gone."

"What?"

"Get dressed. We have to go find her."

"Gone?"

I was lost. How could she be gone? She couldn't get past me. I had the key in the door. Somehow she found a way and the front door was left wide open. I stumbled into my clothes and we went out into what was left of the October night. Outside, the wind was moving the bottles and the rats.

Three a.m. and the bars had shut. We couldn't even tell which direction she would have gone. Would she turn right toward Crotona Park? No. Then left toward 3rd Avenue?

She didn't have a coat with her. I could feel her. She tells me that I'm losing her if I go that way. But then Rhoden started talking because he needed someone to explain to:

"You see, that's why I tie she up, so she can't go and do sheself harm like this. Now look what happen."

Outside in the street with dark all around him and nothing but a cigarette to hold on to, he looked small to me for the first time. I wanted to tell him to stop talking and shut up. I'm losing her. I'm losing the scent of her.

I looked down the street past the square and noticed some cars blowing their horns at the intersection. There was something in the road which they were swerving around and trying to avoid. An animal? Then I spotted her there in the middle of the street, trembling, dressed in a yellow nightgown that rises and falls, rises and falls with the wind. The lights of cars and the South Bronx night struck luminous in her hair, which was grey, but which she still wore in plaits like a child. Transfigured, her face was so beautiful, so still, it frightened me. The drivers swerved to avoid her because she walked straight down the middle of the road, one slippered foot following the other along the chalk line. All along the pavement the broken glass shone like diamonds.

At first, the drivers (mostly Puerto Ricans) cursed at her and then they stared in wonder for a moment, a wonder they give only to the mad and the sacred.

"There she is."

Rhoden stopped the traffic and walked up to her and took her in his arms. He called her name for the first time.

"Irene, Irene, why you do this to me? You know how worried you have me? What would me a do? Come, girl, come!"

He'd gathered her in his arms but she only kept staring past him. She'd gone to that place again. The ambulance stopped and he tried to keep them from taking her, but she'd attracted too much attention for them to just go away. They had to take her, so we followed her inside. It smelled of rubbing alcohol.

I thought maybe I'd redeemed myself because I'd spotted her first, like a dolphin in the sea, but no; it didn't matter. It wasn't enough and it was my fault still. I wasn't good enough yet, because it was me who set her free, me who lost her.

I still heard screams and still saw pain. Guards shouldn't do that. But soon, I too would get better, like the others.

GOD'S MERCIES

I spent the first fourteen years of my life without ever living in the same place for more than a year. My mother had vanished by the time I was two, and I was raised by my Montserrat aunt who had to board me out to places because she worked as a slave (alias live-in domestic). Unfortunately, the people she chose to have me stay with kept dying, so by the time I got to know them, they were dead. This gave me more material than I could ever write in one lifetime. Most of them were Montserratians and so I never really left Montserrat.

Like St. Paul, I could talk about lashes and stripes beyond measure, but I won't. Suffice to say: all that good correction served to do was make me into a criminal. I was not a good thief. A good thief is one who never gets caught and ends up as president, premier of some country or chair of some global corporation. Me, I got caught; hence all the beatings . But then God got around to giving me some mercy and landed me with someone who didn't drop dead inside a year. She was named Marilyn, Marilyn Dyer; she lived with her elderly mother, Lantha. Now what was funny was that at the time, I didn't know that my name was Dyer – never having met my father or even my mother.

Marilyn was about thirty and was therefore one of the youngest adults I'd ever known. She was disabled – she'd had some form of polio – but she was totally independent and had a job with the Internal Revenue where many West Indians found employment. Now Montserratians don't like cripples, although they pretend they do. We find them bad-lucky and even my own mother (when I got to meet her) told me that if a girl is pregnant, she should stay far away from cripples lest it affect the unborn baby in the womb.

Marilyn Dyer was the only reason I'm not in prison today. She showed me the first sign of love I found in America. I remember she had the softest hands. No one had ever touched me since I came to that cesspool (well, not in love anyway). She could see immediately why I was a nervous wreck and could never trust anyone or anything, because anything I had was going to be taken away from me sooner rather than later. She knew why I stole things and squirrelled them away (the same way old people do in nursing homes), hiding candy bars or anything shiny. I remember once I stole a cross; it wasn't even gold.

Her cure was never to hide anything, to leave everything in the open, including her pocketbook. Once I stole a pen and when she found out, all she said was that I could just have asked, and then she let me keep it, which made me feel ashamed and foolish. Unlike other fosterers, she didn't report me to my aunt. When my aunt asked what I had done wrong since the last time, Marilyn would say: "Nothing, he hasn't done anything wrong."

Auntie couldn't believe it. She'd come prepared as always with her leather strap (a dog's leash bound in twine).

Marilyn said, "All he needs is some love, that's all."

"Love? The boy a damn tief and a scamp, that's all. He way-wad and too lie. Is the devil in him but I go drive he out. Believe me."

Yes, Marilyn was good. Even the heart murmur I had started to go away. I could never repay her for what she did. But here's the thing. Years later when I started writing plays, I wrote a play about her to try to show her what she meant to my life, a play I called *Les Femmes Noires*. She came to see it and although it was a big success, she hated it. You see, she had never seen herself as a cripple, never. The road to hell is filled with good intentions. She forgave me, but it took some time.

When my mother felt safe enough to surface, as I tell in more detail elsewhere, we didn't have a hell of a lot to say to each other except the obvious:

"Where the hell have you been?"

"Well, that's a long story, my son."

All Montserrat stories are long. And I didn't want to hear it. It took ten more years before I could even stand to listen to her.

Let's skip to the good part now, where the light from heaven shines on my doorstep and these wise men come and tell me I'm a star. I had my first book written at nineteen and my first play produced by twenty-one. By twenty-three, *The New York Times* was giving me write-ups and using dangerous words like talented and genius. It took me a while to learn that fame has nothing to do with *you* at all.

It's other people that make you famous and they do it for themselves, not you. Like Shakespeare is talented yes, but he's famous because Britain, in its wisdom, knew how to send in armies, conquer people, and then impose their culture on their subjects. Culture can be a very lucrative enterprise and, of course, it helps if the person really has something lasting to say about the world. He helped to make English the dominant language in the world. When you read the King James Version of the Bible, you're reading Shakespeare.

Which leads me very nicely to Joe Papp, one of America's most successful producer-directors. It was Joe Papp who started the New York Shakespeare Festival Theatre. The son of Jewish immigrants from Russia, he changed his name from Papirofsky to Papp. He always said of me that I reminded him of the boys who used to beat him up at school in Brooklyn. I told him it wasn't me, that I was too busy dodging the gangs in the South Bronx; I never got to Brooklyn.

It was Joe Papp who explained what theatre was all about in one minute. "Edgar, theatre is about getting asses into chairs and making them pay for it."

"That's it?"

"That's it."

We never had long conversations, Joe and I. We had a peculiar love-hate relation. But he had an amazing secretary named Gail Merrifield. She typed up my first plays that I wrote in ragged notebooks and brought to her. That's how it started. Gail would later go on to become Joe's second and final wife. She gave me a lot of encouragement and had one of the sharpest minds in theatre (including Joe, who went by instinct mostly).

When my daughter (Nicole) was born, I celebrated by buying him a five-dollar cigar, which I thought was a substantial outlay. He was gracious and accepted. We smoked together (two puffs) and then he offered me one of his real Cuban cigars (El Rey del Mundo), which cost fifty dollars because Cuba and America weren't talking at the time. These were hand-rolled by virgins in Cuba. It was because they were virgins that they cost so much.

I'll just say this. It's hard to tell anyone who has tasted success in their early twenties anything. You start believing your own press. Joe asked me what it was I wanted to do as a writer.

"I want to get all this stuff out of my head so I can breathe." I don't think that was the answer he wanted to hear, but I knew even then that if you start writing what anyone else wants to hear, you might as well put a gun to your head because it's already over for you as a writer. (Joe Papp made a lot of people famous. He also destroyed a lot of people along the way. Rest in peace, my friend.)

LAUGHTER LIKE RAIN

I was fourteen when I met her, the woman who was my mother. I'd met her before, of course, but that was in the womb and I couldn't speak and so didn't ask anything of her except birth and she could forgive that. The problem came later when I had no name for her. She wasn't part of anything – not the walls, not the pictures, not the "Amens" that took place on Sunday when old and overdressed women wept and awaited a coming that wasn't mine.

Others raised me and I never asked why. These were either women who were old and West Indian and smelled of Limacol or Vick's Vapor Rub or else men, and their smell was of rum and tobacco, which stayed behind in rooms after they'd left, or else you'd smell it on their hands if they slapped you.

Many of the children I knew were like me. They, too, were raised by some stand-in, some surrogate, a grandmother or an aunt, or a stranger who stood in for them. And if you had a two-in-one, a grandmother and an aunt in one package, what would you call that – a grand-aunt? What difference does it make what they're called? Who feeds you, names you. They name you and give you a name to call them by – and obey.

"You'll call me Nana. Go on, say it."

"Nana."

What difference – Nana, Tan-tan, whatever – as long as there's food and shelter, and at night when you close your eyes, a red darkness falls around you.

So you listen and you await that time, that perfect time when you're old enough to open a door and not have to close it behind you, ever. You wait.

And in America, to help you wait, there's television, which is part of the magic along with White Christmases and Collie dogs that lived in houses like people, not like anything you saw in Montserrat where you were born to a mother you never met. At the movies, anyone who looked like you tap-danced up and down stairs in musicals or else served food on trains as Redcaps. They also helped little blond girls made of silver onto lollipop ships, which was good.

Hollywood was good, too. It could make Africa for Tarzan, a tree grow in Brooklyn or a rose in Spanish Harlem. There was your *Island in the Sun* with Belafonte, but that was romance and fantasy. Meanwhile, I had to try to keep from being pushed from a rooftop in the South Bronx night that could eat you when police cars snatched you from street corners and made friends disappear. This was before Bob Marley, when all West Indians still lived in trees and had tails to hang by.

So, no, a mother I never asked about, never once. And maybe I never would have if it wasn't for that car – the one that knocked Nana down in Park Avenue, where she worked, not danced, as a domestic. She worked from sun to sun and took sleep where she found it: in church or trains or buses, always carrying shopping bags or pulling her cart.

Now, the car that knocked her down finally brought her the sleep she always searched for. But she didn't want it. She gets up quickly. First, she worries about her *business* being exposed to the world, then her groceries, scattered all over the street like ungrateful children that have somehow gotten away from her. She tries to gather them up and rush home to fix Mrs. Bancroft's dinner. Her mistress is having guests. So glad is the driver to see her get to her feet and not ask anything about witnesses or a driver's license that he gets out of his car to help her as she struggles to retrieve the cans of food along the Park Avenue street. He, no doubt, makes soothing noises: "You all right? Here, let me help you with that, lady."

He feels sorry for her as he watches her limp to the curb, so he waits all of five minutes before quietly driving away, promising himself to light a candle at St. Patrick's Cathedral, which is close, and to cut down on the drink, which is always closer still.

And so Nana, the good servant from Montserrat, limps along, her cart following behind her like the train of a bride's wedding dress. When she reaches her building, 103 East 77th Street, she uses the service elevator because, good Montserratian that she is, she knows the difference between resident and help, knows which she is. So imagine her surprise when she sees the floor coming up to her like a lover. Sleep at last. Fade to black.

When she wakes, here she is in this hospital bed, smell of Lysol, sound of voices on the intercom and the scrape of wheels of a cart not her own. She can't comprehend anything except the nervous eyes of the nurse who is trying to find a vein in this arm that looks so foreign to her. Could it really be hers? As she watches the nurse drawing blood, her first thought is how much she always wanted to be a nurse, not a domestic. But when she applied, so many years ago, now lost in the fog of emigration, they told her that they didn't need nurses. They had enough. What jobs there were would be scattered to the Irish. (It was funny that she had arrived in New York after the Irish, just as slaves had followed the same Irish back home in Montserrat. Maybe that was her destiny.)

What they did need, though, were nurses' aides, not nurses, to lift and carry patients. They wanted her strong arms. The question I always asked about Nana: did her arms make her life or had life made her arms, arms thin and strong and silver-braceleted in the Caribbean way? Back home, in Montserrat, you'd see them dancing masquerade as they rested on her hips, akimbo, or else lifted to God's sky to call a spirit down.

Now only the nurse held that arm; they had taken away her bracelets and ring, her mother's ring, her sister's bracelets of real Guyanese gold and her two of silver.

"Wait. Who take them?"

"It's alright. We put them away for you. You were in an accident. Can you remember? Do you remember a car hitting you?"

She can't remember the car or anything about it. All she can think of is Mrs. Bancroft's dinner, which is unmade. So she lies there preparing it over and over in her mind; going over, step by step, how she would do the lamb and the artichokes. She knew just how her mistress liked them: just enough so the leaves could be pulled off and dipped in the mint sauce. Over and over, she prepares this meal and moves about the kitchen on East 77th Street, her kitchen, where she ruled with the small window-fan spinning and drawing away the smoke out into the courtyard.

I was not the first one she raised. I was the seventh. All the others had ended as betrayers. I knew this, because she told me how all of the others had left her the moment they didn't need her anymore. They'd left for mothers or had run off with some girl. None had come back to find her when they'd started families of their own. Why? It was her lot in life to care for other people's children because she had none of her own and God had given her this task, even though she knew that the memories of children are short – short as love and need. The betrayers – ungrateful; it was just a matter of time before I too would join them.

"Not me, Nana!"

"Not you!?" (She just sucks her teeth and laughs at me.) "As for you, if I had was to depend on you for anything, dog would eat me supper." Then she'd give her little laugh which was bitter and not really a laugh at all.

So I didn't ever want to think of it (a mother), for even to think was to betray. I didn't want to prove her right. I'd defy her by staying until the end just to show her that I was different than the others. But then that day came when the car licked her down and inside of her was my mother, hiding, waiting to come out. That day I became the seventh of the betrayers.

We – all of us children – had come small to America, but I never wanted to. Was this what made me different in her eyes? I seemed to bother her more. I fought her every step of the way. While still in Montserrat, I'd tried to lock the door and hide so they wouldn't find me, slept out in the old sugar-mill one night, but they still found me.

She was more determined. She hadn't just sent for me from America.

She'd come down herself to fetch me. She'd brought her leather suitcases and a metal trunk with two locks and the smell of camphor. And though I tried to hide from her at Glen Mohr and Cork Hill, they still found me when I got hungry.

"You'll like it there. They have trains that go under the ground, and buildings so high up they to go the sky."

But what I wanted was the sea, a sea that was always within running distance. Anywhere you looked from on the island, you could see it, calling you, a salt sea you could float in and be held up safe by, by spirits that always held you up – or took you for themselves, and that was alright too.

All I wanted was never to leave, never to lose the piercing smell of ripe fruit in the garden: mango trees hanging heavy, and orange, genip and soursop and the pomegranate they said that Eve had eaten. In the morning, I wanted real cocoa from the plant, thick and safe as my grandmother's house in Cork Hill, with the servant girls from country who would make goat water, the thick stew with rice that the Irish had left us along with their madness. (These were the girls who would cook and bake for us until their bellies got big with babies and they ran away to England, Canada or America – if they knew somebody there the way Nana had.)

So no, I never wanted to leave. What did you need toys for when you could make a slingshot and bring down birds, or enemies? What did you need television for when you had girls who were much more mysterious and had more to show?

So, when she did capture me with her promises and her luggage and I woke to find myself in America, I ran away three times. But all I found was Central Park, which surrounded me. And though there was a lake and a zoo with animals they said were happy, I couldn't get away from it. I'd run and run trying to lose myself, but whenever I stopped, exhausted, I'd find myself still there in Central Park. When I looked up, there would be the statue of Hans Christian Anderson still looking down, delivering a sentence.

But Nana hadn't lied. The trains did go under the earth in a tunnel. The buildings did stand up to the sky like Babel. But it was what she hadn't said: that here you'd work in other people's kitchens, other people's dreams. That here she was the servant and always had been since she'd arrived. And this was where the money came from that had bought the house I was born in. Or was that a dream too?

So, after the third time I'd run away, I realized there would be no getting back home to Montserrat, because you couldn't walk there on water. America was a "two-water" journey, two waters away from the islands of our birth. You crossed salt water and then fresh water to come here. I understood that America was the place from which everything came and that, even before I'd seen it, was what controlled my life.

It was only when Nana got struck down that the woman who was my mother stood up and walked. She walked right through the door and into the living room, and sat on the couch before she used the word "mother". She sat and folded her long Montserrat legs, one over the other, and tried hard to be sincere. I knew this by the way she kept pausing after she said things, like:

"I guess you were probably wondering about me, right?"

"No, I didn't wonder about you at all."

"You didn't?"

"No."

She seemed confused.

"Why didn't you wonder? Did they tell you I was dead?"

She must mean Nana. I wasn't going to make it easy for her.

"No, they just said you didn't care about me."

"Well that's not true. I did come. I was there but you didn't see me."

Didn't see her? How was that possible? People lie and when they grow up, they lie better. I was trying to make sense of everything, but there wasn't enough time because now we had to visit Nana in the hospital, which would be tricky, because if we went in together it would look like conspiracy and betrayal. We would have to enter one at a time. Would she go first and then me?

In the end it didn't matter. Nana had made up her mind not to talk to either of us. She turned her face to the wall.

The hospital room was private. There was a second bed but no one was using it. It was clean and quiet here, so different from hospitals I had seen in the South Bronx. This was Lenox Hill, not Lincoln Hospital. Here there were no patients dying in hallways while beds and rooms were being searched for, red blanket cases with gunshot and stab wounds. Here, people moved about quietly and whispered.

I wondered who was paying for all this since this wasn't a City hospital. Then I saw Mrs. Bancroft in her open fur coat, her thin Hermes silk scarf. She was speaking with a doctor who, despite thick glasses and balding head, was still an intern. The answers he was giving did not satisfy her. Someone senior would have to be brought.

"Well, where is Dr. Slattery?"

"I'm afraid he's gone for the day. He won't be available until tomorrow morning."

"Well reach him through his office."

Mrs. Bancroft didn't suffer fools gladly. If there were any fools about it was they who suffered, not she. She always made it a point to deal only with those in charge. Why waste time with those in the middle?

Nana had been with her for over twenty years, had helped her raise her

children and to bury her husband, Frank. In fact, it had been Nana's kitchen
where both her husband and children came for solace. There was always
food and talk and touch there. Mrs. Bancroft never touched anything but
her clothes. She loved the feel of good fabric, silk or cashmere, linen or
llama. But she found it difficult to touch or be touched by others. Her
husband had come to understand this, called it her nature. His daughter,
Lisbeth, who looked so very like her mother, he expected would become
the same. But she surprised him by volunteering for the Peace Corps and
going to Africa after graduation because, she said, there it was alright to
touch. How much of it came from those days spent in the kitchen with
Nana? Yet for a year I had lived, hidden and secret, in the tiny room behind
the kitchen, Nana's room, because she wasn't allowed to have anyone there
and so I was made silent and moved like a ghost. The only sound I heard
was the radio when Nana listened to her radio soap operas like *I Remember
Mama*.

It was funny because while Nana loved to touch them, the only touch
I remember was the touch of the strap she delivered every other Thursday,
on her day off. (She couldn't beat me at work because if I cried, I would
make too much noise, so she had to take me to the Bronx to administer
punishment).

But with the Bancroft children, Nana was always gentle, and with Frank
Bancroft, too, she could be patient because she knew he needed healing.
His wife had been the single driving force in his life and made him achieve.
Without her, he would still have been some middle management accountant in Harrisburg, Pennsylvania. Instead, here he was, a banker living on
Park Avenue. The effort and all the overtime he had put in had been worth
it. There was even a picture of him with Eisenhower at a dinner. Of course,
Mrs. Bancroft had helped to organize those social evenings and presenta-
tions. Over and over she'd drilled into him that it was not what, but how
a thing was presented that made it memorable, that extra touch, although
not by her hand. She'd guided him well, Nana had said, even if it was to an
early grave.

Nana would say this only to her friend, Ruth. Ruth was my aunt, too,
although by proxy. Aunt Ruth started as Nana's Thursday friend. Every
other Thursday was the day West Indian women came together to laugh
and dance at the Renaissance Ball Room in Harlem, called the Renny. Or
maybe even, luxury of luxuries, go to a movie and spend the day, the *whole*
day, just being entertained. This was the one day when they didn't have to
work for anyone but themselves, didn't have to wash the agony from the
clothes of their white mistresses. Every second Thursday was the day of the
West Indian maids.

There were building societies where they could meet island men who worked as cooks for Horn & Hardart Automat (or as West Indians called it, Horn & Hardass, because of the heavy workloads), or as tailors. As tailors, they bent like Jews over their sewing machines and were much in demand because West Indians would rather mend than buy.

Death was a thing that women worried about, and because they worried, they made men worry too.

"Who go bury us when we fall here in this wilderness? Who here even know we well enough to bury?"

This was a question that only women asked, because they knew for certain there was death to come – while we men only suspected it.

So, Thursday was the day Nana and Ruth first met and agreed on each other. That had been thirty years before. I don't know what it was they did in each other's arms because love was too large a word for them. They slept together every other Thursday for thirty years, must have overheard each other's dreams sleeping that close.

Ruth had fallen from the cable car that used to run along Third Avenue & 149th Street in the Bronx. She was on her way to Alexander's Department Store. She ended up with a limp in her left leg. She had never sued them. Nana said that was why the limp never left.

"If you'd a sue them, the limp would of go."

As a result she couldn't walk as fast as Nana, which made Nana the leader in the relationship.

But first, to become close, they had to exchange some secret, something they would never share with anyone else. Ruth told about her father who had raped her when she was twelve. She cried and wondered if she should have revealed it to her. Nana just looked at her and took her in her arms.

"Well, I never knew my father so he never get to rape me, but there's not too much a man won't chase. If it name 'gel' they want it."

With that they laughed, healed it, and never mentioned it again.

Nana had loved a man once. I know this because I saw a photograph of her when she was eighteen. Her eyes were still clear and full of light, before taking on the Montserrat face of a woman that hides so much sadness and secrets. She was wearing earrings, her hair was pressed and parted down the middle, and the way she faced the camera was direct with expectation. A man was coming for her, I'm certain of it. This was back home before America, before doubt, when she still wore the body her mother had given her. That was the only photograph I ever saw of her where she looked as if she felt she deserved a life.

Now Aunt Ruth bent over Nana. She gave her ice water to sip through a straw. This Nana accepted. She had turned her face from the wall. We were all staring, trying to smile. Aunt Ruth alone seemed comfortable, as though she belonged. She alone knew what to do and where things were, knew how to find a vase for the flowers that Mrs. Bancroft had brought. We went downstairs to the gift shop but I couldn't get anything but a red balloon that said, "Get well soon". I stood there, holding it in my hand. Nana looked at me: the foolish child of a foolish child.

As for Mrs. Bancroft, she didn't know what to say to me. She was never certain if I was the same child, or yet another of Nana's projects. She only saw me at intervals, and had trouble keeping track.

The silence in the room was parted when Aunt Ruth stood on her thin bird legs and said: "Well, look at that. And you have a television too. See, you just push this button here and turn it on so, from your bed. Soon you go get spoil, Nana. You not go want to leave."

She had placed the vase with Mrs. Bancroft's flowers on the cabinet beside Nana's bed. She seemed to be measuring the place as if she was deciding on a vacation home. She did the same thing at cemeteries, always comparing one with another for comfort. I never saw anyone like her for sitting on tombstones and distributing Ritz crackers and cheese from her bag, speaking to the living and the dead alike.

"You know, they could wheel me right in here. I could use the rest."

Nana whispered something to her.

"What she say?" asked Mrs. Bancroft, "Is she in pain?"

"No, she say she want me bring her some fish and dumpling when next I come. She say she can't go with the food they serve here. No taste. She don't understand she go get me in trouble. They go stop me from coming. Girl, behave youself. What you do?"

Everyone laughed, even Nana. Then my chair was given to Mrs. Bancroft, which she at first refused, then accepted as it was well cushioned.

"You mustn't feel that you have to rush yourself, you know, Nana. To get better I mean. I know that it will probably take a few weeks before you feel like your old self again."

No one said anything, least of all Nana. We all knew just how good that old self had been. She'd done everything: the cooking, the laundry, the raising of the two children, now adults. She was, in fact, three servants in one body, a trinity. Quietly, Mrs. Bancroft was already considering her alternatives. She realized just how difficult it was going to be to replace her.

Who else knew just the right amount of starch to use on her clothes to keep the shape but not cause irritation? Mrs. Bancroft, her skin was so sensitive. Her husband Frank had been the same way. She'd tried sending things out to the laundry, but it wasn't the same. Inevitably, a rash would happen. But with Nan (as they called her) this was never a problem.

And then there was the issue of trust. She would never feel comfortable leaving her valuables about with other servants. There had been that business with the South American girl who, although she did actually get down on her knees to scrub the bathroom tiles, the way Nana did, and this very much impressed her, still when her watch, her Elgin watch, went missing, her first thought was theft. She was even tempted to call Immigration to have the girl arrested. And even when the watch was found in her bathrobe, where she'd forgotten she'd left it, she still resented the anxiety the incident had caused her. It had been her own fault, but still she never could get herself to ask the girl back. Who needed that anxiety? With Nana you never had to worry.

"As the eyes of servants look unto… the hand of her mistress…" the Bible had said.

What a bother change was. Why couldn't things remain the same? A clockwork Nana who never gave out, just like the Eveready bunny. And, of course, there was the cooking, too. Nana knew just how she liked her things done: the seasoning, the food never too dry or too bland. She had a special gift when it came to making soufflés. Over the years she'd gotten even better. She'd learned from her sister, Frances, in Canada. They'd come over together on the *S.S. Lady Hawkins* and landed in Boston (the landing place of so many Montserratians). The recipes that Nana learned she'd share with no one, not even Aunt Ruth, who had no patience for soufflés anyway.

But it wasn't just the cooking either. Nana had another gift that was special. She could make herself invisible. Once the dishes were cleared away from the table, she vanished. No loud clutter of cutlery or plates to disrupt conversation at dinner parties in the Hamptons or Fire Island, where her friends tried to steal her away. She'd stayed faithful for over twenty years. How could she ever be replaced?

Suddenly, an idea came into her head. She looked at my mother and then at Nana. Why shouldn't the niece share some of Nana's skill? Surely she must have learned something of Nana's magic?

"Excuse me, my dear, but would you be at all interested in coming and filling in for your aunt while she recuperates? You could perhaps do a few days a week, you know…"

Suddenly, my mother was laughing. It was all she could do to keep from falling over. Laughter like rain on a rooftop, she couldn't stop herself.

"Excuse me, have I said something amusing?"

Now even Aunt Ruth joined the laughter.

"Listen, this girl, Phyllis, she don't know nothing name work," said Aunt Ruth.

"I'm afraid I wouldn't be much help to you. Sorry," said my mother.

"She don't even know how to boil water. That's not what she was raised for. Ask her about piano or idleness. Now, *that* she know. She never had to scuffle for nothing. She went to boarding school, like some princess."

Aunt Ruth felt entitled to make fun of her. Nana had given her the right.

"Oh, really?" said Mrs. Bancroft.

"Yes, you better just put she to sit in some chair. *You* woulda do better in a kitchen than she."

"I see."

But she didn't, really. Mrs. Bancroft couldn't fathom the fact that her servant's niece had been brought up like a debutante, which she – née Moira Baker – had not been. Although her husband believed she'd come from a privileged background in Grosse Pointe, Michigan, the truth was that her mother had worked in those houses as a domestic.

Whatever she'd learned about privilege she'd learned from the magazines her mother brought her from the coffee tables of her employers. From an early age, Moira had decided this was the life she wanted. She became the figures she saw in *Vogue* and *Vanity Fair*. She worked endlessly at recreating herself; she studied typing and went to secretarial school and no one who knew her was at all surprised to hear that she'd moved to Philadelphia, and then New York, or that she married well. She had always had an eye for fashion and good taste. *That* she'd been born with. You couldn't cheat that. Still, it bothered her that this girl had been to boarding school and was laughing at her. She couldn't even recall if she had signed for the girl's immigration papers. There'd been so many Nana had asked her to sponsor.

But having failed with the niece, she now turned her attention to Aunt Ruth.

"And how about you, Ruth? Do you think you might want to come and work for a while?"

Aunt Ruth just looked at her.

"I could never cook like Nana, you know. Me good with meat, but I could never do them pastry business the way she do."

"Well, I wouldn't expect you to."

"And you see all them hours she do, I could never do that."

"I wouldn't expect you to be a live-in maid like Nana."

"You know what me think? You go have a hard time finding a next one like she."

"I'll be myself again soon," said Nana.

But things were never the same again. Nana never returned to work. She came home; she got a stroke on her left side and finally got tired of her body because it wouldn't do what she told it to do. She died of disgust. They found she had put money in three different banks and had told no one, not even Aunt Ruth. The government ended up taking most of it. She had a deposit box with a key and no one knew. A key which no one could find.

Now, everyone could understand Nana not telling my mother, who she treated as a child until the day she died. But how could she not have told Aunt Ruth, who she slept with? How did she keep from revealing it even in her dreams? And so Aunt Ruth became Nana, began to send money and clothes to Montserrat and sponsored others to come when they sent the pleading letters that always began with "Greeting, in the name of the Lord", but she never forgave Nana and rehearsed the one question she would ask when next they'd meet, in paradise.

"Why, Nana? Why didn't you trust me?"

As for me, that day changed my life, too. The day Nana got "licked down" by the car, I found my mother hiding inside her like one of those Russian dolls that have endless dolls inside them, one inside another.

My mother lived on an avenue called Tinton in the South Bronx. She kept a room there, not an apartment, just a room. When I asked her why, she said it was because back home she'd lived in a house large with servants and it had meant nothing, nothing at all, because all they did was whisper and gossip and grudge her with bad mind and envy. Where I saw paradise, she saw prison. When my father had touched her, leaning her against a tree, the same tree her mother Frances had leaned against, she fell from grace because he was Kinsale, and she was Cork Hill.

He'd given her a transistor radio so they could carry their world with them, as much of it as they cared about, anyway. Now, here she was in New York on an Avenue called Tinton, where she kept dolls for company, actually spoke to them. Set them up in separate communities because they wouldn't always deal with each other, some on the bed, some on chairs.

Here, she worked in a movie theatre, pierced the dark with her search-light and led people to their seats. It was the perfect place for her. She loved the flickering shadows, the silver screen. She'd invite me to her job and joy. But even after Nana died, I felt guilty about going to meet her. Guilty, because it was like a tryst, like meeting some secret lover and Nana would get to know. What better place than a movie house? She'd get me free tickets and seat me in the last row, bring me franks and popcorn from the concession stand and then, just when I felt safe, she'd come and sit beside me.

"I did come and look for you, you know."

"What?"

"Back when you were small, I would come to see you when you played in the park."

"Which park?"

"Central Park."

Of course, but she never saw when I tried to lose myself there.

"Why?"

"They only let me watch you from behind the fence."

"They" must have meant Nana. I remember a woman watching by the fence, a woman in a grey coat. She never spoke. Sometimes, she'd sit on a bench and watch me. If she tried to approach, Nana would take me away.

"Do you love anybody?" she asked.

I thought it was a trick question. Why should she want to know that? I was just fourteen, more hand-sinned than sinner.

"Sometimes," I said.

"Don't look at me," she said. "Watch the movie. Do you love anyone?"

"Why do you want to know?"

"If you never loved anything or anyone, you wouldn't understand about your father yet, so never mind."

The thing between my mother and Nana was me; the thing that she'd never be forgiven for was me.

She frightened me with her questions, this woman, but I liked her laughter; it was soft and safe there in the dark, although a mother was a dangerous thing to have. Still, without her, there was no memory and no laughter like rain.

ON BEING SENT DOWN FROM YALE

It was a peculiar time, the seventies. More this than that, depending on who and what you were and what colour. Although they said race didn't matter, it did and still does. It was a peculiar time. Paradoxes packed tightly together can make truth.

By the early seventies we had seen in quick succession the deaths of the two Kennedys and Martin Luther King (all televised). Death seen is different from death read. We saw also some sudden corporate gestures made on the part of academia and government working together. One such gesture was Yale University's School of Drama admitting, for the first time, a significant number of black students.

One could be cynical and say that these gestures had more to do with greed for grants than genuine remorse over disparity of opportunities. I'll leave that question to be decided upon by more objective minds than my own. Suffice to say that Yale Drama School found itself in a very peculiar situation. For the first time in the history of the institution, there would be a graduating class of mostly black faces.

Problem: what to do with so many Blacks with nothing to do but be spear-carriers in Shakespearean dramas, all of which must be as distant as possible from reality? (No Blacks must play Othello, for example.) It must be remembered that this was still the reign of Robert Brustein, then czar of the Drama School

So it was that one young playwright (me) decided it would be a good time to take advantage of the opportunity and form a company. The result was the birth of the Yale Black Players, a company formed and christened on the stage of the Yale Playhouse, a former church. Of course, we used the entire school, but in the main the core of actors, stage designers and directors were black. Even our very own theatre administrator, who was a recent graduate of the school and had done her apprenticeship in England (her name Helen Marie Jones), was black. The two plays that we opened and eventually toured with were *The Ode to Charlie Parker* and *The Crucificado*.

I remember there was a feeling of elation of at last being able to show what we were capable of. The actors gave everything of themselves without complaint. There was no such thing as sleep. When we were not performing, we were rehearsing. We were not the only ones who were afire with a sense of mission and purpose. The School of Art and Architecture was near the Drama School. It was impossible to pass it without colliding with someone's vision or rapture. There was tremendous energy on campus, a feeling that anything was possible and that this generation would be an agent of change.

The city of New Haven was electric with social action programmes. The Black Panther Party was alive, well and very active. The population of New Haven was made up largely of those who had migrated from the rural south to work in the many arms factories that existed there during World War II. By the sixties, however, the main employer was Yale University itself and so the inner city, functioned as a fiefdom to provide labour to maintain the smooth running of the campus.

Meanwhile, our theatre company was moving from strength to strength. Imagine our giddy state when we were invited to perform in New York. This we did, over midterm recess and all was well until we received reviews in *The Village Voice*. One day, I was called in to Robert Brustein's office. I entered, certain that we would be congratulated on our success. Surprisingly, there were no handshakes, no smiles, only icy silence. I remember mostly the table. Seated around it were a group of trustees. They seemed like portraits that had somehow managed to step down from their resting places on the university walls and come alive. These elderly bodies, clothed in tweeds, sat silently staring, their gaze fixed on one object: me.

"How dare you. How dare you form a company and call yourselves the Yale Black Players? There is no such thing. Who gave you permission?"

"Well, no one... but I thought..."

"You thought what?"

"I thought there was a need so I answered it."

"What the hell are you talking about?"

"Well, I saw there were actors and no scripts."

"Don't be ridiculous! What do you mean no scripts? We have whole libraries of scripts." Indeed it was true; it seemed that acres of trees had perished in sacrifice to become Yale scripts.

"No Black scripts. There was nothing for our actors to relate to and so..."

"Well, let me tell you something, my good man, the reason for that is because the majority of the world is white, a simple fact of life."

"No, I'm afraid you're wrong about that."

At this point one of Brustein's minions whispered something into his ear, informing him that he was, in fact, incorrect – if not in his world view, at least in his demographics.

"Well, be that as it may, you are still students, and students are forbidden from performing professionally. Didn't you know this?"

No, I hadn't known this. No one had taken the trouble to inform us of this before. I looked at the portrait faces. None of them had said a word, asked a question, queried a custom.

"Well, in any case, it is the decision of this board that you be expelled from school for your blatant disregard of school policy. You seem bent on causing disruption and conflict. If after 24 hours you are found within a hundred yards of this campus, you will be arrested."

The entire meeting took less than half an hour and was a remarkable demonstration of the efficiency and the power of Yale University. Within a day I had, in effect, ceased to exist. Access to housing, library and even the bookstore was closed to me. More interesting still was the fact that I could be arrested if seen. I had become *persona non grata* which is Latin for "one more black face that can be arrested if seen beyond the pale".

The question was what would I do now? Was there life after Yale? It was then that the city of New Haven really opened up to me; the neighbourhood of Dixwell Avenue – which is less than five minutes away from the campus and yet remains unknown to most students for their entire stay – provided me with home and love. Amazingly, Dixwell also provided me with a performance space in the many churches in the area and an exciting audience that was hungry for theatre.

The strangest thing of all was that the School of Divinity turned out to be the most socially active and relevant branch of the University. They provided lighting when we built sets. They never once attempted to censor our scripts or influence our performance. Long after the radicalism of the School of Art had subsided and all the architects turned from revolution to designing golf courses in Japan and Hawaii, the School of Divinity continued to be the one group that tried to defend New Haven from the twin plagues of drugs and unemployment that have left the inner city a wasteland. It was true what that Greek boy, Thucydides, talking about the Peloponnesian War, had to say: Death seen is worse than Death read. What you see with your eyes pierces your heart.

A decade later there would be a new black Dean at the School of Drama. Lloyd Richards would enter and with him came actors such as Angela Basset and Charles Dutton, and writers such as August Wilson, who achieved three Pulitzers before he died. They would make it possible for black students to emerge from Yale Drama School without being regarded as freaks or anomalies.

What I find ironic, though, is that it is still possible for a student to emerge from three years at Yale unaware of the presence of its host community – i.e., the black ghetto (such as circumscribe all the ivy league universities – think Harvard and the slums of Cambridge, think Columbia surrounded by Harlem). Two worlds perfectly sealed and separated one from another. Why do the rich always live within running distance of the poor?

It was a peculiar time, more this than that.

STAGS OF GOD

To know a man's heart you first have to enter his chest. Hammer or saw will do. The body won't forgive you though, and you still won't know what he feels. Only words can do that, so let me try words.

The garment district is still the one place in New York where no one asks where you've come from or why. All they ask is your sweat and that you push their chariots through the labyrinth of the streets. Here only man and cart matter. Man and cart and time, since nothing else can move there. Trucks stall still, like elephants dying. Only the bent body of a man can thread through traffic and so there's always work there, though there's the finding.

To get employment you have to go through an agency. You can't just see a job and beg work or walk up to a truck and offer to unload her like a tanker ship in a port. Here, it's not the unions that stop you; it's the fear that you'll vanish into the ether with all you can carry. You need an agency to vouch for you, but they'll only do that after keeping you around long enough to know your smell. This takes some time, before they send you out.

The one I went to was called Stags and it was on 8th Ave. in the shadow of the city. No matter how early in the morning you arrived, there was already a queue waiting, a queue of those even more desperate. Whether I came at 5:00 or 4:30 a.m., when the streets were in darkness and the rats were still fleeing the spray of the sanitation trucks, there would be others there before me. The office itself didn't open until 6:00, but that didn't matter. We would stand and wait for the galvanized gate to lift and then we'd enter what was a converted loading depot with rows of benches. On the platform, which was above us, sat the foreman, Moose. His desk was there and his swivel chair, where he spent a lot of time. But most important of all were the three telephones on his desk: the Trinity. This was the centre of power because it was by means of these phones that the summons for workers came.

The calls would not start coming in until 7:00, but of course, you wanted to let Moose know that you were there early and that you were willing and able to go. People did everything to gain his affection. It was amazing how many cups of coffee would suddenly appear before him:

"Hey, got a coffee for you, Moose. Just the way you like it, black with three sugars."

He might cross his legs and play with the toothpick escaping from his mouth, and then announce: "No thanks; got two cups already."

Then magically donuts would start appearing or else offers to run to the store for him.

Then you'd wait. If you were lucky you would get a seat against a wall which meant you could doze for a while without falling over. There in the dimness, dreams were free. You could barely make out the outlines of faces, each man in his darkness. Our dreams were projected on the back walls like phantoms; a womb-like hum of conversation and then drift.

And who were we among the shadows, we who waited? Some were Africans who for one reason or another couldn't go home. Perhaps their name was in someone's pocket (be that in a khaki soldier's uniform or the silk suit of a cabinet minister). They couldn't return for *reasons of health*. Then there were Haitians who had little to return to and could do much more for those on the other side by sending remittances. The same for some Latinos, and so we all sat waiting in different languages. Some sat reading newspapers, but you had to be careful not to be caught reading anything heavier than *The Post* or *The Daily News*, otherwise they might think you were a union organizer and you'd never get work.

But come seven o'clock, everything changed with the first phone-call. Now it was Moose's time. He would wait for the fifth ring and then pick up. All of our eyes would be following his hand:

"Morning, Stags Agency. Talk to me."

He would take down the information on a yellow note pad and then transfer the names onto memo slips. At that point the accountant, Silverman, would enter with the key to his little office. Now the day would really begin. Work was assigned according to names in the ledger. In other words, how much a man owed and how much a man brought into the agency determined who was picked first. By eight o'clock everything was pretty much over for the day as far as assignments were concerned. You stayed on and waited regardless, either out of defiance or ennui. What was good was that Moose never looked at you, never even acknowledged your existence until he was ready. When the phone rang he would always look up at the ceiling as if watching the ascent of some insect.

We played the game together for weeks, me appearing and he dismissing. Was he waiting for me to grovel? Of course, the only question was how much. I would sit there and stare at his throat, watch the Adam's apple moving up and down, up and down. Then finally one day he called me. So surprised was I that I pointed to myself to make certain, so as not to embarrass myself by walking up to his desk and then having to sit back down. Yes, it was me he meant. The Haitians have a saying: "God has a branch for every bird."

He wanted me and a Trinidadian named Goodwin. I was trying to decipher the address on the slip he gave me. Fortunately, Goodwin knew the place. We went outside into the blinding sunlight. I was in shock. The world had suddenly changed. I had come out from the cave and the world of shadows and was too stunned to move.

"You better put something in your belly, man, you'll need it," said Goodwin.

I didn't want to take an advance on pay so I settled for a coffee. Ten minutes later we entered the depot which was just three streets away. There I encountered my first chariot. I was assigned a cart piled so high there was no way to see over it.

"So high, you can't get over it. So low that you can't get under."

They gave me a sheet of paper and a destination

"Deliver, get a receipt and get your ass back here. We'll have another one waiting for you, okay?"

I bend, start to push. Nothing moves but me. I bend again, push harder. Nothing – at which point I notice people watching me and shaking their heads. The first thing you have to do is get up the ramp, negotiate it and then the street. Goodwin gives me the initial push (the breath of life). Once in motion, stay in motion. The world is simple, so simple it's frightening. In the mechanistic universe, everything is either push or pull, all else is illusion.

Goodwin, he likes me (well as much as you can like anyone you know for two weeks and may never see again in life). He makes it crystal clear, though: "Hey brother, me can't walk for you."

Meaning he couldn't push my cart and his too. So I had to learn to walk all over again, like a blind man. It's only by walking that you learn to walk.

Streets are different with a cart because a cart has its own mind. It doesn't follow like a lover. It's only the luck of the draw you find one that functions at all without collapsing on you. Each street has a little incline from curb to road. You never notice them – those little inclines – until you need to. It took me three days to commit to the street and not the sidewalk. Three days I kept battling with myself, because to travel in the street against traffic you can't even see, while bent double, is dangerous. The sidewalk is safer but then you have to stop at every corner, step down into the street and then lift again at the next curb. Finally I'd had enough. My back gave out and so I stepped into the road regardless of the danger.

In life, only pain overcomes fear. Pain and hunger. Get hungry enough and you'll eat any dragon. So here you are together in this street, you and your dragon and the only ally you really have is rhythm, both ally and enemy. You have to learn the rhythm of the streets to catch the traffic lights, otherwise you lose and they catch you.

An object once in motion stays in motion unless stopped by another object (say your foot for example). It took me three days to learn that. But then it took three hundred years for us to evolve from goods to services. From slaves to Stags.

Suddenly it was Friday and we got our paycheck. Grumbling, we took it and they explained what the deductions were for. If somehow you'd forgotten about all those advances you'd asked for food and carfare, Silverman (the accountant) was only too willing to show where you'd signed for them.

"This is your signature, right, or do you want to claim identity theft?"

The best part, though, is when they tell you that you can cash your paycheck at this liquor store on 38th street. A check-cash/liquor store (they know that most of us don't have bank accounts), so now you needn't walk too far to find your dragon. It's there waiting. One-stop shopping.

Friday has its own rhythm, one of anticipation and lazy disappointment. Businesses shut down early (before the Jewish sunset) so there's a lot of quick-quick followed by slow-slow motion. Now that you know how to move through streets and negotiate pathways like a big boy, you can make more runs in half the time, which means that you can get back to the dispatch office and get more assignments. But then you reach the phase of the bottleneck: those offices they save for the last because you can only get in through the freight elevator, which is located at the service entrance in the basement.

The elevators can only fit two carts at a time. Two carts and the operator who is in no rush because he knows what you don't: that you can't move without him. So the arguments start now because everyone says "next", but there's no next because everything's stopped dead. There's only one way in and one way out. If no exit then no entrance. Soon the sweat is pouring and we're stealing each other's air like men stuck in a mineshaft. Eventually you surrender.

The elevator operator has proved his point and so people start backing out into the street and let those leaving get by. If worse comes to worst you can always talk back-pain. It's the one topic that unites all men. Even the greatest racist supervisor will give you a five-minute monologue about his lower back. It transcends race and class. The back is the great equalizer because it gives the first whisper of mortality.

Finally, you find yourself back at the dispatch office; you have all your paperwork turned in and now, as you walk that last block towards Stags, you take the weightlifter's belt from around your waist. You lift and lower your shoulders just to see if you still can. There, standing outside Stags is Goodwin, who you haven't seen in days. He's been working loading a truck in Jersey. You want to tell him about the belt that he suggested you get; only he's not listening to you. He's pacing back and forth outside the office, muttering, talking to himself, not too loudly, just enough; a quiet mutter.

"What the hell they take me for?"

"What?"

"Man; not a dog, not a goat, not a child. A man!"

Now I see that he has something in his hand and flings it through the pane glass window at the Stags logo. Everything shatters and now Moose comes out raging.

"You paying for that, hear me? You paying for that. I don't care how long it takes, you paying."

"I done pay already," he says as he crosses the street.

Yes, Friday has its own rhythm. In a million offices along 34th Street, bosses were rehearsing *Death of a Salesman*, while in the twilight streets you could see men following behind their empty chariots back to the depot. Goodwin vanished. He'd flung the bottle and destroyed the Stags window. Now all that was visible was the sign of the previous owner of the warehouse, "Guaranteed Overnight Delivery" (G.O.D.). From Stags to God.

So now Monday, I find myself in my first truck. It feels as foreign as a tanker. Moose told them that I would be replacing Goodwin. They can tell I'm a novice by the way I walk all the way around the back of the truck just to get in the booth. We are three together: Marco, who is the driver and Puerto Rican, and Rufus and myself who aren't. People look smaller from the booth of a truck. Because I'm the novice I have to sit in the middle between two sets of elbows to remind me that I'm not worth the prize of the window seat. Marco only asks one question of me:

"Can you hang?"

When I'm slow in answering, he knows I can't. He's totally disgusted because it means delay while I learn.

Now when I heard the term "hang", I thought he was asking if I could hang out, meaning carry my weight and endure, which in a manner he was. Only later did I learn that hanging is a particular skill in placing garments in a truck at speed, with all items being placed according to size, colour and destination and, of course, having them all face the same direction for easy unloading. To do this means that you have to hold upwards of twenty or more garments in each hand without dropping even one, because dropping anything would interfere with the flow of the assembly line and the next thing you know you have chaos. (Rhythm is your ally or your enemy, remember?)

You have an itinerary of ten or more stops. Every inch of space must therefore be utilized to the maximum and, at the same time, you don't want to mess the crease, or worse, get anything dirty. And most important of all, you have to count every piece accurately because if anything went missing you'd be responsible for it. Of course, moving under that kind of pressure inevitably causes accidents, especially to fingers, since you're dealing with wire hangers and hanging on a wire clothesline (wire to wire equals pain). Take your choice: wear gloves, you lose flexibility; go gloveless and your hands get cut.

Marco was all right as long as everything was flowing. You might even get a smile and a song, but when things started backing-up he'd fly into a rage and there would be no song. That's when the accidents would happen.

"Just don't bleed on the clothes. Blood's hard to clean off."

Since blood was expensive I tried to keep mine.

We covered the entire city from The Bronx to Queens. The garment district was the hub, but because the real estate was so expensive most of the factories and the warehouses were in the outer boroughs. The problem was always time. The dream was to arrive, pick-up, load and exit (like the dream of coming to America, getting rich quick and leaving) but of course it never quite went like that and, most of the time, you had to stand around and wait while the items were still being sewn or ironed. Sometimes you had to load the truck directly from the window of the factory by means of a clothes line. That's very tricky because if anything falls, you're responsible. So you have to send a small batch at a time and monitor the descent. Stand ready to catch everything.

Now Marco was from the paranoid school of trucking. He felt that anyone approaching the truck had robbery in mind. To this end, he always kept a metal baseball bat by the steering wheel, which he would cradle lovingly in his arms. Marco was from the swing-first-and-ask-later school. Anyone even turning their head in the direction of the truck must be challenged and we're expected to back him up. Once I disagreed with him that a passer-by had even noticed our truck. We were driving along and getting ready to approach the Midtown tunnel. He suddenly stopped.

"Get the hell out of my truck! In this truck I'm the captain, understand?"

"Okay, Jefe," I said, getting out. "Since you're willing to die for Stags, you expect everybody else to, right?"

"It ain't about Stags, it's about respect."

I start walking but he pulls up soon and takes me back in.

Marco's strange. He'd retired from boxing after he'd killed a man in the ring who turned out to be a cousin of his. The family never let him forget what he'd done. Now he'd found his way to the garment district where no one asks you why.

I got better at hanging and learned not to bleed so much. I felt good.

One of our main stops was Chinatown. It was there that the invisible became visible. What seemed little more than abandoned bricks and walls

for hanging advertisement posters, turned out to be factories teeming with
workers on each floor. Families lived there. There were elevators oper-
ated by ropes that had to be a hundred years old. We only see the things
we look for. All else is invisible to us in our parallel universes. Now,
suddenly, I realized that the Great Wall of China was still being built – it's
not over. The elevator operator who smokes his cigarette solemnly as
only the Chinese can (meaning that once it's lit, it never leaves the lips
until it dies), takes you to the fifth floor and then places a pin in a hole.
He draws back the metal gate to allow you to step out. But he has to come
out first.

Now you meet a factory floor where women are seated at their sewing
machines, some with children kneeling beside them on the wood floor.
The radio, above on a shelf, broadcasts in Chinese and English. In the
centre of the room is an electric hotplate on which a huge pot of rice is
boiling. Every few minutes eyes glance in the direction of the boiling pot,
the high point of the day. Everyone has their personal vegetables and bits
of fish and pork to have with their meal, but the rice takes pride of place;
it's communal.

Marco goes inside the office with his order sheet, while I go looking
for the water fountain and find instead a water hose and a basin. While
bending over, I notice the rotten floorboards and light shining through
from the office below, which is in full swing. The thought occurs that if
a fire breaks out in this building, the only one getting out alive is the
elevator operator, who probably won't be coming back up for anybody.

Then suddenly you hear the approaching footsteps of a woman in boots.
She looks remarkably like Madame Chiang Kai-shek. She pauses to
examine the work of a girl seated at a sewing machine. There's a quick
exchange of conversation and then suddenly she gives the girl two sharp
precise slaps across the face and flings the garment at her. The girl runs off
in tears with her silent scream. No one says a word or even looks up at
anything except their sewing machine. Only the children's eyes follow
everything. Then Madame leaves to the sound of her boots, the boiling rice
and the voice broadcasting on the radio:

"Today we will learn how we greet someone. Say, hello, Mr. Smith, how
are you today?"

Marco wheels the carts across the floor toward the elevator. He's seen
it all before. He checks his watch as he waits for the slow creaking sound
of the ancient elevator's rising. We load our truck.

Now I know that even cloth cries. Everything costs, but people least of
all. The garment industry is built by the hands of women and on the backs
of men.

The truck is loaded and we head for First Avenue. We stop for lunch because work makes you hungry, except when it makes you sad. I don't want to eat, so while Marco settles down to rice and beans and chocha, I walk over to Second Avenue. There's a theatre there where I have some memories still running: La Mama, Ellen Stewart. The stage door is open and I can't resist looking in, just for a minute.

Theatres when dark are always cold. They have ghosts in them. There's usually one stage light left on, a solitary lamp like a beacon from a lighthouse on a night sea. There's wood from a recent set waiting to be recycled. I can still hear voices: my words in someone else's mouth, suspended, drifting in the ether like time.

Time, what time is it? Suddenly you remember the waiting truck and so you run back to First Avenue, only there is no truck, no Marco. There's nothing, not even the Chinese girl's silent scream. How strange everyone looks to you. Now you find yourself running, running first along the sidewalk and then into the middle of the street. Inside the truck, you never felt this alone. So you run, you run, but chase as you will you never quite catch up to your heart.

OF CLASS

The Cape Verde Islands are located in the mid-Atlantic Ocean some 300 miles off the west coast of Africa. The Portuguese brought their slaves there to breed them, much the way the British brought theirs to Barbuda for the same purpose. Breed them like cattle or sheep. The Portuguese were very good colonizers and kept their empire going well into the 20th century. Now how the slaves and ex-slaves of Cape Verde ended up in Massachusetts is a mystery that only the sea can explain. Just know this: wherever there is sea there is slavery, because wherever there is sea there is piracy and the daughter of piracy is slavery.

All of this history is unimportant. All you need know is that the Cape Verde islands have some of the most beautiful women in the world. One of them was Noelle. Cape Verde, by way of Boston and Roxbury slums and present day slavery and plantations. Then God saw to it that she came to New York and to me. Noelle had a body that made men tremble and women pout. So unique was she that she made even my mother stand when she entered the room. It was as though Queen Elizabeth had entered the Albert Hall. I couldn't believe it. My entire family – blind uncles, paralyzed aunts, all of them – now had only one question when they saw me:

"Where is Noelle?"

It was as if I, who had never done anything right in my entire life, was suddenly given the gift of grace. And what was it they saw? She was the perfect trophy wife. She was the gift, the award of excellence in the black community. The one you married when you became pastor of a major mega-church (think Coretta Scott King, or Lena Horne or Dorothy Dandridge). My mother explained it all to me in a simple sentence:

"You marry her and you children will have the blessing." Meaning they would be light-skinned with good hair and less African features. For everything since the days of slavery has been about getting closer and closer to the big plantation house. The closer to the house you get, the lighter the children and therefore the easier their lives. Of course, the ultimate dream is to enter the Plantation House itself, even if it calls itself The White House. The same rule applies in the Caribbean; the closer you are to the centre of (urban) power, the lighter the people, the better the houses and roads, and the more Anglicised the culture. The more remote ("country people", "people from bush"), the darker and less educated. In Jamaica they call them "The Dungle and Back-a-Yard people".

This, then, was the Noelle who had caused such a sea-change in my life. As my mother, in her wisdom, had said, it was because of Noelle that everyone else around me was suddenly getting pregnant and I became like Krishna among the Gopi girls.

So the question now was what to do. I couldn't marry any of them, because whichever one I married would resent and be resented by the others. Sometimes the best thing to do is just to stand still. So I stood still, but you can get yourself into a world of trouble doing that, especially if you stand beneath the wrong tree. In my case it was the Tree of Life. I had to decide what to do with the trophy woman I was living with. Should I marry her in truth, and make everyone in my family happy – my mother, aunts and cousins, the living and the dead – everybody, except my daughter and my son, who although not yet old enough to talk, already knew her to be the enemy?

Among the unhappy would have to be listed Noelle's family, who wasted no time in making clear to me that they were Cape Verdeans and therefore not the descendants of slaves. When asked how the hell they got to Massachusetts in the first place, they would quickly wheel out the old set-piece about working as sailors on a ship. Working is different from labouring, you see. Slaves laboured but free men worked. So needless to say Noelle's family did not consider themselves black, nor ever dealt with the fact that they were specifically bred by the Portuguese to be house slaves and whores. As I say, the Portuguese were excellent colonizers.

But what do you do with a trophy wife except display her and then torture her in private? Or else she tortures you by making you feel that you don't deserve her. It is only later that you come to find that God doesn't make mistakes; she is exactly what you deserve, just as daughters are exactly what you deserve. It was easy for my mother to be philosophical and detached. She could already see the wedding album on her coffee table.

My mother had an active fantasy life. I've mentioned her dolls. When I told her that she would not need the dolls because I was giving her grandchildren to put on her couch, she gave a loving glance at the dolls and said she preferred to keep them. Of course, if it was Noelle's dynasty that would be different. The dolls would be replaced by long-haired Cape Verdeans and these could sit any damn place they wanted. Not that my mother didn't love her grandchildren, both girl and boy, but she was a product of Caribbean hypnosis.

She was raised to be someone's daughter, eternally.

OF DAUGHTERS AND FATHERS

Daughters are God's irony on man. Not His vengeance or His revenge on us, but surely His irony. Daughters, when they come, are never expected and seldom asked for by men, especially as a first child. Always a surprise – usually more for the father than the mother, who – if she suspects at all – keeps it to herself and devises consolation strategies.

Take me for example. In my innocent mind, I had already seen myself in the park with my son at weekends. The birth of a son is the perfect excuse for going crazy and buying that leather catcher's glove (the good one you could never afford when you were small). I had already been to the sport's store and priced it, together with the leather World Cup soccer ball. (What the hell! Nothing's too good for my boy.) So imagine my surprise that day on the Lower East Side when I entered the hospital room at Mt. Sinai and found there this tiny, sleep-ridden face with eyes closed and wrapped in pink, her mother looking up at me from the bed a little defensively:

"Well, it's a girl. You're not sorry are you? I know you wanted a boy."

I tried to make the appropriate noises: "Oh no, that's cool, just so she's healthy."

But my heart wasn't in it. My mind started drifting around the room. Bye-bye baseball glove. Soccer? Well girls do play soccer, but usually it's with their mothers.

"Well, you want to hold her?"

Now what are you going to say? "No thanks" or "I'd rather not"?

So you fall into automatic mode and your hands go out and hold something tiny and frighteningly fragile, and when suddenly eyes open, your fingers quiver, and you find something looking up at you, and she is tired from all that swimming and crossing over – and she was already two days late in arriving, as most daughters are. They don't rush out of the womb like sons. Daughters take their time, as though they are having second thoughts about whether they want to come.

From the opening of her Pisces' eyes, so filled with tears and sea water, she had me, for she was an immigrant like me. She, too, had come to this city by water. It makes a difference how you enter America. It determines, forever, how you will think of her. For the next two weeks we circled each other – she not altogether sure of me and I frightened of something taking her in the night. Then, after the struggle to lug the crib and the bassinette up five flights of stairs, she decided that she would not spend one night in the crib. Not one. She slept with us every night in the bed, half the night facing her mother, half the night facing me. During the day she didn't mind the crib, but definitely not at night. She breathed on me and with me. Her breath smelled of milk and she kept my terror away.

In the afternoons I'd walk to the park with her. She fit just right atop my head or around my neck and learned early how to cling and not fall. It was usually between two and three o'clock that we might feel adventurous and walk all the way to Central Park from East 10th Street. And since three o'clock is the hour of the Haitian nannies, we might watch them as they walked their white charges; they would often be asked to walk the dog at the same time and so we would watch them as they skilfully navigated their way, pram in one hand and dog leash in the other. I could feel my daughter's head spinning from side to side as she tried to follow all the action.

Usually, on the way up to the park, I would make a pit stop at my drug dealer's apartment. He was from Belize, which the British called British Honduras but the Hondurans called Belize. His name was Enrique and he loved Garifuna music as much as me. He knew quality and sold good drugs. I called him El Maestro and wanted to make him my daughter's godfather since I spent so much time there and she seemed to like him. But he looked at me with his tragic Spanish eyes and said quietly:

"You know, maybe it's not such a good idea to make your dealer the godfather to your daughter. I'm no priest, you know. And maybe you should think twice about even bringing her here, because… hey you never know."

We never spoke about it again, and a little after that somebody showed up at his house with a sawn-off shotgun and there's not too much conversation you have with a sawn-off shotgun pointed in your face; it's not an ideal occasion chit chat. They took everything they wanted but left him with his life that time. The word *grace* comes to mind. It was by grace that I wasn't there with my daughter. And when I think of grace I think of St. Augustine. He used it a lot.

He's my favourite philosopher. I loved him even before I knew he was a black man from North Africa. He was from Carthage (present day Libya, though some say Tunisia) the place the Romans tried to wipe out of existence by spreading salt. Because he was a black man from North Africa, he liked his cockfighting and his women but he also liked God, and so spent a goodly part of his life figuring out in which order he should love them (In *De Ordine*). But what I liked most about him was that he was always asking the question: *How do we know what is real and what is illusion? How can we be sure even of our own existence?* He finally came to the realization that even our

doubt is proof of our existence, for if we did not exist we could not doubt
– which made sense to me at the time. He had a mother, Monica was her
name. I had one too and she was asking me questions much like Augustine's, namely: "So what do you plan on doing with your life now that you
have a child?"

It was by grace, in the first place, that the child was born a girl. Everyone
had expected an exact replica of myself complete with dreadlocked hair,
dark shades and clenched-fist salute. Instead they got this calm angel child
with dimples and eyes you swam in. They couldn't burn me in the pit as
they had longed to do, not quite yet anyway. I'm speaking of the maternal
grandparents who noticed the fact that I had not married their daughter, but
seemed quite happy to impregnate her.

Time helps with seeing and so now I can better understand how they
must have felt to see their one daughter, in whom they had invested so
much hope and struggle, the daughter who had defined them as good
parents because they had managed to send her to Yale – which was no little
thing for a black man who worked as a chauffeur in racist Columbus, Ohio,
where eight out of ten people they knew had children either in or on their
way not to college but prison – and now, just as they were about to retire
and enjoy the sleep of the good, here comes Satan in the form of some
dreadlocked West Indian boy, from a Caribbean island that they had never
heard of, to ruin everything.

But daughters, as I say, are God's irony. The parents were willing to cut
their loss and retrieve her and take her back before I gave her yet more
babies, for a daughter with one child born out of wedlock was still a saleable
item, especially with a degree from Yale. Two or more, however, now that
would have been a disaster.

"Girl, come home to your parents. There's no future with him. The
boy's a dreamer and we've heard things about those West Indians; they
make babies all over the place."

Nor were they too thrilled with the strange African name I had given
their granddaughter: Onika.

"What the hell is that? Why couldn't he give her a good Christian name
like Mary or Martha?"

But they soon fixed that. After a week, Onika became Nikki and then
Nicole, something they could live with. This done, they returned to Ohio
to pray and await the inevitable.

The inevitable didn't take long in arriving, for a year later, just as she
began walking and climbing steps and opening doors and drawers and
touching anything and everything you said not to, I found that I was about
to be a daddy again, only this time it was not with her mother but with
another girl. Saint Paul speaks of the thorn in the flesh; perhaps what he

really meant was the thorn *of* the flesh. So, finding myself in a dilemma as how best to deal with the situation (for situation it was), I decided that if all else failed it was best to tell the truth, especially if you have no choice, having just got the news very late in the pregnancy.

What sealed it was the birth of my son. I had to try to get all parties together and have a calming and healing session like extended families are supposed do in Africa. The only problem was that this wasn't Africa. Here, in New York, when young unwed mothers hear about other children being fathered by their man, they aren't pleased. So no, there would be no sitting together in unity under a baobab tree. All I remember was a wild piercing scream followed by the question:

"How could you, how could you do that to me and to *your* daughter?"

The unpardonable sin was of having a son with another girl, not even a full year later. Why didn't I, at least, use a condom? Because I'm from the Caribbean and don't want anything to get in the way of my feeling? Because of the thing we have called macho? And since I was macho, then my son must be Machito, or little Macho. I don't remember exactly what more she said, although I remember the word *Bitch!* being frequently used in connection with my son's mother, and what she was going to do to that…

Then the tirade turned to my person, with hands and nails reaching for my face, and what hands couldn't reach, feet could. Suddenly there was no Yale, no anything but street, and she was doing what any of her friends would have done if they had felt themselves played and disrespected. She was going to make me have to hit her, begged me to, while she scratched and clawed and ripped my clothes and reached for anything that her hands could capture. So Africa did come into it after all, because she leapt like a Wolof princess right into my face and told me to kill her. Then I realized that she was serious, that this was what she wanted me to have to do. My hands were around her neck, and I was seconds away from cancelling two lives, when somewhere in the horizontal blur of the floor I saw this figure moving and realized that those Piscean eyes staring at me were witnessing everything. Our daughter was watching me kill her mother and she wasn't even crying. Pisces don't cry out loud, they use the silent scream.

Grace is Augustine's favourite word. After that day it became mine too. It wasn't two lives that were saved that day, it was three. Disaster only takes a moment to enter. After that, I never let myself be alone with my daughter's mother again, because I never had known anyone who could get me so out of control. But this was someone's daughter and the mother of a daughter, *our* daughter.

It was time to seek some succour and advice from someone, and my mother was the closest thing I had, so I went to inform her about the birth of her grandson. She was less than enthusiastic and I had a difficult time getting her to turn away from the television. She watched it religiously, from Perry Mason to Colombo. It was her one treat since she could no longer go on long bus rides to Niagara Falls with her old friends from the Montserrat Progressive Society. Diabetes had been plaguing her for some time now. She waited until the commercials to question me:

"So now, what you plan on doing? You now have a daughter and a son. I can't understand why you so foolish and stubborn. I think I must have drop you on you head when you small. Didn't I tell you a million times Noelle is the one you should marry. Leave the rest of those girls alone. They can't do a thing for you. Noelle, she is class. Don't you see that these others just get themselves pregnant to try and take you from her?"

My mother was no Monica, mother of St. Augustine, but she had her moments. She gave me pause to think. Now I must admit that I have always had trouble seeing the obvious. Whether it was from a fall I had from a rooftop when I was a child in Montserrat or not, it had really never occurred to my ten-watt brain – before my mother mentioned it – that anyone would really plot to get themselves pregnant by me in order to get me away from Noelle. But given who Noelle was, it did begin to make sense – the whole chess game that was being played out while I was busy dealing with St. Augustine and his Confessions.

OF ENGLAND II

Fortunately, one of the things that I wrote found its way to England and got me an invitation to follow it, which I did, and this too is what Augustine meant by grace and gift. Plays sometimes travel and run.

I went to England for a week and ten years later I found myself still there. That had something to do with the fact that every time I phoned America they kept telling me about another friend who was in detention for political offences, who had died of gunshot wounds or, in even greater numbers, from something they called AIDS. What this was no one could explain to me, except that its presence resulted in death. First they said drug addicts got it from dirty needles, then it was just gays who had it – and I was all right so far – but then they said it had to do with having unprotected sex. I started to have less and less desire to return to America any time soon.

I was also completely addicted to the BBC and to news, real news, not entertainment. The more I heard about America and the CIA involvement everywhere in the world, and how the World Bank and the IMF were working diligently to make sure that the so-called Third World would be in debt forever, and that the most brutal US-supported dictators remained in power until their last geriatric days – the more I learned about the States, the less eager I was to return. Yes, England is a good place to get information about anything except itself (for example, that it is the second largest arms dealer in the world). To learn that about England you had to return to America which, as I said, I was in no rush to do.

What England also gives you, in abundance, is history, especially British history – as they like to see it. And fair enough, no one is ever eager to hear too much truth about themselves; it's never quite the right time for a writer who is only interested in doing that. It's like trying to sell a book to a blind man and the book's not in Braille. But England remains a good place to either read or write a book, because its other attribute is boredom.

I missed my daughter, but did I miss her enough to want to die for her? I told myself that when she was old enough I would send for her – though her grandparents would never let her go unescorted to live with some crazy West Indian father in darkest London.

Even so, England is a good place to heal. It's a postwar country, by which I mean it's a good country to come to recover after a war. Its two primary colours are green and grey: green in its spring from constant rain and grey from its continuing dampness. Eventually, it becomes calming to the eye. All in all, there is the atmosphere of an asylum, an asylum in which the patients, having become totally familiar with its wards and corridors, are content to walk and read. Actually, reading while walking is quite a common activity. This way no one has to actually look at anybody else and this ability to navigate around others without seeing is itself a very British thing – this and the obsession with detail. They say the smaller the island, the madder the mind. England is a very small island. That is why they needed to rule the world.

So here I was, nicely settled into my English asylum, thanking God for His grace in letting me get away from America for an entire decade and thus saving my life, for there's no doubt that had I been in America in the 80s, living the way I was living with my condom-less self, I would surely have contracted something interesting enough to move me off this planet. As it was, my activities in England were very quiet, quiet for me anyway. England had its share of AIDS, but it avoided me. As I say, by grace.

Just then I got a letter that focused my mind:

"You better come and see about your son. He's at that age."

And what age is that? That age when he is a large enough target for both police and street gangs to see and shoot. My mother summed everything up for me when she said:

"It's been ten years. Whatever book you were reading or writing you should've read it by now. Come home. See to your children."

She didn't mention that she, too, needed some seeing to. And so I left England and came home to America.

OF THE REMNANT

When they asked Augustine who it was that he was writing for he said, "For God and the remnant." But then he had a rich mother. I didn't. I had a poor one who had once enjoyed privilege but who now looked from her South Bronx window and more and more considered jumping, and perhaps would have, were it not for the scandal she knew it would cause back home in Montserrat.

When I came home to New York/Carthage, I found a city gone strange with homelessness and the new poor, whole families camping out in the shadow of City Hall, people calmly foraging in garbage cans, and not an eyebrow raised in amazement. This was not the city I left ten years before. People were totally selfish without apology. I remember at Penn Station on 34th Street seeing a mother asleep under a blanket on the subway floor with her child in her arms, and people walked around and over her and continued conversations without missing a beat. They saw nothing, felt nothing. You couldn't tell the people from the garbage. In front of an office marked Human Resources, the junkies bent like trees and waited.

I went in search of my son and his mother, who were living on Riverside Drive among the new Dominicans. He was growing fast and had already cut his dreadlocks because he was tired of people mistaking him for a girl. It was a time for street gangs and video games. The two went together because to the street gangs, violence and war were just video games – the taking and giving of a life nothing more than the flex of hand on the throttle of a play station. No more real than that. I saw with my own eyes a Dominican youth calmly step out of a car (a car that had been slowly driving on the sidewalk) and go up behind a man he was following and shoot him three times at point blank range in the back of the head. Everybody looked away and tried to go for cover. The youth, just as calmly, went down into the subway. Next stop, Dominican Republic, to the house and land that hit earned him. I realized it was time now to get my son.

But that's not easy after years away, because you don't know who he is or who he might be. The best thing to do is find some neutral ground, some street you can walk to together and talk and not talk. First thing you notice is that he looks like his mother; this is good – if daughters favour their fathers, that's another instance of God's irony. So you walk with this boy and the second thing you notice is that he has big feet, like you. And the weary way he bends his back in concentration, that's you too. You start to think, "Damn, genes are strong. You can run but you can't hide."

So you walk along, talking and not talking. You ask about sports, and no, he's not big into sports. Little basketball, that's it. He wonders if you'll hold that against him and you swear that you won't. This is a different generation. They spend as little time as possible outside. Why? Because they're lazy? No, Pop, because outside is where you can get shot.

You tell him about growing up in the South Bronx and he says he knows about it and that's where both his grandmothers live. It shocks you to know that he's been visiting your mother regularly, taking your place. You've never really thought of her as the boy's grandmother. Women are wise. His mother made sure that while you were away in some place called England, contact was being made here at home. As I've mentioned, my mother never saw me much as a child. She was only allowed to glance at me from behind a fence in Central Park. My son she could at least touch.

So I'm learning him, this young man who is my shadow, extended before me. I want to look good to him. You want to look good for your son. He meets a friend and doesn't introduce me as his father. The word feels strange in his mouth so he doesn't use it. We walk some more and then we enter the building at 800 Riverside, and as we are walking up the steps to the apartment I trip and fall.

You trip because half of your mind is back there in Central Park on that woman, your mother, watching behind the fence. The other half is thinking about the day he got born and that house. So you trip on a stair and watch him come to help with that look of worry and love, and yes you're fine, fine but what's in your eyes now is tears and you… and you can't think why. It was that 7th step that you tripped on. It's some twenty years later and they still haven't fixed it. It's like the step in some ancient cathedral worn by the knees of peasants, or even by their kisses. Maybe they're just too cheap to fix that seventh step at 800 Riverside.

It was an interesting season to return to America – unapologetic America where the gospel of prosperity was still being preached loudly from pulpits by both black and white pastors. It had to be shouted from pulpits and the White House in order to drown out the noise of starvation – all those homeless people sleeping in subways and lining up for soup kitchens. The pastors had to convince those who had homes and money that they were God's elect.

"God wants you rich; that's why you are. And don't forget that this America is God's country; that is why He has so richly blessed us."

This said, they pulled away in their limousines to their suburban homes.

I was amazed, when I returned, to find two things: firstly, that hardly any black ministers with a church in Harlem actually lived in Harlem. They all lived in the suburbs and merely came to work in Harlem. Secondly, that all the construction work in Harlem was being done by Eastern Europeans (mostly Polish or Serbian) and beneath them, doing the actual grunt work, were Chicanos. No Blacks could get in the unions. Not even in Harlem, never mind the rest of the city. Those working on the highways were invariably either Italian or Irish. Those who worked as firemen, even in Harlem, were almost to a man Irish. The only work available for Blacks was in the police department, security, or underground on the railway, though sanitation was beginning to open up as more and more Whites abandoned these professions.

Did I want to go under the earth for the next twenty years? The answer was no. So I stayed home and helped raise my son. What I didn't realize was that most of his friends hadn't seen much of their fathers either – and they hadn't been away in darkest England. They were in places like Riker's Island, Sing Sing, Green Haven and other exciting "correctional" facilities. There was also a whole generation who only went outside to go back and forth to school. Other than that they hardly ever dared to venture out.

The police, meantime, were busy with sweeps in which they would descend on a given area where they suspected drug trafficking and just arrest van loads of people, thus fulfilling their quota of arrests. It worked in Harlem among the Blacks, and in the South Bronx among the Blacks and the Puerto Ricans, but when they got to Washington Heights, the Domini-cans didn't want to dance. They had decided that not just police should have guns. So when the police started using helicopters on roof tops, I didn't need CNN to tell me I was living in a battle zone. It started to look like Lebanon or Bosnia.

So went my first year back in America.

Soon the apartment at 800 Riverside started looking like a cadet barracks. We were doing work-out sessions and homework and it was just a safe hang spot, and soon word spread (since nobody wanted to venture to the park and get shot). Soon I was teaching reading and literacy (once you teach one, the others get jealous so you have to teach everybody). There was even a new definition of father. A father is anyone who sticks around. God is a father because he does that. Sons are good things to have. Good things to come back to.

But daughters are more complex because they look more like you but they don't speak. They don't say what they fear. So the only way you know them is by who they stray to.

While I was away "reading my book", as my mother said, my daughter was being raised by her grandparents and her uncle. Her grandparents thanked God, not me, for making her possible, for she turned out to be the one bright light in their last years. Me they never had too much use for. One day when Nicole was in elementary school, they read one of my books over the school intercom and when she told them that it was her daddy's book they were reading, none of them believed her. Said she was a liar. Her mother had to come to school to prove it. Nobody knew what a writer was. They knew what a cop was. They knew what a prisoner was. They knew what a soldier was, but not a writer. If St. Augustine said he wrote for God and the remnant, I say, if asked, I write for a living and for my children, who will never read my work unless they stumble across it on their way somewhere else.

As I say, daughters are strange things. They come as a surprise and part of God's irony and then they hold time against you. If you have a son they hold him against you too. If they ever forgive you at all, it is if the two meet and see themselves in each other's eyes, away from mothers, away from fathers: always away from you.

I wrote once that if a man was to come upon his daughter by the side of a dark road he would no more know her than he would the night around her. But that's not necessarily so. He might know her by the shadow she makes on the ground before her. There are things you can say to a son that you can never say to a daughter. You can ask him, when he makes love to his girlfriend, whether she laughs or cries when she comes. He will look at you with the disgust with which all youth looks at any age greater than theirs. He will never answer you because that remains in the realm of intimacy that cannot be shared. But the question does get him thinking:

"Why would you ask that, Pop?"

"Because some women laugh and some cry. Some women do neither. There's no correct way; it's just that if you can get a woman to laugh with you, then you can usually get her to love you. You are more than half way there. Some are so grateful for laughter that they find their release right there"

But the truth is that he probably can't tell if her eyes are open or not because he isn't looking at her. It takes years to look at a woman and really see her. For the most part, all we see is ourselves. With our eyes closed we see the woman we want, not the one that we're with.

I married once. It wasn't the one my mother wanted, but it was one whose eyes I liked to look into when she came. She was someone who had come from the same Caribbean island as me, and so I thought I wouldn't have to explain myself as much (as if I could, in any case). We had the same humour and, as I've said, if you can make a woman laugh… She had the strong arrogant body of a Senegalese and the dark skin to match. What was good was that loving her was like loving myself. She had the audacity to announce that she would take me away from all the women that I'd ever known. I asked her why she thought so, was her loving so strong? She answered simply:

"Because I have more imagination than they do."

She was right, she had. To meet a woman who tells you in advance exactly what her desire is and what she will do to you, without guile or coyness, is amazing. It can be frightening if you feel in anyway timid. It is like stepping into the ring with the young Mohammed Ali, who loved to tell you exactly where he would hit you next and in what round he intended to knock you out, and you were utterly helpless to prevent it.

It was a refreshingly new stratagem and it got me, because male arrogance is a woman's greatest weapon. We always feel we are in control, but she was a PhD in just how much women keep hidden from men because they know how threatened men are by the potential loss of power. How many private secretaries actually run businesses for their bosses, but never take the credit and, of course, are never paid equal to their worth? The question becomes: is the whole gender issue in society really about economics when all is said and done? And this just leads to the next big gorilla in the room that is never mentioned, race.

I suspect that white women in particular are masters of stroking and lying to their men because they, more than any other, know just how explosive that whole issue is. The role of the white woman to her mate is that of cheerleader and silent accomplice. Women have traditionally been one step away from slavery. In early America, for example, women were regarded as chattels (and a woman was certainly moveable). Upon marriage the wealth of the woman was assumed by the man. So you have George Washington becoming instantly wealthy upon marriage to Martha, taking over everything, including her slaves. He then uses the excuse that he would free the slaves were they his, but alas, they are really his wife's property (which of course he owns and exploits to the maximum). Then we have Jefferson who does a similar thing with his dead wife's slave, and goes one better because he impregnates her and makes several generations of mixed-race slaves with Sally Hemmings – whom he never acknowledges as his concubine. What is most interesting of all is that his daughter (his white daughter) witnesses everything and yet says nothing. So what is that peculiar relationship of daughter/father as she watches him slip nightly through the secret passageway (not for nothing was Jefferson an architect) that connected his room with that of his Negress? Daughters always know. They know first as daughters and then as wives. They know to see and not see. They know the cost of things.

Yes, we don't want to stumble and fall before our daughters, whereas we can be vulnerable before our sons who, we feel, should somehow be better able to understand, because sons have the same third legs and can therefore be expected to understand that a father can trip over it. A man's greatest fear is to become senile and incontinent, and have to be changed by his daughter. I know that I pray nightly that this never befalls me.

America is the land of the disposable parent as well as the disposable diaper, and the two are connected. There are more nursing homes in America than anywhere on earth. Parents now live longer than at any time in history. In previous centuries, there was always either a predator, an illness or an affliction that solved the problem of old age. Certainly among the enslaved, there was no such problem, especially in the Caribbean when the average working life was seven years. Seven years of labour as a cane cutter was usually enough to solve any problem about growing old. But in the present day plantation you can, and very often do, grow old and labour for longer periods, even with diabetes and prostate cancer and the myriad of other goodies that are common afflictions of black males, either in or out of prison.

One day I decided to deal with one of my fears. I got my son and my daughter to meet. I introduced them and sat back with a teddy bear that I had purchased. When my daughter tried to take it from me, because she thought it was a gift for her, I explained that, no, this was in fact for me and it was the only protection I had and therefore couldn't part with it because he (Augustine I'd named him) was at least on my side. My daughter looked at my son (Machito or little Macho, since I was big Macho) for confirmation of what she had long suspected – that her father was totally insane. They got on very well and found they had a lot in common, besides a father. It was good to see them. Good to see myself in them, the best and the worst of myself.

Daughters really are God's irony because we bring them into the world just to give them away. We give them away so that they bring back grandchildren to humanize us. Perhaps by the time of grandchildren, we have learned to be parents. No other animal has offspring which return after leaving the nest. Only man returns on holidays with offspring. The Caribbean is littered with broken and extended families, alliances more complex than any UN gathering. You will find every shade and every accent within one family, which might extend to twelve or more islands. It is always the daughters who make the connections and thread the tapestry that was her father's life, not the sons, because they are too busy trying to comprehend their own spider's webs to make any sense of the larger pattern. This is true regardless of what economic system we live under.

In plantation life it was usually the son who was driven off first, like a young lion. He either escapes or is sold. The daughters tend to stay with the mothers for a longer time. When it comes to present day immigration, it is the son who tends to leave first to find his fortune in the new world; the daughters after.

The relationship of daughters and their fathers is a strange one. As a result, there are two things that you can never hope to do. The first is to rival a dead father in a wife's or partner's affections. You can never better a memory, for memory adds perfection to every portrait. That lesson cost me a wife, for I could never equal a man who had become a legend in his daughter's mind. The second impossibility with the daughter in a wife is to try to achieve forgiveness for a man who you've never met and yet are held responsible for. For with daughters all wounds are fresh and the blood still flows, although unseen. The bed you sleep in with her is always a very crowded one, filled with all these unseen ghosts (fathers, uncles and even grandfathers). Do you understand now why there's so little room left under the blanket for you? You can never rival a father nor clean up the damage done by one.

I remember how jealous my daughter's uncle was of me; he over protected her, preventing her from visiting her strange West Indian father because he didn't trust people who came from the islands. All that he could picture was a wild man wielding a machete and lighting voodoo candles. Well, I was fresh out of candles but he managed to keep my daughter away from me for a good bit of her childhood. Of course, the rest was my doing. Yes, daughters and their fathers are funny things – and the surrogates who take the place of fathers and become protectors.

And yet in lives that are sometimes stunted with fog and fear, daughters have always been our greatest grace and our greatest chance for salvation. When you ask Augustine's question: how do we know that we really exist? The answer is that we exist through our children and it's really only because they exist that we begin to know why we do.

SLAVE SHIPS AND PRISONS

There are two things in the world for which there is no disinfectant: slave ships and prisons. The smell of want and fear, sex and despair seeps into the walls and never can be gotten rid of.

America has the highest prison population in the world. There's a place called Riker's Island and it's the largest prison facility in the universe, the "home of New York's boldest". (It was there that Dominique Strauss-Kahn, the former head of the IMF, was held while awaiting bail when charged with raping that African chambermaid in his pricey hotel room.)

I made a visit to Riker's, not to see Strauss-Kahn, but Tariq, a Haitian friend of mine. But when I arrived he had been moved, like a package, to Woodbourne, another prison facility. I had a play that I had written for him. The theatre saved me and I hoped it would save him. In prison you either use time or do time. The play was about Iraq on the eve of the invasion. I called it *The Birds of Baghdad*.

I first became involved with prison when I was teaching Creative Writing at City College. It was a good fit because the education system taught me a lot about prisons and vice versa. I found that the prisoners I dealt with had one thing in common: illiteracy.

The most common sight you'll see in any black neighbourhood, be it the Bronx, Harlem or Brooklyn, is the presence of no less than four armed police at every entrance to a public school. It's mind control for students. This way they have no problem adapting to prison. They get used to daily searches. It's in fact, a self-fulfilling prophecy. It sends a signal. But no matter what form power assumes, youth will find a way to subvert it. When you see those young girl students, even in the charter schools, wearing their clean and clinging uniforms, you realize they will never be subdued.

At City College all I was asked to do was to help students to become literate enough to become good wage-slaves, and if possible keep them out of prison. Together with students you share a conspiracy. Together you pretend that you want them to read and question everything. In truth, both you and the students know what's really required. Translation: it's possible to survive quite well in America knowing nothing more than how to read and write your name and being able to make sense of the front page headlines of any tabloid newspaper.

Before I jumped ship I was an adjunct professor. If you check the dictionary you'll find that "adjunct" means something added on, like an appendage – in other words, something unnecessary, an afterthought. The Holy Grail is to make tenure. You see, without tenure there is no health insurance, which means that if you come down with cancer you're on your own. So professors kill for tenure, but they mostly kill themselves

Where I did find a hunger and thirst for books was in the prisons, because only there did the lights go on and reality set in. At first I didn't want to go. I refused requests for three years to start a writing workshop. Once I started, I couldn't stop. You can get addicted to anything, even prison. I got caught up in their lives. Once an inmate reads his first book, he can't stop either. It takes him places not even drugs can. They keep asking for more books. I couldn't fulfil all the requests I got once the lights were turned on. They keep asking, "Why was it I never read nothing when I was outside?"

"Because you didn't need to."

"They told me all my life I was too stupid to read anything. Then here you come along and tell me books can set me free. You right, though. Once I start reading I don't even see this place."

They even started reading poetry. Poetry is big in prisons because you can pass poems easy, like cigarettes.

Teaching in prisons can be the most rewarding thing anyone can do in this life. The only problem is the blood. Every time I left a prison with some of the writing samples, my briefcase would grow heavy with the weight of blood.

Working with prisoners kept me in touch with reality. The greatest resistance I encountered was not from the inmates. It was the guards who were jealous of the fact that prisoners were getting a free education. I soon realized that I would have to teach them too.

There was the fascination, too, of all were the people visiting prisoners: not only the wives and girlfriends, who were probably glad that their men were in some facility and that they couldn't spend the night playing on other women's drums, but the parents of prisoners.

Question: What do you do when you encounter the pastor from your church visiting his son? You know for certain that this is no ordinary prison ministry visit because you see him throwing up outside the gate. He has had to step out of his Cadillac car in order to perform this operation and you suddenly realise that he hates prisons more than you do. It is then that you thank God for that basic training that you've gotten from Montserrat back home. Montserrat, that land of denial, where you learn to see and not see; hear and not hear. For example, when you see a woman cussing her man in the street:

"See you, you just a damn scamp and a waste of space. You feel you a bad man, right? Big time lover."

"Me tell you, me barely know the gal!"

"Lie you a tell 'bout you barely know she. Is there you sleep last night. Me watch you and she leave the club together so please, jus stop lie. Don't insult me and play me for no fool. You feel you is lover? Well hear now, two can play the game. Me knuckling you and you no even know."

"Wa?"

"Me say me a knuckle you and you no even know, and what's more, it not even you that take me head. He could last all night, and you, (sucks her teeth) you just a dribble. So go back a sleep where you sleep last night. Me kyarn go wid you no more."

She exits, leaving him stranded, and he turns to me shamefaced knowing I witnessed the scene. That's when you take out a copy of *The Montserrat Reporter* and start to read, leaving him time enough to make an orderly retreat and go after her without actually running.

But what could I say to put my pastor at ease? The answer was nothing. Sometimes there is no chit of chat that solves anything. So I said: "Hello Pastor" and let it go at that. The truth was that he was an arrogant son of a bitch who owned a Cadillac car and a yacht – a small yacht but a yacht none the less. He liked to see his name carved into the side of buildings. He knew that *Ebony* magazine had named him as one of the ten most influential pastors in the Southern Baptist Convention. But all this still couldn't get his son out of prison or save him from having to go visit him because his wife was more powerful and she had probably threatened to leave him if he didn't make the visit. He knew damn well she'd do it, too. So he was forced to leave his solid gold cross and his several gold rings at the gate. He'd never felt more naked.

Once inside, he knew he had to take the seat at the table facing the guard. His body language would have told everything. He would never once have looked at his son directly. Their conversation I can imagine.

"You did all this just to shame me, right?"

"To shame you? That's what you think? Listen, Pop, not everything is about you."

"Sent you to the best school. Gave you everything. Your mother spoiled you rotten and then you turn around and rob us blind."

"I had a $300-a-day heroin habit. What the hell else could I do? You stopped giving me money!"

"You could try working for a living like everybody else."

"Doing what, being a preacher like you? Rob from the collection plate, right?"

Pastor turns to slap his son but he knows he might just slap him back. So instead, he signals to the guard that this visit is terminated. He's fulfilled his obligation. He'd promised his wife that he'd come, not that he'd stay. This isn't worth a heart attack. Uneasy is the neck that wears the cross.

If the new radical movements like Occupy are to be relevant they have to address the prison problem. There is no one in the black community (and I assume Occupy wants the black community) who, in one way or another, is not affected by the prison industry. Everyone has some experience, if not as an inmate then through family members or employment as guards. We either feed it or feed off it. Closely related to this is homelessness. Believe it or not, more vets die in prison than die in battle. They return from Iraq or Afghanistan and find themselves homeless and abandoned by society. Next stop: prison.

ALWAYS OCCUPY

And so I left Montserrat yet again for America. I recalled an earlier return and the thought that it was like returning to the scene of a crime. I don't know why but it felt like that. Unlike volcanoes, which don't use passports and don't waste time going through customs, each time I returned I was made to do the "immigrant shuffle", one step forward, two steps back, then you shake your backside along with the others, we the people of baggage. When they asked me what country I was from, and I answered Montserrat, they would always correct me and inform me that Montserrat was not a country. It was a British dependency. Britain was a country. To which I'd respond: "But I wasn't born in Britain, I was born in Montserrat."

They would look at me as a mother does her demented child, shake their heads but wave me through.

I see now that God was merciful when I was a child, when He saw to it that I started my exile in America and not England. England is a land without dreams. What you're born to, you stay with. Instead of dreams, England has pride and that pride helped her conquer the world. On the other hand, America is a land of dreams and dreamers to dream them.

But on one earlier return I had found myself back in America for the next ten years, without any dreams of going to my island in the sun, which would always be waiting for me as if I'd never left. On that return, the money tree, supposedly so abundant in America, had taken its time sprouting and so I found myself, as I have described, doing things like "pushing the Jewish chariots", as they called working in the garment district of Manhattan at 34th Street.

Now I was returning to perform three of my plays in New York. It was almost a year I'd been away and New York, the city of cities, had changed. A year is a long time in New York. I learned that as soon as I went in search of Borders bookstore on 59th and Columbus Circle. Borders no longer existed; it was gone, gone not only from there but everywhere in the city. Borders had been sodomized and then eaten whole by Barnes and Noble and other bigger aggregates. They no longer existed in New York, and if you don't exist in New York you don't exist.

Fair enough. I went to Barnes and Noble instead. It gave me a refuge to gather myself before the battle ahead. I had burned my bridges and changed plantations before. My last return home to Montserrat was something of a desertion, an unpardonable sin. Not that they loved me in Montserrat either, but people always love you more when you're somewhere else. I had given the wrong answers to girlfriends and wives and so found myself homeless. I was a man without keys. But I'd rather be keyless in the world than clueless.

Now, back in New York it was spring and there was even hope of summer. Barnes and Noble was a good place to start. There, among the overpriced Starbuck's café-latte with exotic sounding names, there were endless books and magazines that would help me catch up on changes, and there were the inhabitants of Barnes and Noble itself, a microcosm of New York.

You had tourists (those who dipped their snouts into their coffee cups), and the Blacks and Latinos who serviced them and for this received carfare allowance disguised as pay checks. You had the literate homeless as distinct from the illiterate who spent their day in parks. Then you had those who still had homes and so spent their time reading biographies of the rich and famous, mainly movie stars or singers. You also had the young students from Juilliard, the premier music school just a few blocks and several auditions away. Most of them were children of concert orchestra musicians, some of whom got to play at the Lincoln Center, which was directly across the street from Barnes and Noble. All of this made the place ideal for gathering your forces. It was also a good place from which to make phone calls to friends who wished you dead.

Now, it's important when you're calling friends and seeking refuge not to sound desperate. This is more easily done as you watch young nymphets (of which Barnes and Noble has an abundance) who already have fame in their eyes. And despite the fact that they have no money yet, their parents do, and their bodies give even the poor hope. It's easy then to forget that a quarter of the population is surviving on dog and cat food. Scarcity makes these young girls even more appealing.

You see, Barnes and Noble exists on the Hollywood system – where only ten percent of actors actually work. Yet this ten percent is enough to carry the other ninety. Likewise in the bookstore, only ten percent of people actually buy books and magazines, yet this is sufficient to keep the store open.

Now although most of my friends were vague, some stayed true, which was good because I didn't want to have to sleep in that park across from Barnes and Noble where, somewhere between fame and famine, I'd spent many a night half-dreaming.

Although I'd been away only a year, a lot had taken place. Wall Street had
collapsed and managed to take half the world with it. Never before in the
history of the world had so few mad men with power managed to affect the
lives of so many. So this, then, was post-Armageddon America.

I wanted to see for myself if what I'd read was true. So on my second day
in New York I took The 1 Train to Wall Street. Wall Street is a very personal
thing with me because the first commodity sold there was me. Consider
Wall Street as a betting shop where they made wagers on everything, even
the Middle Passage. The stock market is that great game of chance that
started with slavery but now dealt in houses as well as lives. Now, thanks
to Alfred Jones, something mystical had been created, called *hedge funds*,
made from tears and misery.

Banks closed and men grew richer. Wall Street itself is an irony because
it was once the first black ghetto, the first Harlem. There, graveyards
abound. So you can understand why I wanted to see their faces, this new
crop of traders. I wanted to see if there was any sign of panic or remorse; but
no, there was nothing. They were absolutely the same. They were still
certain in their certainties; still wore the same Brooks Brothers suits, still
arrogant masters of the universe.

There was no cutting back in their lifestyles. The young lions still went
outside at lunchtime in their shirt sleeves and suspenders and bought ganja
from the young Blacks and Latinos who dealt and dwelt there. They still
gathered in front of office buildings, Goldman Sachs and 666 (the biblical
number of the beast) and still called themselves: "The big swinging dicks."

The only thing that was different was the small gathering of youthful
protesters who called themselves *Occupy*. The traders didn't like them
because they brought too much attention. The common thinking was that
Occupy would exist only for a few days and then go away. They were just
young, after all, and so they'd soon grow bored. Impatience is a young
man's vice and patience an old man's solace. But they didn't go away as
expected and so the problem now was how to make them disappear. With
most groups you simply find the leaders and either buy or kill them. Wasn't
that what the '60s was all about, assassinations and betrayals and govern-
ment-sponsored infiltrations?

But this movement had no leader. So, how do you assassinate an idea?
Still the Wall Street moguls were defiant. They had time and limitless
resources, not just the entire New York Police Department, but their own
private security as well, made up of Blackwater forces, fresh from Iraq and
mayhem. Now they stood guard behind the glass doors and made certain
that the young barbarians wouldn't get past the gate. Nothing could stop
the Stock Market bell from ringing, not even Bin Laden.

So, yes, their faces were still arrogant, the traders, but I'd seen that same arrogance on the faces of the elite on my own island of Montserrat before the volcano erupted – those who had power and a sense of entitlement, mostly the result of the estate system where wealthy land owners left property to their offspring of colour. They, too, had been certain in their certainties. They lived their many-mansioned lives in the sun, but what they hadn't reckoned on was a volcano erupting impolitely. Not even the Mafia (and yes, Dorothy, there really is such a thing as the Mafia), who had big plans for Montserrat, had imagined lava or pyroclastic flows coming down on you at over a hundred miles an hour and forcing people to evacuate over half the island. Now those same mansion houses were being occupied by feral pigs, goats and cattle – like some vision from Orwell's *Animal Farm*.

The Occupy movement had its base at Zuccotti Park, a space no larger than a school yard and yet it managed to attract worldwide attention. What was so unusual was that you could actually hear the sound of thought going on there, a forcefield of energy.

Everyone had a chance to express an opinion without censure. It was a university without walls and it amazed me. There was a hopefulness and expectation that I hadn't seen since the '60s. It was the kind of awakening you get the first time you hear a solo by Charlie Parker or Ornette Coleman with his *Free Jazz*. Or the first time you saw an action painting by Jackson Pollock, a sense that anything was possible. (Pollock was the first American to take his instruction from the Vodou art of Haiti, instead of trying to copy dead European geniuses. He realized that it was the power released by the attack of paint on canvas that was the main thing and not just slavish imitation or reproduction.)

So what happened to that '60's hope and energy? I think it died at Kent State with the shooting down of students and the entrance of reality: the sudden realization that these people in uniform really didn't wish you well. In fact, they might even kill you, even with those pretty flowers in your hand.

The response was the '70s. Students, when forced to choose between becoming their fathers or being killed, chose the former. Wouldn't you? It's no accident that enrolment in humanities courses plummeted and students chose accounting instead. Wall Street is the result of all those bright young ones coming to the realization that money is what the world is all about. And, of course, the neo-liberal economists helped by offering Wall Street the ideological weapons. They used all the good intentions of the American dream of owning your own home and turned it into an excuse for foreclosure and hedge funds. It was cleverly done, and greed helped, as it always does. The very nature of capitalism is "all you can get away with". *Laissez faire* has more to do with the basic nature of man, which is, as Hobbes said, "brutish". All this came to me in Zuccotti Park as I searched in vain for a toilet.

I watched the Occupiers. I would have stayed there with them but I'd already slept in too many parks, and not always willingly. So I left them and went to Boston to rest and gather, but Occupy was there too.

Boston is a secret and subtle place. It's never obvious like New York. They like to leave lights on and curtains drawn in Boston. It's no wonder that the highest concentration of Montserratians in America live there. That's because Boston has the three things Montserratians are obsessed with most: education, religion and crime. Boston offers all three in abundance. There were more than three hundred bank robberies in Charlestown in one year alone, almost one a day (the Irish finding their own solution to the banking crisis) and so it was a perfect place for a Montserrat man to hide.

Boston is divided between the Irish and the Italians. They keep the crime and power between them. Not that the Irish and the Italians like each other; they don't, but they can at least unite in religion and meet in Roman Catholic churches (which also provide excellent opportunities for money laundering). While the two groups may not like each other, they do on occasion marry. The second thing the two agree on, beside Catholicism, is their total hatred of Blacks.

Isn't it amazing how Blacks cause so many people to unite? This is an irony of God. Everyone hates us (including and especially we Blacks ourselves). As such, we've united the world. Even Chinese learn the word "Nigger" at a tender age. It may be the first word they learn in English and I think it's a requirement for proof of citizenship.

But to return to Boston: the Irish and the Italians owned almost everything; whatever was left belonged to the Poles. There is still a remnant of the old Boston money, of course – Beacon Hill and all that good stuff. They're dying off slowly, though, and are seldom seen in public. However, their grandchildren are and a lot of them are in Occupy.

I had to put a play together, but it's funny, this writing business. You can only do it apart and alone; you have to be careful when committing acts of art. You need darkness but still enough light to see the page, like at a jazz club.

I neither drank rum nor smoked herb all the time I was in exile. Why waste God's gifts if there's nothing of beauty to look at? Not that Boston wasn't pretty; it even tried dawns and sunsets, and what it lacked in love it made up for in history. But I never felt at home there. I played no drums there but the flute instead. The flute is an instrument people can forgive. The drums bring too many spirits.

Boston had its own spirits to deal with: its tidy colonial houses with witchcraft in the woodwork, houses tight as Christianity. Perhaps they brought it with them on the Mayflower. I don't know, but witchcraft was definitely there along with the remnants of piracy. Whenever I see water and ships I think of slavery. Boston has a lot of water and a lot of ships. The American Revolution started there but ended in New York. You can transform slavery into many things: sometimes into universities, sometimes into banks and even sometimes into churches and museums.

It was interesting to see how many times the name Winthrop came up in Massachusetts. He was the first governor and a good slaver. Then, as now, you needed money to run for office and we were everyone's opportunity but our own, like sand upon the shore. Winthrop owned much of the land along the Charles River and the Commons.

Boston is a very healthy city, unlike New York. Sports abound. So it's easy for a not-so-young man from the Caribbean to get lost there among the Lotus-eaters and the healthy young white girls jogging along the Charles River. It takes a while to learn that the ivy-league universities are really just another plantation. Reality is always just beyond the gate, always just a ghetto away.

But as well as a lot of thought, sport and crime, there was also drugs. I suspect there always has been. Oxycondon was the drug of choice; it came in from Canada and Amsterdam. It had almost replaced heroin, almost, but not quite. Nothing will ever replace heroin, not as long as we're in Afghanistan where poppy is as easily available and plentiful as yachts sailing along the Charles River. But now it was time to leave Boston and go deal with my play in New York.

I had no yacht, so instead I took one of those Chinese buses that charge half the price of Greyhound, and will soon drive them out of business. I started rehearsals at New Federal Theatre which was, thank God, just a few streets away from Chinatown. I didn't have far to walk and there was always the food for solace. The producer was Woodie King, the last of the giants of Black Theatre in America. It was he who started people like Denzel Washington, Morgan Freeman and Billy Dee Williams (whose mother, by the way, is also from Montserrat). Woodie King gave them all a stage to act on. As for me, he knew me before I did.

So I was performing my play *Trance*, which was about Langston Hughes. It was a producer's dream because they only had to pay one actor: me.

Now, my first (and best) agent, Helen Merrill, taught me some interesting things about theatre. Helen, who had known both Brecht and Paul Robeson personally, had experienced the madness of Germany during World War II. Maybe that was why she chain-smoked Camel cigarettes every waking moment of her life. She always said: "Listen Edgar, to hell with dialectics. People will do anything for a piece of meat, even kill each other. Never forget that when you write. Don't get lost in the clouds."

Well, Langston Hughes had spent a lot of time in the kitchens of the world. He always wrote about food. He always talked about food in his writing because he lived the early part of his life searching for it: "Amazing what you can do with mustard greens seven days a week. You see life differently."

When theatre is done right, a power is unleashed. That unleashing of power I call "Trance". I wanted a director because a good director gives the actor permission to be better than he is. He functions like a priest in a ceremony and focuses energy and light. I chose Ronnie Clanton from The Actor's Studio. The simple set consisted of a huge photograph of Langston Hughes and the sound of the sea.

My first experience of theatre was the church. Maybe that's why I take it so seriously. I saw that something happened when the priest raised the chalice. He was more than himself. The priest occupies the church. The lifting of the host is the transformation of man to spirit. As in Vodou, there is always a war taking place between spirit and the body, a struggle between rider and the horse. When the rider takes control the spirit is freed. It's no accident that most theatres started in churches. There is The Actors Studio, New Dramatists and New Federal Theatre, which is still housed in an active church.

I found a room in Brooklyn to park myself. It was somewhere in the desert of East New York, Vermont Avenue. I travelled there by night. Like a thief. This was good because I got a chance to see the homeless who slept clothed in newspapers and black plastic bags on subway platforms. They were bent like wire or else they lay prostrate, feet propped on the seats, hands clutching their crotches in an effort to protect the one bit of real estate they still owned. I kept thinking of what Brendan Behan, the Irish writer, said: "You want to help the poor, don't join them."

So I lived in this rooming house with four other cell-mates who were all West Indian. What made it bearable was that most worked nights and mostly in hospitals. (West Indians occupy hospitals like bees a hive. The Health Industry is primarily Caribbean. We do stoop work as nurses or orderlies scrubbing floors. Fortunately, Caribbean people stoop with grace, whether retrieving a cricket ball or emptying a dustbin).

I'd never lived in a rooming house before. We were all as celibate as monks because the landlady allowed no women to enter. As she said, "Women are trouble. I should know; I am one." Couldn't argue with that. She also said that not everything in life is "pum-pum".

I travelled mostly by night and soon got used to the grammar of the lonely Brooklyn streets and the sadness of the all-night Arab groceries with their bullet-proof glass and the half-shut eyes of the Arabs who occupied them.

One night, I came home, fell in bed, turned on the radio to WBAI and found out that the police had surrounded Zuccotti Park and were about to dislodge the Occupiers.

It was 2:00 a.m. (It's always best to attack before dawn, as in Iraq – before you can tell a white thread from a black, as the Koran says.) An hour later I was there. I hadn't seen so many police since 9/11 and the fall of the Twin Towers. Mayor Bloomberg had had enough. It was beginning to look like the Paris Commune. He sent in police from all five boroughs. They gave the Occupiers ten minutes to evacuate. He promised that whatever items were left would be returned the following day at the Center Street Police Station. Then they sent in the sanitation trucks, which crushed and demolished everything – tents, lap-tops and books. (The Occupiers had started a free library.) Of course, the assurance of items being returned was nonsense. Laptops don't respond well to trucks driving over them. The night was grim with drizzle and the swirling lights of police vans. Just the cover of Fanon's *The Wretched of The Earth* lay at my feet.

Mayor Bloomberg is the perfect poster child for money and power. He's the only mayor of New York who managed to triple his net worth while in office. Not even "Gentleman" Jimmy Walker from the good old Irish Tammany Hall days, who had to flee to Europe rather than go to prison, not even he had managed to go from 7 to 22 billion dollars while in office. This mayor simply bought himself an office and a city. He rewrote all the election rules so that he could run for a third term and if he chose to, could even run three more terms, virtually unopposed.

A good clear message was sent: the Occupiers were nothing more than refuse. What do you do with refuse? You remove it. But then, so is the majority of the population irrelevant and crushable. When faced with a judge who dared to oppose him, the mayor simply bought himself another judge, just as they would do in any Middle Eastern country or Africa. I couldn't believe that Occupy was so naïve that they didn't expect it. They had let their guard down because they had started to believe that they were accepted, like lovable stray pets. The media acceptance had lulled them into complacency.

The mayor spoke through his commissioner, Kelly, who is an Irishman. The Irish have always found that the best survival technique is to make yourself indispensable to those in power (as on Montserrat where they functioned as brutal overseers). (Just take a look at the both the police and fire department of New York or Boston if you want to see what occupation looks like). The irony is that this same police, as reactionary as they are, will still fund the IRA on the side, because rebellion is still part of their DNA.

They see no contradiction in supplying the industrial prison complex on the one hand and supporting armed struggle on the other.

I performed *The Birds of Baghdad* at City College and watched the students get the shock of recognition. There are two things that I like about City College: It's not NYU and it's not Columbia University. It's not busy swallowing up New York City property for corporate interest. Not yet, anyway. I like performing for students because they're always astonished and have to put what they witness into another part of their brain – somewhere they've never been. Students are so used to lies. That's what successful education is: learning to package lies better.

The Birds of Baghdad just drops you in Iraq right before the invasion. I tell what I saw with my eyes and make the audience walk with me. I'd gone to Baghdad expecting to see camels and genies in lamps. What I found instead was babies dying in incubators from uranium poisoning. And money, more money than I had ever seen in my life. You see, in Baghdad, money isn't counted, it's weighed.

My play tells how when I looked into the children's eyes, I knew we could never win in Iraq. They know their history. You can't defeat an enemy that has a history. I understood then why it was so important to Europe that African history be destroyed. Napoléon understood that and therefore made certain to disfigure all the faces of the statues in Egypt. He disfigured the noses so you couldn't see the African connection. God rewarded him with the Rosetta Stone. That is why, during the recent Iraq war, the museums were looted and libraries destroyed.

The students were amazed that I went to see for myself and bear witness. Why didn't I just stay safe in New York and await the blessings of Social Security? Then they wanted to know what I thought about the Occupy movement. I had just a few simple things to say.

The reason Socialism has never really caught on in America is mainly because no one in America really thinks of themselves as *the poor* since the possibility of wealth is always just a Lotto ticket away. Not even those in the Deep South or Appalachia, where coal mining has long died and left the earth an open grave, consider themselves "the poor".

There really still is a thing called the American dream. Everyone expects that their life can change in a day if they just scratch the right card, answer the right question or spin the right wheel. So, the anger of the poor is never against the billionaire who breezes by in a chauffeur-driven limousine. No, the anger of the poor will be directed against his neighbour who is sleeping on the park bench beside him. Why? Maybe because that neighbour has a cigarette that makes him a property owner. That's where their fight will be. That's about as deep as the class warfare will go.

One phrase in the Declaration of Independence, "And the pursuit of happiness", makes America truly unique. No other nation on earth would have dared to suggest that men have a right to happiness. Of course, it was brilliantly crafted by Thomas Jefferson (another good slaver who despised blacks but fathered many).

So what do I think of Occupy? Occupy is a thing greater than itself and that's why it's important. It's a different way of seeing. America has always been about the process by which the "*They*" becomes the "*We*". In other words, we always aspire to be let into an exclusive club that won't have us. This wish to be let in is at the very heart of capitalism. This is what makes it work.

A Chinese curse is to wish that someone live in interesting times. Well this is that interesting time.

Some occupy property. Some occupy the soul. There was a time when English was important because of Shakespeare. Now, English is important, not because of Shakespeare but because the language of the revolution is American. Rap music, especially, has penetrated the entire world. Not bad for a despised people. We have managed to unite the world in a way that the UN never could. We have claimed the youth of the entire world.

It was time for my third and perhaps most important play, *The Scottsboro Boys*. If you take nine black boys from Alabama in the depths of the Depression, and add two white girls who work in a cotton mill and add the ingredient of accused rape, you have the story of the Scottsboro Boys. What fascinated me most about the case was the fact that only two of the nine actually knew each other (because they were brothers); the other seven were total strangers.

The main motif of the play is the train. Trains (as I learned from Langston Hughes) are always present in our music (the blues). The sound of the train's moan can most clearly be heard on the harmonica and is echoed in the saxophone.

Why were trains so important to us? Was it because of A. Philip Randolph and the Sleeping Car Porters? No, it's because trains were the only means of flight from the South to the supposed refuge of the North. The problem was that we seldom had the money for passage and so we had to stow away as hobos. If you were caught, you were beaten and sometimes killed.

So it was that these nine boys came together on a train. Unfortunately for them, there happened to be two white girls (Ruby Bates and Victoria Price) who were supplementing their income by prostitution, also on board and unknown to the nine. The boys never even got to enjoy the pleasure of these young ladies. In an effort to save themselves from prosecution, the two vestal virgins concocted a story of rape. Sex and economics has always been at the heart of slavery. Call slavery a full-employment miracle.

For me, the Scottsboro case is a microcosm of America and the American Dream. Victoria Price saw an opportunity for celebrity status and rode it – a way out of the cotton mill, for then as now the economy had collapsed. The second girl, Ruby Bates recanted her testimony, yet the wheel of fate was already in operation. The testimony of these women managed to destroy the lives of nine people, managed to eat their youth; two women and nine young men who never met at any point in their lives, except in court.

Resistance to the destruction of youth is for me what is at the heart of the Occupy movement. It's an attempt to reclaim life and to resist in the face of power. I performed *The Scottsboro Boys* at the New Federal Theatre and asked Alice Spivak of the Bergoff Studio to direct. It's easier when you have a director who has known your work. The play is essentially to do with redemption, or at least, the search for it.

The play was well received but I needed to return home. I missed the Montserrat Sundays with their untidy choirs. I needed to come home. Sometimes when you go searching for family, you find famine instead, but that's alright.

It was in the stillness of the night when I stole away. I needed to come home, my real home. One good thing about Brooklyn is that it's near Kennedy Airport. I was frightened to walk away from New York, but I was more frightened to stay.

It's only by walking you learn to walk. Never lose the love. Once you lose the love the game's over. Only amateurs despair. I was lonely so I brought a drum. Drum and dream together make drama. Where ever you find yourself in the world, always occupy.

3. UNDER THE VOLCANO

DEPORTED TO PARADISE

Safe to say that Montserrat is a very peculiar place, as full of contradictions and paradoxes as a pomegranate has seeds. Chief among these is our love/hate relationship both with Britain and with ourselves. As a result of this conflict we never quite know whether to call ourselves a British colony or not. Our response seems to depend on the time of day and circumstance when asked. On the one hand we like to be independent and on the other we like to be secure. In life in general it's difficult to be both independent and secure, never mind when there's the threat of a volcano looming above your head. We resent having to take instruction or reprimand from authority figures and will quickly challenge the rule of law. We resent the exploitative nature of our colonial past and find no romance in Sea Island cotton or limes. History has left us with a deep distrust of Rule Britannia and what it really means.

While we may love to sue government and are often called confrontational, litigious and always in opposition, we, at the same time, desire all the pomp and ceremony of Britain and would hate to have to abandon it. So you see how this duality causes a certain paradox and strangeness of thought that is often described as *Montserratian*. There is also a peculiar shortness of memory that allows us to deny the fact that a mere two generations ago we were all bound to the estate system. This convenient ability to forget is part of our inheritance; it allows us to delude ourselves with class consciousness and hypocrisy, a very useful gift to have.

Next, although we profess a love of Africa and our native ancestry, I think you would be hard put to find many Montserratians who would willingly call themselves African. Now Irish – that's something else. Many would more quickly claim Irish ancestry by virtue of the prevalence of Irish last names on the island than any other. The fact that so many of the parishes bear the name of the estate plantation owners is a constant reminder of a massive Irish presence on the island. This incidence of history is not rejected; its persistence is – if anything – embraced and celebrated. I have already argued that there is no evidence that the Irish were any less brutal in their approach to slavery than the British. Indeed, the evidence points to the contrary. The Irish for the most part were reluctant to think of Montserrat as home. It was a means of amassing enough wealth to return to their true home (Ireland) transformed as lords of the manor. It was poverty, after all, that had brought the Irish to Montserrat in the first place: indenture and servitude and flight from oppression. They entered Montserrat as either property or deportees. Some were able to move from worker to overseer and eventually to land owner. It would be nice to believe that this upward mobility was achieved gently, but very probably, the lower the origin the more desperate the desire. The Irish, therefore, didn't have the time to be either gentle or casual in their approach.

All of this becomes quite interesting at present, for Montserrat is the only island that embraces the title, the Emerald Isle of the Caribbean. There is a week-long festival on the island called Saint Patrick's. Not even Ireland does this much commemoration. Still more interesting is the fact that recently Montserrat has added the component of an African music festival as part of the week of celebration. Through this synthesis of Africa and Ireland one can witness history. It is a very curious thing to watch the Irish visitors to the festival, who hitherto were totally unaware of this strange island or this peculiar aspect of their own history. The belief was that they were far too busy being oppressed and staving off hunger in the potato famine to ever have time to oppress others. To learn otherwise is a revelation to them and one that they are quite keen to comprehend.

From the Montserrat standpoint there is much to learn from our music. There is its healing aspect and the fact that what can be denied in the written word cannot be hidden in the much more visceral dynamism of music and dance. No matter the self-loathing that comes from colonialism, we can't help but feel the pulse or deny the heartbeat of the music. I think this is the reason for the current success of African Gospel music in the Caribbean. All of these various forces coming together at the same time produce an amazing synergy. The Africans who come to perform at the Montserrat Festival are shocked by the similarities they find. There is, for example, a direct relationship between the kora (the stringed harp of Senegal and Gambia) and the banjo and ukulele of Montserrat string band music. Then there are the masquerade dancers in costumes that are so undeniably African: the movements that interpret life and death; spirits of ancestors that are, as always, watching and witnessing us.

When we think of how the first Africans arrived on the island, we have to recognise that slavery could not be achieved in the New World without the tacit agreement of the Old. In other words, we weren't merely taken, we were given. Deportation from your homeland can be very cruel. The autobiography of Equiano, the one time slave, attests to that. But what of deportation back to your homeland, what is that process like? There are those who, as a result of encounters with the prison system abroad, get deported back to Montserrat. What does that feel like, without benefit of family, funds or raiment?

The fact is that if you return to Montserrat and are male, and if you remain too long to be a tourist, you are immediately perceived as a deportee, until you prove otherwise. You are tried, scorned and convicted in the eyes of others until a history and a name is attached to you: "Is who he be?" You will be judged and rejected unless verified a celebrity on radio or some form of the media. We each of us seek uniqueness in our captivity, some aspect that singles us out, defines us and sets us apart from others. I suspect that is why we, as a people, are so eager to attach ourselves to an Irish connection. There is, after all, nothing unique about having an English master, but an Irish master is quite another matter.

But if I were asked to design a new flag for Montserrat, instead of the pale Celtic woman with the harp that we now have, I'd have a sugar mill. Our mills are built to withstand everything – hurricanes and even volcanoes because of their design and the eggs and lime in the mortar. As an icon, the sugar mill more fittingly represents us as a people, built for struggle. The sugar mill and the donkey are our legacy.

Yes, it's a curious thing to find yourself deported to Paradise. But we've made an art of it and a history.

ON WHY MONTSERRAT IS UNIQUE

(For John Allen, the Man from Baker Hill)

If Montserrat were not unique, I would never have chosen to be born here and certainly would have denied my homeland long ago. Of course, Jamaica was tempting, especially in the '70s and '80s when so many Montserratians were passing for Jamaican and even living there. But although the Blue Mountains are wondrous, they don't have the same spirits as the Silver Hills. Trust me!

So let's deal with what is the real problem with Montserrat: few really believe that we are unique. If you ask us, we answer, "Well, we lived with an active volcano, and when others ran we stayed." This is of course true, but Montserrat was unique long before the eruption. All the eruption did was to give us a better excuse to run.

As for me, I love Montserrat bad. I love Montserrat the way a young man loves the girl in the corner of the dance floor who is "wining" by herself and wearing those high heels that she knows show her to good advantage and yet are comfortable enough for her to go all night if she wants to. Of course, the young man wants her and all he can think of is "Get she panty off!" This is the form of love where you are in love with the same person: yourself!

Then there's a next form of love. Think of two elderly people in the same nursing home, a couple, but now they live in separate wards. Almost every day, when he remembers her, he puts on his white cap and takes his cane and goes in search of her through all the rooms. When at last he finds her, he calls out to her: "Come gal, get you things them, le' a-we go home!"

She walks to him and touches him on the left side of his face where the cap doesn't cover. "But Jonnie, this we home now. You forget?"

"For true? Oh yes, that's right." And tears come to his eyes and he walks away. But tomorrow he'll come in search of her again.

Now this kind of love no young man can comprehend, because it's incomprehensible, this finding and losing, finding and losing. Well, it's so I love Montserrat. Bad!

Then Montserrat is a very religious place and full of hypocrisy at the same time. The two things are not mutually exclusive. Is that what makes us unique? I doubt it. We have a far way to go to beat Barbados on a Sunday morning around church time, with all the big hats and looks of disdain on the faces of parishioners. (As they say, if looks could kill, me would a dead long time.) So no, Montserrat does not own the market in hypocrisy and church going.

How about homosexuality and the fear of corruption through education and the Internet (that minefield of wickedness and depravity)? Is Montserrat unique here? Again we have to say, no. Because although we have a long tradition of man bulling man (and woman bulling woman) we are still in the minor leagues when compared to Barbados, which wears the undisputed crown when it comes to being the bull capital of the Caribbean. (It's not for nothing that Barbados is known as "Little England", followed, of course, by Trinidad. (Remember Trinidad has all those petro-dollars to play with). Montserrat is still small change when it comes to sodomy and the like.

No, what makes Montserrat unique is the second of the two words I have never heard uttered from the mouths of politicians: dignity and graciousness – the ability to let big people alone to do as they would, and pretend that you don't know. In fact, in Montserrat everyone knows everything, even before it happens. Nothing in Montserrat moves faster than gossip. It arrives on the wings of angels.

That might be the only explanation of how, before the volcano days, information travelled so swiftly from Town (Plymouth) to the mountains. Here, let me pop a popular myth, the one that says that all Montserratians gathered in Town in joyous harmony and ate hand-made ice-cream together and partied. There were, in fact, large numbers of people who seldom ever came to Town. Some went their whole lives and didn't see it once, would not be caught dead there. "Damn people there, too wicked. Piss 'pon you head and tell you say it raining."

The reason was not distance or lack of transport. There were people who travelled the entire island, twice in a day, without fainting. The reason is that some people hated Town with all its pretentions and snobbery. In the mountains everyone smells the same – of animals and manure. Anyone who has spent a life following behind goats and sheep knows what I'm talking about. The goat is the most useful animal on earth because every part of its body is useful – from its meat to its skin. It is a profitable animal. But it stinks and if you play a drum with goat-skin, after three hours of serious playing, the spirit of the goat will enter you through your hands and you will smell of goat. Spirit is the only explanation of how people stayed away from Town and yet still knew who was bulling who, instantly.

Again, it is graciousness that allows Montserrat's "live and let live" attitude to endure. "Let he go on with 'e chupidness. As long as he no touch me or mine, no problem, but if he ever cross that line, is dead he dead and me not waiting fu no police either!" There is no lack of rocks in Montserrat, and failing that there is always the cutlass, since every man is a farmer (in some form or other). This solution is known as settling out of court. It is why Montserratians can afford to be gracious.

Let's move on now to the good ladies of Montserrat, church-bred all. We'll start with the general and move to the specific. Montserrat is unique because of its women, fiercely independent. Not all of them are as eloquent as Shirley Osborne (our current Speaker of the House), but then the Honourable Shirley is a child of privilege. Although there are not many of her ilk in my little Montserrat, poor women still manage to get their point across – and with less chat.

Scholars have tried to explain what made the Montserrat woman the way she is. Some say it is because she survived slavery intact (and if alive means intact, then that is certainly true). Some even say that it was the influence of the Irish and the Brehon Law.

Brehon Law? Well, long before God created the British to civilize the world, the Celts were the first scholars, creating thirty-one Druid universities in Britain and Ireland, long before the Christians came. The Druids were not just academics, but poets and keepers of the oral tradition (just as the griots in Africa). In Ireland, the Celts also created the Brehon laws. The main thing to know is that there was no police force, no law courts and an unusual degree of gender equality. Women were allowed to divorce their husbands with no loss of property, whereas in England women had no rights at all. They existed simply as chattels. If you married, your husband owned everything, including you. Whatever you brought to the marriage – property and money – were his forever. When the British started to take over Ireland, the first thing they did was to revoke all such rights for women and subject them to Common Law.

My theory is that the indentured Irish women who were sent to Montserrat, because they wouldn't submit to the English colonisers, still had the Brehon Law in their souls. Some say that is why Montserrat women are so rebellious. They may have mastered the art of disguising it, but, trust me, it's there.

Now to the specific. All I need do is look at my own family. My aunt was known in Montserrat as "Marse Ann". I had the blessing of spending some time with her. Marse Ann certainly qualified as fiercely independent. She determined at an early age never to subject herself to any man. Now how much this had to do with her own upbringing, I can't say, but this much I know. She was in competition with her brother (my father, the notorious Toomer Dyer) from childhood on. She couldn't hope to outrun, out-drink, or out-gamble him, but he could never outfight her, ever. She married early, had a child and then decided that she preferred women to men. Instead of hiding the fact (she never liked living in closets), she announced it boldly.

She next determined how she could raise a child and make an independent living. She decided upon house painting, a thing no woman did in Montserrat. She was soon known as the undisputed best painter in the island. I don't think she had ever heard of the Brehon Law. She didn't need to. She *was* the living Brehon Law. Bless her (she died recently) and it's only now I realize what a warrior and pathfinder she was.

But what I know about her makes me curious about the slavery period itself. How many women went with women? There are, of course, no figures on this because who the hell knows what slaves did in their free time? The day belonged to the master but night belonged to the slaves. Under cover of darkness, the slaves travelled from estate to estate. Montserratians still have a love of night travel (moon or no moon) – but you better know where you walking.

One last note regarding my aunt, Marse Ann: She had a lifelong grudge against my father. She once stated clearly that she looked forward to seeing him in his grave. Montserrat's unique graciousness? Yes, because what I did not know then was that despite their conflict, it was she who went to fetch him from Antigua when he got stricken with a stroke. I had always thought that it was my sister who went to fetch him and found a house for him in Montserrat.

Was it a love-hate relationship? She explained this gesture of kindness in classic Marse Ann fashion: "The only reason I come look for you is because I don't want you to dead easy. I want you to live long so you could suffer!" And true to her word, she made certain to send a hot meal for him daily, always on time. She looked after him until his death. She then outlived him by some thirty years. What must he have done to her to cause such a lifelong anger? Evidently, he hurt her to her soul. Montserrat is unique in anger and love.

Now I have been accused many times of only loving the Montserrat sea. This is not true. There are some trees in Montserrat that I've made love to (the silk cotton tree at Cudjoe Head for example), but the sea is the most faithful and has never betrayed me. There were times she could have taken my life when I used to swim out to the Leviathan ships, but she didn't. Times when she could have taken me at night as I slept on my cannon at Carr's Bay, but again she didn't. But there are other women I love in Montserrat, too, but me not go call names. I'll only say this: I've learned far more from the women of Montserrat than from the men.

Let's deal now with the women of "class". My auntie Marse Ann would never have called herself a woman of class. A woman of class would never walk directly up to a next woman and tell her boldly that she wanted her. She would do it by the more convoluted way of applying pressure. Let's see how this works. Let's take a young innocent girl who has just graduated from university with top honours. Let's call her Alice.

Come Alice, come, a new interviewee for her first job in government, full of innocence on her long Montserrat legs (gift of her mother). She arrives secure in the knowledge that her glowing résumé will get her through: the letters of endorsement, her success in debating teams representing Montserrat, her many prizes in sports.

She rises early, but not before her mother. Mommy has risen earlier to iron Alice's white shirt meticulously – the same one Alice wears to Pentecostal church on Sunday. So our Alice enters full of hope and well brushed teeth. She wears the black suit she wears for special events like funerals – and her new panty, also ironed by Mommy.

> There's a brown girl in the ring
> Tra-la-la-la-la
> There's a brown girl in the ring
> Tra-la-la-la-la-la
> And she looks like a sugar in the plum.

The interviewer is a woman, so our Alice feels safe. When she's asked the trick question as to why she feels that she is best qualified for this particular position, our Alice gives her most Pentecostal smile and her well-rehearsed speech about wanting to give back to Montserrat. Meanwhile, the interviewer-woman smiles from across her mahogany desk, thinking: *This poor fool really thinks life is all about résumés and qualifications.*

Now our Alice wonders why she feels so uncomfortable. Could it be the way that her interviewer is staring at her legs? Only men do that. This is a woman after all, and only men have those thoughts. Of course, it doesn't help that her interrogator keeps asking her about her love life. Why should her personal life matter?

"Well, we like to know that if you get this position you won't disappear on us and start a family."

"No, I have no intentions of getting married at the moment."

"Good, I can tell from your resume that you are very goal-oriented. You like to win. I just wonder if you are willing to do what it takes to succeed."

"Oh, I'm not afraid of hard work."

"But are you willing to make certain accommodations?" And again she stares at Alice's legs.

"Well, yes, certainly." She wisely doesn't ask: *Like what?*

Our Alice gets the job, but getting a job is not the same as getting a career, and she soon learns what they mean by accommodations. She sees that in Montserrat, for certain women, failure is often rewarded with success. Girls with half her skills are moved up the ladder, and Alice is baffled as to why: "She doesn't even know QuickBooks or Power Point!"

Her friend, Latoya, explains. "Maybe not, but she know fu heist up she skirt and bend over. She do that very good and you don't!"

So Alice learns what they mean by accommodations. She also learns that a lot of professional women marry, not for passion but simply because it's the safest way to keep other men (and other women) from off you.

Women of a certain class marry and stay married regardless. Having found success, they have new issues to deal with. It's not the "Heist up you skirt and bend over" problem anymore. It's the problem of rising up the corporate ladder faster than your husband or significant other. Don't tell anyone, but we Montserrat men are insecure. We don't like it when our women earn more than we do.

Men react in different ways. Some take to "cuffing she about", just to remind she that you the man here. Others take to drink (and I'm not talking after-dinner sherry, I mean come home and piss-in-the-kitchen-sink kind of drunk or all over the couch (where she now makes you sleep). But you stay together because that's what women of a certain class do.

Even the wives of known sexual abusers (those who attack young girls and make them do things that they would like to do to at home but dare not) give the man the benefit of the doubt the first time and say, "The girl must be lying." How about the second and the third? Is everybody lying? And yet she stays.

How about a woman pastor of a church staying on in an abusive relationship with a man she knows is a compulsive liar, drunkard and thief? She knows he has a mistress, knows where the mistress lives and that he bought the house for her. She knows the car and the number. She's even parked outside his mistress's house to haunt him. Yet she stays with him. Why? Because that's what Montserrat women of a certain class do. Is it because they need his money? No, these women could easily support themselves. They stay, not out of love but out of denial, the refusal to admit that they made a bad choice. "I couldn't have married such an animal. If I did that I would have to be a fool. I couldn't have made such a mistake."

So they stay and walk with their heads held high, swanning around from place to place, tending their lovely gardens, just the way their mothers did, as if there's not a cloud in the sky. Montserrat women can do denial better than anyone in the world. Now there are ways to get back at a man. She can have babies outside that clearly look nothing like him. This may work to shock him back into submission. If he, too, is of a certain class, he dare not say a word. He continues sleeping on the couch.

Praise must be given here to the prostitutes of my Montserrat. How many marriages have they saved or murders have they prevented? Bless them. They, at least, are perfectly clear about what they are. They screw men for money and women for power – on request, just like everyone else in government.

It all works so well, it's a shame that the university runs no courses on this. That's why our Alice can graduate and still walk with rose-tinted spectacles.

The last reason why I find Montserrat unique is that we never admit anger: anger at God for sending the volcano; anger at ourselves for losing the two homes and two cars of pre-eruption Montserrat, anger at those who left and now return (the gentle Diaspora). We can't ever admit that we hate them for returning.

Montserratians are "resilient", remember? We walk about on permanent automatic. What do I mean? Check your children. Any child over the age of ten knows how to stare at you with eyes wide open and attentive as you waffle on with some long diatribe about what they should be doing with their lives. And if you ask them what you just said, they can give you back your last sentence. They learnt this skill at school. Meanwhile, their minds are ten thousand miles away, playing some video game, texting a friend or surfing the net for porn. Yet there they are, right in front of you. That is Montserrat. We know how to give the appropriate response to questions. Smile, go to jobs we hate and at the end of the day return home to our little hells, all on automatic. I think the only time we are not on automatic is when we are home sitting on the toilet. It's the only time of the day when we allow ourselves to think.

I'll end this journey into the uniqueness of Montserrat with those who return to their homeland, full of great expectations and hope. Those who come to save us, welcome! The part I like is the shock when they discover that no one gives a damn about their good intentions and qualifications from foreign universities. We grudge you leaving and we grudge you returning. We may love you on holiday, but when we find that you've come back to live and work, that's a whole other story (and all stories in Montserrat are long because the roads are).

Now some people can't handle rejection. For me, fortunately, it's as natural to me as walking. As I've written elsewhere, God, in his kindness, had me raised in the exciting cesspool of New York, the city where every day is rejection and so you are always being tested to prove yourself over and over again. I learnt two things about Montserrat's uniqueness there. When I saw Montserratians working as servants I had to wonder whether there was any island on earth that loves and serves white people more. I also learnt that Montserrat was unique because people leave it but never forget it.

Even so, I knew that what I wanted to find I would have to come home to. It was my mother who told me I should go home to Montserrat if I wanted answers about my father, because she couldn't give me any. She could barely give me answers about herself. Like what would make a mother abandon her child? There was an answer to that one: fear and not wanting to cross her mother's will.

"What you know about child?" her mother would have said. "You a child youself. You leave him here and we'll see to him." So, of course, she did. And what they said was true. She didn't know what to do with a child. I understood that they were right in theory, but I was still pissed.

When I found my father. I found he had nothing to tell me either. Nothing I wanted to hear anyway. The trees had more to say than him – at least they danced. Then I found the Montserrat sea and everything changed. People were alright, but then they changed too.

Montserrat people are different by day and by night. By day they will feed you river-fish and maybe their daughters. But by night they watch you and hide away the light.

When I returned to the States my mother wanted to know what I thought of him.

"Not much!" I said.

"Does he still have that dimple in his chin?"

"Yes Mom, he still has the dimple."

"And his skin still smooth like chocolate?"

"Yes." I didn't want to tell her that "he" had a stroke in Antigua and the side of his face was slightly twisted. She didn't need to know all that. Better she remembered him as he was. What I couldn't fathom was what the two of them had in common? They were from different worlds. Was a dimple and smooth skin enough?

Meanwhile, I went back and forth to Montserrat, but I wasn't there when my father died. I figured he could do that without me. I got married to a girl my mother didn't have much use for, so she never attended the wedding. In phone conversations she managed not to mention her at all.

"You have two babies with two different women, why you didn't marry one of them?"

"Because the other one would kill me; that's why, Mom."

"And you think this Montserrat one won't?"

Not much I could say to that.

My mother started to suffer badly from diabetes and when she went into hospital she always wanted me to smuggle in all the food that she shouldn't be eating. She loved MacDonald's hamburgers and fries. The nurses looked the other way, and of course the aides would come in for their share. My mother and I had our best times together during those hospital visits. I knew the hospital so well that people thought I worked there. Then the cycle started happening. She would be good for a few months and then she'd have to enter hospital again.

One day I went to visit her and found her on the floor, crying. I was worried that she'd hurt herself but she hadn't. She was embarrassed that she'd wet herself. I lifted her up with strength I didn't know I had and put her in the bath tub and washed her, which made her more embarrassed.

I said, "Don't be silly, you washed me when I was a baby", which of course was nonsense. She never washed me once. That's what servants were for, the girls from country, Annie and Sis. But we played the game as if she really had. Then, finally, one time she went in the hospital and never came out. They called me to collect her things and arrange for the body to be taken to Benta's funeral Home, Benta's who buried most Montserratians.

But here's the thing, I was totally on automatic. *Resilient.*

I wouldn't let anyone help me. I didn't shed one tear. I was totally in control all the way through the funeral. It was only three months later when I was cleaning out the apartment that I came upon a barrel, one of those barrels that we use to ship things home to Montserrat. I found all my books and papers, books in Spanish and Greek and Russian poems by Pushkin. Even some books that I'd written. She saved everything, even my music books. She wouldn't let anyone in that room. That was her message to me. She'd saved everything. That's when I lost it. That's when the tears came and I couldn't stop. That's when I knew I had to come back to Montserrat.

Why is Montserrat unique? Because once you're born here you never really leave it, try as you will. It's like trying to escape my father and finding out that people who have never met me walk up to me, even in Antigua, and say: "Toomer Dyer's son". Not a question, a certainty. So strong is his mark on me. It's like a friend of mine, Ponteen, says about his restaurant made of stone facing the sea at Little Bay. "Stone stays. And the only way me a go leave this place, me have to dead."

That's why Montserrat is unique. Once we know who we really are, no one can conquer us but ourselves. But first, we have to accept ourselves as I accept my father in me, in order to be free of him because freedom can never be given; it has to be taken.

Buy truth and sell it not.

LIVING BENEATH VOLCANOES

The only thing wrong with volcanoes is that they don't behave themselves. They act up and don't stay where they belong and every now and again, they get attitudes and kill you. That aside, volcanoes are pretty. They're nice to visit and spend a day watching, as you might watch birds. The only problem is, long after you put away your binoculars and go home, they keep happening, and more and more they follow us across continents and enter our lives.

I was born beneath a volcano. The Soufrière volcano in Montserrat is one of three volcanoes in the Caribbean called Soufrière, but there is only one Montserrat. It was cute when I was small to go climbing the huge hills and go to see it, my volcano. Tourists would come, too, and it was said that the heated springs were good for your health. So people came to "take the waters". Then one day I was taken away to "prosper" in America. The Soufrière volcano grew up, too. But then the volcano went bad like a truant child and turned from teddy bear to terrorist overnight. But that was some time later.

I'd come back home to see her, my as yet unerupted volcano. Well not so much to see her as to find my father. And not so much to find my father as to see about my family house and land. Montserrat and the Caribbean as a whole is really about land and the ownership of land. Now people will play games and try to tell you that's not so. That the Caribbean is about golden sunsets and rum on the beach and the taste of coconut water, which is nice, but spend any time there and you'll soon see that after the tourists go home and the cute masquerade costumes are put away for another year, the bottom line is land: who owns it, how much will be left to whom when so-and-so dies, and what's left after taxes. If there is any doubt in your mind about this, just reach up your hand and try to help yourself to some fruit from a tree that you think is "free" and comes from God, like the rights of man. You do this and you'll soon find out what Eden is really all about. In Montserrat someone is always watching you.

Montserrat can best be described as a tiny Caribbean island of few people and many lawyers. There are now just five thousand people on island (there used to be twelve thousand), which is the perfect number for an asylum with just enough space to keep us from doing each other too much bodily harm. For although all of these five thousand are mad, no two are mad in exactly the same way.

So anyway, I'd come home in search of the house and the land that I remembered so well. The memory, the taste, the smell was what had sustained me for the many years I was away. I returned to find that my land had been taken and sold and now all that was left was a huge hole in the ground, a pit, in fact, that I wanted very much to fall in but merely peed into instead.

So the one good thing about going home was the chance to meet my father and spend some time with him. It's nice to find a father and meet him late in life; that way you have less of a chance to hate him.

I had many questions I wanted to ask him, but when I was with him I couldn't think of any. Which was fine with him as he never trusted either words or people. I was not a problem to him. My father lived life one cigarette at a time and all that really interested him was if there was one more left in his shirt pocket that he could reach with his good hand. (His stroke had made reaching difficult, although he managed to pitch stones at stray dogs and people pretty well when he was of a mind to.)

Now I couldn't complain to him about my house and land being stolen because it had nothing to do with him anyway. The inheritance had to do with my mother and her side of the family. All he had was a shack that the government, in its kindness, had awarded to him as a gift of grace for his many years of service hanging cables all over the island from dizzying heights (which no sane person would attempt to climb), bringing electricity and radio to the island. For this, a disused jetty, which was where ships once landed goods, was given to him. It was already rotting by then and it now seemed past decay. It was the perfect solution, they thought. Now, when the sea came in too much, he either had to go out or drown. This was the same jetty from which I left the island as a child, so it was fitting that I should return and watch it crumble all around him. So every day, I, the good son, would bring him cigarettes and listen to the sound of the sea quarrelling at his door (like Montserrat people, he'd say, as he sat and smoked).

I learned a lot from my father, although I doubt if we ever said more than a hundred words to each other in total. Words beneath a volcano are precious.

Then there was Solo, my friend. We were children together and swore we'd never, never stop being friends or ever part. We cut each other and shared a blood allegiance that was stronger than any flag. But then I betrayed him and went away while he stayed, and now he had the advantage over me because he saw me first and remembered me, whereas I didn't recognize him because he'd lost his front teeth.

"Is life take them."

He never questioned life. When I told him how they had stolen my house and land from me he just shrugged.

"At least you had house and land to tief."

He wasn't impressed. I'd grown up soft and so expected things, whereas he was from the north of the island and never knew anything but rough. I'd left him barefoot in Montserrat beneath a volcano and now he was still barefoot: my doppelganger, my other self. He expected nothing from life and was therefore seldom disappointed when he got just that.

This was a general understanding on the island. Some had much and some had little and some had none at all. If those who had nothing learned to work for those who had, then all could get along. Only those foolish enough to try and upset the natural order of things would get in trouble and come to grief. Solo was willing to work, but never for long and never if he had to wear shoes. Solo's gift was machines. They talked to him and he understood them; he liked them much better than people. As long as he could "hear" machines he would always eat.

But by now I'd had enough of the island, so I left and went landless back to America to pout.

HOW TO LOSE A WIFE (QUICKLY)

Funny how it all came together at once – the spewing of the volcano and my decision. That very night on the television, pictures of an island, eruptions and pyroclastic flows. When I made sense of it all, what I realized they were saying was that half my island had disappeared and that something had happened 30,000 feet in the air, sending ash as far as Puerto Rico (over a hundred and fifty miles away). Montserrat would soon be no more, and if Montserrat didn't exist, would I? The next month, *National Geographic* devoted half its issue to showing pictures of the island, before and after. The lush green had become a lunar landscape. The heat from the pyroclastic flows had destroyed everything in its path, including nineteen people. Most of those who perished were farmers producing food for evacuees in the emergency shelters. The town, the airport: everything gone; people living in cars (some of whom once had two homes), sleeping in churches and in the harbour. A British ship (the *Leviathan*) had been sent to evacuate the few lunatics who still were refusing to leave. It was then I knew that I had to go home. I told my wife.

Wives are peculiar when it comes to volcanoes. They take them personally. Somehow they sense a sexual threat. I remember that it all began calmly enough when I mentioned, as matter-of-factly as I could, that I was going home.

"What do you mean you're going home? Going home to what? There's nothing there. It's not like you own property or something. They already stole that, remember, so why on earth would you want to go back? Everyone's leaving!"

"That's exactly why I have to go back."

I found myself on a boat to the island because the airport no longer existed. The ferry from Antigua was almost empty. The sea rose and fell beneath me; I imagined I was on a camel; it frightened me how calm I was.

Once I reached the island, I walked past the stares of the people and found a perfect spot on the waterfront and laid down when night came beneath the stars and slept like a dead man. The best sleep I'd had in years.

My father was now dead but the sea still quarrelled. I thought of taking over his shack but that had gone too. Like a dream. When I woke it was to the sound of thunder and I thought that the volcano was erupting. But no, it was only the hooves of cattle, the feral cattle roaming the island in search of food and shelter now that they no longer had owners to feed them. They banded together like terrorists and took what they could. Many of them had hooves burned from the ash and now they, too, were refugees. When I awoke they were all around my head and so I jumped up and shooed them away, making a motion I remembered from childhood that I'd seen farmers do. It was still there in my unconscious. Now I went in search of Solo for I knew he would never leave. They would never let him board a ship to England, barefoot. But when he saw me, would he accept me or turn his face against me?

There are certain expectations among people in the West (the so-called First World). They are very comfortable with the eruption of volcanoes in Third World countries. It is, after all, part of our heritage along with voodoo and carnival and siesta time. What they are not comfortable with is volcanoes in blonde countries, drifting blight and devastation. Take for example, Iceland.

Several years ago Iceland was flourishing, filled with millionaires, luxury cars and international banking. Then something strange happened. The Wall Street bubble burst and Iceland found itself holding the useless loans of people from as far away as the South Bronx where I grew up all those many years ago.

Although Iceland has the oldest continuous parliament in the world (The Althing), no one asked any questions when they were seated in their limousines or private jets. Only when the collapse happened did Iceland ask: what the hell are we doing with junk bonds from America? We can neither eat them nor grow them. What use are they to us? Then the volcano erupted and shut down all of Europe, made the skies so still that only birds could fly.

Captains of industry don't like volcanoes because they don't like uncertainty. They don't like being told *No* in any form, such as in: "No flights allowed today." A sky where nothing moves but birds is frightening. What they like is a name and a number. Who can we negotiate with and how soon will this end? But God seems to be a non-negotiable item and access to private numbers doesn't help.

I was very sorry for Iceland because they suddenly found themselves possessing nothing but bits of paper on which were written the names of dead souls in the South Bronx and New Jersey. The country woke up one day and wondered how it had strayed so far from its true path as an island of fishers and farmers.

The same questions arise in Montserrat: who will feed the people? It always comes back to the fishermen and farmers – eyes looking out to a white foaming sea or up to a steaming and fire-capped volcano. Among the

Nuba people in Africa, ash is considered sacred, especially ash from the acacia tree. It's smeared on the faces of warriors or wrestlers who go forth to wrestle with God. Now ash is feared because of the danger of emphysema and cancer; the word carcinogenic appears again and again. This is no longer the business of warriors and dreams. This is not manna from heaven, this is death by breathing.

I'll end with a fable. Once upon a time there was a Montserrat woman who every day would rise and clean away the ash that had fallen while she slept. She would wash her clothes white until they wept clean and there was no stain of ash or history. But over and over, just when she'd finished and placed her clothes on the line, the ash would start to fall again and she would have to start the process all over. Like the monks she would say: "Always we begin again."

But it's hard to live life like a monk and so one day she decided she'd had enough. Ash was falling even in her dreams, and so she applied for work abroad, as far away from Caribbean volcanoes and their misery as she could get. So it was that she found herself working in a place called Iceland, a country of cold weather and blonde silence. Now the clothes she wore had no stain and though she missed cassava and goat water, she kept this to herself until one day the volcano of Iceland erupted and she looked up at the sky and cried:

"What is it? Is it me, Lord?"

And a voice answered: "No, it's just a volcano."

She had to laugh, even in her terror, for you can't take volcanoes personally. They happen regardless of weddings and births and dreams. They just happen above your head and beneath your feet.

Ash falls, man falls. But only one rises. Once upon a time or yesterday, you choose which.

And somewhere, Solo.

DANCE MASQUERADE

In life, you never know anything much. It is like a play that you enter somewhere in the second act and everyone knows their lines but you. Take me for example. Although I was born in Montserrat I'd never really been there until well into adulthood. The Montserrat I was born in only existed in my mind, wrapped in dream and fantasy, the other Montserrat. The real one I only came to know at the age of twenty-three, when I came back to what I thought was home.

In life, it's important to know, if not where you are, at least where you're not. For example, Antigua is not Jamaica. I found that out five minutes after landing and they took one look at my dreadlocks and offered me a pair of scissors to shear them, a not too thinly disguised metaphor for castration. Humiliation is good for you; it reminds you (just in case you need reminding) of just how powerless you are. Fortunately, I'd come armed with a book that had my name on it. When they saw this they allowed me to continue homeward and un-castrated.

What was interesting is that within fifteen minutes of arrival on Montserrat I saw everyone who would have an impact on my life (although I didn't know it). I had arrived on St. Patrick's Day (a holiday that is taken much more seriously on my island than in either Ireland or America), a fête day when everyone was gathered to eat, drink and tell lies, and so I had the benefit of seeing everyone in one place, at one time.

There was my father (who I'd not yet met), several brothers (also unknown to me), the girl I would later fall in love with (she was pretty, like rice) and the lawyer who would steal my home from me (he would later become a judge, thus proving that God really does reward the wicked whenever possible).

There were also characters like Levons Watts, who would later throw me out of his restaurant (Harbour Court) for entering without a shirt, as well as the Commissioner of Police who would arrest me for possessing ganja, but then later redeemed himself by quitting his post when his own son fell foul of the law (he turned out to be a decent poet).

There was also Maas Bob Griffith who started the first trade union in Montserrat and who would later give me the original speech Marcus Garvey made when he visited Montserrat in 1936.

And lastly, there was my aunt, Maas Ann, my Beatrice, my true guide
to Montserrat society. My aunt, as I have written, has the distinction of
being the only woman in Montserrat to be given the title "Maas". She is
an instantly identifiable figure; the best house-painter in the Emerald
Isle. I thought that I had seen most things in life (everything from
barefoot children walking in snow in Ireland to deadly girl gangs in the
South Bronx) but it was my aunt, Maas Ann, who introduced me to the
padlocked refrigerator door (a thing she did nightly) as well as the two-
minute shower. By the time you entered the shower you had just time
enough to get through one chorus of "Fire in the Mountain": "Fire, fire,
fire in the mountain and nobody there to out 'um." By the time you got
some soap on your body the water would slow to a trickle and then stop,
completely.

"This not New York. They does charge for water here, you know!
Nothing free in Montserrat except cusha."

Indeed, Auntie and I had few conversations that didn't involve money
(then again most conversations in Montserrat are either about money or
land).

Another favourite topic was my father and her brother, Toomer Dyer.
She summed him up for me: "You father be one damn dirty scamp." This
about covered everything. She would send a plate of food to him in Kinsale
daily because she didn't want him to die of hunger.

"Me want he live long so him could suffer."

In Montserrat, the grudge is an art form (grudge and malice, two sisters)
and nothing is sweeter to a Montserratian than vengeance. Time is irrelevant. Take the bull pestle. A bull pestle is made from the penis of a bull.
You cure it in salt, and this requires a great deal of time and patience. The
bull pestle is an excellent instrument for administering punishment because you can break bones without breaking the skin.

When I told Auntie that I was a writer, she immediately thought about
passing bad cheques, which may explain why she impounded my clothes
when I tried to depart her house.

Auntie, Maas Ann, was also an expert on Montserrat women. It was she
who informed me that Montserrat women liked rough sex in order to drive
the religion out of them. She was certainly much more informed than I, so
I had to take her word for it.

After departing her house, I tried my cousin, Tom, who told me that he
wouldn't be able to help me right then because he was busy caring for his
wife, who was at present awaiting Her Majesty's pleasure, having been
arrested for embezzlement. Being a very devoted husband, he would take
meals to her twice daily. (In Montserrat, love is eternal.) And so, no, he
would not be able to receive house guests right now.

The holiday being done, I then set about the business of finding out what had happened to my grandmother's house and land. It was then that the good lawyer informed me that neither house nor land existed any more, that it had been sold and all records had disappeared because of the courthouse fire. This fire seemed to explain everything, like the burning of the Reichstag.

Next, I went in search of the new owner, who turned out to be Hammy White (God's Messenger, and also family). But I arrived to find him in the act of a butchering a three-hundred-pound hog. As I watched him, his meat cleaver held high, it occurred to me that it might not be the best time to discuss matters of real estate. Not that he needed the meat cleaver for he had strength enough in his hand to dismember any animal without it. All I said to him was: "Perhaps another time, yes."

You know, I've always loved math because math, unlike people, never changes. For example, it gives me great comfort to know that the square of 10 plus the square of 11 plus the square of 12, when added together gives you 365, the exact number of days in a year. Math calms me. But Montserrat is not about math; it's about masquerade, a dance in which nothing is ever what it appears to be.

Take, for example, my father, Thomas "Toomer" Dyer, whom I tried next. He lived in the abandoned jetty house in Kinsale. I would have stayed with him, but when the sea came in, you had to come out of the house. I once asked him how many brothers and sisters I had. Or, more directly, how many children did he have. He smiled, enigmatically. I'm still waiting for an answer. My father was only interested in who was with him, because only they could help him. Hypothetical sons or daughters in New York, London or Toronto, he didn't care about.

My father's favourite expression when dealing with women was: "Bathe and come, darling." It is said that as he was breathing his dying breath he tried to lift the skirt of a woman who had been his former lover (with his one good hand). This was the same woman who was reputed to have robbed and betrayed him with another man. He had beaten her senseless with a stick. It was said that this caused his stroke. Ten years later, he still wanted her. In Montserrat, love is eternal.

My mother never had a harsh word to say about my father. She described him as always a loving man; then there would be a pause, and she would add, "to me anyway." Her smile, too, was always enigmatic. If I asked any more, she'd tell me, "Go and see for yourself."

This reminded me of another loving man, another blessed and wounded figure in Montserrat history, James "Bodo" Allen, who was a mason and writer around the early 1900s. He tried to provide work for those who were not fortunate enough to be born of the gentry. He fell in love with three sisters and so loved and bred them equally. One of the offspring was William H. Bramble who became our first Chief Minister. (Thank God Bodo Allen loved women and not sheep, goats or donkeys.) He built the sugar mill at Lookout for one of his offspring, the same sugar mill that was the site of his execution at the hands of the police. It's said that his spirit remains there and there's always a jumbie table set for him.

My father could not help me, so I had to find other accommodation. I tried Johnnie Dublin at Letts Enterprises. He rented me a room upstairs, and although I could not see the sea, I could at least hear it at night. What I didn't know at the time was that one of my brothers had also stayed there and absconded, leaving a bill of several thousand dollars. As I say, you don't know these things if you enter in the second act. It appeared that everyone in my family was either criminal or clergy, and sometimes both. My stay at Letts was not long though, because word soon travelled of the presence of the rich and "successful" writer, Edgar White, and I found a daily procession of cousins and mendicants at my doorstep, all of whom had remarkable stories of need.

By this stage, my aunt, (Maas Ann) decided that what I needed was a wife (in Montserrat, wife means sex). Unfortunately, my aunt and I did not share a similar taste in women. She tended to like them on the large side, too much goat water and provision food for my taste. Actually, the only slender girls in Montserrat tended to be under-age, and since I was neither an ex-Chief Minister nor a Chief Minister's son, I could not get away with sleeping with a minor without facing prosecution. There was a time in Montserrat when mothers prayed only for sons to take care of them in their old age. Now mothers pray for daughters (attractive ones) who are far more lucrative in out-of-court settlements.

I next tried the Wade Inn, which was less accessible to my cousins. I took a room at the end of a dark corridor on the second floor facing a broken mirror. There, I could come and go in secret. There I stayed for the remainder of my time back home in paradise.

I had many interesting discussions with farmers on Montserrat and with my cousin, who was a vet. I was informed that the favourite animal for acts of bestiality was the sheep, with the cow coming a close second (although a few have a preference for donkeys). Apparently, the sheep is favoured because it makes less noise during sex and is more compliant. There is a story of a cabinet minister who was found abed with a sheep. He was threatened with arrest, not so much for the act itself as for the fact that he had put panties on the sheep. This suggested perversion and Montserrat, as we know, is a very religious country. He is said to have pleaded in his defence that he found much more passion and love from the sheep than he did from his wife.

The only person who was not surprised by anything that happened to me in Montserrat was my mother, Phyllis White. She had come of age during that class-conscious, stratified era of estates in Montserrat – for example, Brades, Waterworks and Farrells estates. (It was, in fact, at Farrells Estate where the volcano would do so much harm and devastation in terms of the loss of human life.) In that world, an adult was expected to address even a child of the plantation owner as "Maas", whether or not that child was still in short pants. What must it have felt like for an adult, male or female, to have to address a child as "Maas"?

My mother had long since come to terms with Montserrat and its pretensions and had decided never to return, although she remained secretary to the Montserrat Progressive Society in New York for over twenty years and was always active. As to Montserrat itself, her only comment was: "Too much pretence and poppy show." She was, therefore, not at all surprised to hear about the theft of the family house and land. She merely said, "So they stay." I, on the other hand, was not so forgiving and was determined to wipe the dust from my feet and to never return.

The Montserratian is a curious animal who you can keep a slave by offering him one of three things: (a) a key; (b) a uniform and (c) a title. Any one of these will be enough to keep him in bondage. As long as you give Montserratians a key, they will not only lock themselves in, but will wake up three times during the night to make certain that their cell door is locked securely. The same holds true for uniforms and honorific titles such MBEs.

I came back again fifteen years later. First Hurricane Hugo struck and then, a few years later, the Soufriere Hills volcano erupted. My wife came to me through the hurricane. She was born from it. By this I mean that I met her as a result of the hurricane relief effort in the USA. Apparently, although I was through with Montserrat, I was not through with Montserrat women. As I explain in an earlier piece, I lost her through the volcano.

Volcanoes are very handy things to have on an island because when they erupt they provide the perfect excuse for flight. I learned a great deal on my return. Half the island had disappeared and I was curious to see if I would find the same pretensions that I left. I learned two things. First, that everything I'd known had disappeared. The town of Plymouth, Cork Hill Village, the hotels, the banks, the stores – all were no more, even the memorial clock, beneath which my father first met my mother and "troubled her water". The New Jerusalem would have to be built in the north. Imagine my surprise when I found that much of the goods and clothing we had so diligently collected for relief in the States was now either being sold in the shops, or blissfully rotting away in some ware-house at Carr's Bay.

It was at Carr's Bay that I found refuge. I found a canon facing the sea and made that my home. I learned, too, that there is a lot of money to be made in poverty. I had never witnessed this before. I found that there were those who loved nothing more than a good disaster; in disaster is opportunity. There was Brown & Root who were providing housing and shelter (the same Brown & Root/Halliburton that appeared at every crisis, from Bosnia to Iraq.) Tragedy is always local, profit global.

Although I was homeless among the homeless, there were those who still found me strange, and my choice of sleeping on a canon they saw as slackness. I remember, for example, Murphy, "Rootsman" of Carr's Bay, who found it unforgivable that I didn't provide shelter for myself. To him, the one thing that separates man from animal is the fact that man is able to create shelter for himself. It therefore bothered him to his very being that I failed to do this. So although he would allow me shelter on occasions of severe rain or ash, he wouldn't sanction it. He might let me sleep there, but he never spoke to me and I joined his list of non-persons. He even provided me with a sheet of galvanize that I, of course, being a good city boy, had not the slightest clue what to do with. I used it as a bed to sleep on; this further infuriated him. Soon, however, this problem was solved when someone stole it, having found better use for it than I.

One incident sticks in my mind. It was one night at Brades where temporary housing had been erected. It was a strange night full of moon and jumbies. I saw a seven-year-old boy climbing the steps of the housing project (just like the ones in the South Bronx). People had placed sheets at the windows for privacy, so as not to be seen while eating (as though the very act of eating food was more forbidden than sex). You could see their silhouettes behind the lighted windows. In this peculiar time people dealt with their sadness in different ways. Women tended to talk to themselves and pray. Men, on the other hand, got drunk and danced in the road like Greeks and then lay down and dared cars to run over them. (Only a Montserratian could understand this.)

But it was that seven-year-old boy who interested me, with his thin legs, legs meant for running. He reminded me of myself at that age. I remember when I reached the States I used to love to run barefoot. I joined the track team at school but they would not allow me to run barefoot. I knew nothing about strategy or technique. I only knew "throw you foot 'pon ground and run". You ran until either your heart burst or you won. I've lived my whole life that way. I was a sprinter and I ran for my life. I ran through South Bronx streets in places like Vice Avenue, Freeman Street and the Hunts Point where General Colin Powell grew up. If you gave me a three-foot lead, you would never catch me and if you did, then I deserved to be caught.

This boy was singing Buju Banton's, "Destiny". I remember it was very popular at the time and Rose Willock was always playing it on Radio Montserrat. He sang:

> I wanna rule my destiny
> I and I, I wanna rule my destiny.

But it was when he sang the refrain:

> Destiny, Mama look from when you call me
> Destiny, Mama look from when you calling...

that it all hit me again. It had been two years since my mother's death, and only once in those years had I shed a tear. So much of that time, even carrying her casket together with my friend, Wali, at Woodlawn Cemetery in the Bronx, there was no emotion. (How clearly, I remember that day. Although snow was on the ground I could still see some green grass beneath it.) Like a machine, I fulfilled all obligations, everything from collecting her clothes and dentures from the hospital to the arrangements with the funeral director. Even when I went to the hospital and the nurse didn't know that she had died (and I wanted to slap her for her ignorance), not a tear. Even when she said: "We are not responsible for her personal items..." (like her gold bracelets and rings), still no tears. I asked for nothing from anyone, not even from my then wife. Everything alone. Only once did I cry. This was when I discovered that my mother had kept my books in her room.

I'd keep saying to myself a mathematical formula: one equals a point; two equals a line; (you draw two points together); three points equals a triangle or surface; four, you take a point and put it inside that triangle. If you connect all those points, you have a tetraktys, and all the dimensions of space are represented there and once inside it, you are safe; nothing can harm you. Four, that was me, the number four. But then Montserrat isn't about math, it's about masquerade, like the spin of the Spirit Man that pulls you into trance, like the beat of the drum, like the dancing of the trees, like jumbies.

It was that night, there at Brades, that the whole thing came on me again and I couldn't stop crying. I went back down to Carr's Bay and went into the sea and washed in the sea because in Carr's Bay no one notices tears.

The hardest thing in life is forgiveness – well two things, because first you must forgive your parents and then yourself. Parents are convenient things to have to blame. They answer all questions as to why things are the way they are. But with parents also comes an awareness of time. We see that the past is not real because it no longer exists (like the town of Plymouth), and the future is also unreal because we have no idea what is coming next (like the New Jerusalem). Only the present is real – who and where we are at the moment.

This makes Montserrat a very peculiar place because now, even fifteen years after the eruption began – and the fact that we have a generation for whom any mention of Plymouth is about as meaningless as the "begats" in the bible – yet the reality of the past is stronger than the present. We have people walking about who have visualized in their mind's eye each street, each house, each road, each school, each church – though none remain. We have people who place their favoured photographs on the walls of their restaurants and shops like Harbour Court and the old Lee's Pharmacy. They desperately watch them as they yellow and disappear like jumbies before their eyes from the harsh and cleansing sun. In Montserrat, the past is much more real than any present.

Now, as to forgiveness of self, you can only do that when you have forgiven your parents for having you born at all. A corollary to this is that you can only love your island when you love yourself. No one who doesn't love themselves can possibly love the island from which they've come. As I say, my mother did not need Montserrat. I do. I have many fantasies, many dreams that I like to think of as reality. I call them my swimming to Redondo dreams. Redondo is an island that can be seen from Montserrat. It always appears close. But then in Montserrat, every-thing appears close, mountains and even the moon, but it's all illusion, for behind every mountain another mountain hides.

Among the illusions that I have is that, had I never left Montserrat, I might have become a farmer (you know, living peacefully beneath my vine and fig tree) or perhaps a doctor or a politician. The truth is that the hardest work in the world is farming. It is not casual labour, it's not a sometimes thing. You are chained to the land and if it fails, you fail. There's nothing worse than work in the backbreaking sun and Montserrat is blessed and cursed with abundant sun. As for being a politician, this is equally an illusion, for politics is not a nice person's occupation. The best position to be in is that of the opposition, for then you never have to take responsibility for anything – and taking responsibility is the last thing that an opposition really wants. Some may be willing but no one is *ready* to die for their beliefs.

What I know with absolute certainty is what would have happened to me had my family not taken me out of Montserrat. I would have become Rhadyo (the calypsonian who wrote "The Swordman" and is now per-ceived as mad). The truth is that there is no place in this society for nonconformity. All opposition is either imprisoned, crushed, "sworded" down, driven into exile or tranquillized with medication. These are things for which I cannot blame my parents. The best thing that could have happened to me was leaving in order to return, to return by choice, not by deportation. This must have been God's will for me.

Remember that Montserrat is a peculiar, magical place of masquerade where old men still gather to tell lies to the sea.

IN SEARCH OF SHANGO
(For Pat Ryan)

Be not deceived. There is no such thing as change in the Caribbean. As it was, so it shall be. The plantation house still dwells in us too deeply for us to change. Governments and political parties come and go, but never our minds. Whether it be Guyana, Montserrat, Jamaica or Barbados, it's all the same. So fear not: the Caribbean the way it used to be will always be. So now, having gotten all nonsense of false hope out of the way, we can begin.

The other day the spirit came on me and I wanted to play fife, and because it was a hot day (you know, one of those days when they love to say the sun is out in all its glory), I sheltered in the shadow of the Faith Tabernacle Pentecostal Church in Brades. I was in mid-flight when a woman approached me.

"What that is?"

"A fife," I answered, in my innocence.

"I mean, what that is you a play?"

"Fire in the Mountain," I said, then realized that she was not asking about fire on any mountain, nor about how my fife could sound so sweet. It was about:

"You no bother bring no Benna music here. You crazy or what? You know where you be?"

"Yes, Montserrat, land of my birth."

"So you don't know this is sacred ground?"

Now I thought of summoning the good Mister Wilson who was just across the road selling his ice cream, letting him speak in my defence. Then I remembered where I was: on the tightest and most anal island in the Caribbean, and so I thought better of it, because he might act like he's never seen me before in his life. So although he does like the fife, I decided not to trouble him with moral decisions.

So instead, I had no choice but to plead that I was an ordained minister (a thing I don't easily like to admit). She forgave me and retreated after telling me that she was a Watchman for the Lord. I complimented her and played "How Great thou Art" (in a very subdued version). But I couldn't help wondering what she would have done had I set up my drums and started playing Trinidad Shango or the Big Drum music of Suriname or

Carriacou – for whilst the fife lifts my spirit, it is the drum that gives me life. She might have wet herself and run away in terror, having seen the devil himself.

How quickly people forget. She could not remember how recently the Pentecostal Church itself was considered unrespectable because of all that ecstatic praise and talking in tongues (called glossolalia). I couldn't help but admire those who had been brave enough to set up a Pentecostal ministry in Montserrat. Believe me, they suffered mightily for it. They suffered both persecution and prosecution in this staid place. Yet now, having become established, they became just as stiff-necked as the Anglicans, the Methodists and the Adventists before them. Bless them.

Why I say that the Caribbean will never change is because we hate ourselves. Always have and always will. Or more precisely, what we hate is the African in us, the undeniable Africanness of our bodies. This is especially true in Montserrat. We just don't want to be thought primitive. Fair enough. What I find funny, though, is the number of Montserratians who marry English, but then return to Montserrat and immediately start sleeping with a black partner (usually the same childhood sweetheart from the village they came from). They may even let go of their English spouses. Skin turns red with sunburn. What looked good in the snow and grey of England doesn't look as impressive in the sun. But there's no cause for alarm, because for each mixed marriage that ends in ruin, there is some eager young man or woman ready to replace the fallen. Remember that nothing is as appealing as OPP (other people's property). It's what keeps the Caribbean going.

Fortunately, no one is recording any of this except gossipy rum-shop owners:

"Yeah man, he take one look at the bamsey and next thing you know, he let go the wife hand. She had was to go back a England by sheself. Me tell you! Me feel sorry for she because she can't understand wha happen. She feel she did know he, but she can't go with Mon'srat, 'tall."

Anyway, to return to where I started, the poorer the people, the more the need for God; the greater the joy and sorrow, the louder the music. This is why the rich distance themselves from the poor as quickly as possible. They can't go with the noise. But then the rich have no great need of God (until, say, a volcano erupts and then they need Him for the length of time it takes to relocate). Their relationship to God is always negotiable. The poor, on the other hand, take God very seriously because it's the one thing that the rich can't steal from them.

As for me, I have a huge appetite for everything, and so I need more than just a single wafer placed on my tongue on a Sunday morning to be filled. It was because of my hunger and thirst that, some years ago, I went to Trinidad in search of Shango.

Shango can't be contained in a single room in a dull, two-hour church service. Now in Trinidad there is Shango Baptist that is Bible based, whose worshippers wear similar headdresses and worship in churches. But Shango itself is Yoruba African based and there is no Bible present. It mostly takes place outside and there is ritual sacrifice of animals (usually a goat for the feast table). There is also rum present, used as a libation. You quickly realise the difference between the two. There are always three drums present at Shango, one to keep the heartbeat, another played with sticks (the repeater drum) and a third to play the counter rhythm. The drummers have to be strong because the ceremony lasts all night. One last thing: it's not a good idea to close your eyes at a Shango Feast because when the spirit enters, machetes can start flying. Shango is after all the God of lightning and fire and he's not an easy god. You know this when you see people go into trance and start to writhe.

Following the spirit is not easy; it is like unto a man who leaves his house at first light and goes to the mountain. In the mist, the trees look like they're dancing jumbies and the leaves spin like a woman heisting her skirt and dancing, always just a short distance before you. You try and reach her and she takes you deeper and deeper into the mountain and leads you finally to a stream. Call her Oshun. Sometimes as you approach her she vanishes or you drown.

There was a man who they called the greatest Orisha drummer in Trinidad. Andrew Beddoe. He had the power. There were stories of him causing lightning to come suddenly. I went in search of him. I had only heard him on tapes when people had recorded him. He was not an easy man to find because you couldn't just hop in a taxi from Port of Spain to his house.

To find Beddoe, I had to go to Tunapuna and find one of the few men who could show me the way. A lot of Indians live in Tunapuna. It's a good place to drink coconut water because this is where the best coconuts on island are found. But be careful, because they have a lot of women there and the coconut water is smoother than Fernandes' rum and goes straight to your hood. Before long you find yourself "bazodie" and saying words like "forever" and you feel you want to climb her like a tree. You wonder whether this woman is really La Diablesse, the Woman in White.

> Drink Coconut water
> It good for you daughter
> Coconut water got a lot of iron
> Make you strong like a lion

The Indians who were living in Tunapuna were the descendants of people who came as indentured workers. After slavery was abolished, the

British contributed their usual mischief. Having seen that the newly freed blacks were now demanding living wages and were all too willing to set fire to the cane-fields at the very height of the season, they did two things: first they sent to India for workers who, because of widespread famine, were willing to work for pennies a day. This did not endear them to the Africans. Secondly, they outlawed Shango because they noticed that whereas Christianity extolled submission, Shango urged revolt. Soon they were locking up followers. This led to worshippers becoming even more remote and secretive.

As to the East Indians, their labour backed up the power of the plantation owners to control the economy and deny the African ex-slaves access to the land. This divide and rule tactic kept the two groups apart in mutual suspicions that are still used by the politicians of today to control their communities.

One good thing that the Indians did was introducing ganja to the Caribbean. It was they, not the Africans who brought it over. They were obviously not searched with as close a scrutiny as the slaves had been. As to whether the two groups will ever be able to really get on together, I don't know. I'll have to leave that to better and deeper minds (like Naipaul) to figure out. Where they do connect is in music and forms of stickfighting such as African kalinda and Indian gatka. They each have influenced the other, the presence of flags in Shango, for example, and more recently the connections between soca and chutney.

But as for me, all I wanted was Shango and Andrew Beddoe because he was the link between past and present, the keeper of the chants. It took me three days to reach his house because it was the rainy season and you needed a jeep to even approach where he lived. Even then you had to walk because there was nothing approaching a path. This was in Laventille, the place that has fought the hardest to maintain the authenticity of the culture (as, too, did John-John where Beddoe originally came from). When we found his shack and knocked (forget telephone), a woman answered and said he wasn't there. Not only that, she hadn't seen him in days but she was sure at least that he would return because his drums were still there.

"He'll be back when the rum and the money done."

You could see that she wasn't too happy with his doings. She gave us that look that a woman gives when she's wondering what new problems we might be bringing her. My friend understood the situation and was able to put something in her hand that would help her get through until Beddoe's return. She was the sensible one. She had to be. In time, he did, in fact, return, his drum strapped to his shoulder and complaining about how things had changed and how the Feast wasn't the same anymore. People weren't honouring the ancestors the way they used to.

"Them not respecting themselves. Even goat for the feast them tiefing!"

The woman didn't want to hear it because she'd heard it all before. She knew that he needed rest and wouldn't bother to question him about whether he had any money left from all this time away. That would be behind closed doors – and the questions about what he was killing himself so for?

But this was what he was born to do. She would have preferred it if he stayed home and just went out to do recordings in studios. But that wasn't Shango or Andrew. Shango wasn't coming to a studio or a wine and cheese evening at a Culture Centre. He was outside in the unsafe world where people cried out in their joy and sorrow.

I never got to hear Andrew Beddoe play live. I never got to see him bring lightning down from out the sky. I wasn't meant to. I only got to touch his calloused hands with the long fingers, strong like sticks. But that was enough. He had been ill for some time but he was well enough to know what he wanted. Better he died there in Trinidad – as he did – than in England like so many I'd known who'd gone before, anonymously, waiting on the mercy of the National Health Service.

In this world, if you follow your heart, they will come after you with rods. Not because they hate you. It's themselves they hate, not you. It's the freedom of you that angers people, so don't take it personal.

Don't be deceived into thinking it's you. It's Shango they see and they can never forgive you for opening the door to their hearts and entering.

ON BEING *THE OTHER*

History, to me, has as much to do with the things that didn't happen as the things that did. This is a very different view from that of the so-called realists who say that history is only about success and victory since it is only the victorious who get to record it, and so all else is irrelevant. The British royal family, for example, always makes certain that their children major in history, as well they might, since for them history reads like a family portrait. If, on the other hand, you come from a small Caribbean island like Montserrat, you learn to glory more in gesture and defiance than conquest. Or to put it another way, you learn to share the victory of mere survival.

Montserrat has never been exactly a hotbed of insurrection. Subversion has always been our meat rather than revolt. Being colonised by both the Irish and the British tends to instil in you a certain guile; faced with captivity and forced labour, you soon learn that not every nail must be driven straight. We could never hope to equal Haiti in open rebellion. We had neither the numbers nor the terrain to engage in prolonged guerrilla warfare like Jamaica with its Maroons or Brazil with its Quilombo societies that could strike at will and then vanish into the hills, sometimes for years at a time. When you lack such numbers and terrain (and, dare I say, such will?), you have to make do with intent.

For example, we celebrate St. Patrick's Day here every year, not in celebration of the saint who supposedly Christianized Ireland and drove away its snakes, but more in memory of the attempted slave uprising on Montserrat on that day, hoping to use the occasion of the holiday as cover. It was a good plan. All it lacked was success and silence. Life at that time was sharp as a needle and brief as thread. Any attempt at revolt resulted in execution by hanging because an example had to be made. For the master, it involved the concept of treason. But was it treasonable for a slave to attempt freedom? When you are *The Other*, the alien, the threatening presence in midst of any community, you're made to pay the price.

Do you see what I mean when I say that history is a very peculiar tale depending on what lens it's viewed through? In such an environment, the greatest fear was that a slave would go unaccounted for any length of time. The first institutionalisation of surveillance in the Americas had to do with keeping accurate records of the presence and absence of slaves, for it wouldn't do to have random comings and goings, especially after dark (though they happened). It was for this reason that the pass system was instituted in pre-emancipation days. After emancipation this became the passport.

The difference between pre- and post-slavery was the introduction of money into our lives. Not that money was not always present during the slavery period because of course it was, although we had little contact with it. Money floated somewhere in the ether above our heads and was seldom seen in quantity. It remained a tantalizing promise that, when amassed in sufficient quantity, might be used to purchase freedom. This usually took a lifetime to do. A few pence could be made here and there from selling produce from provision land, but money was not the absolute necessity it became after Emancipation, because then a master had no need to feed or clothe you. It was no longer in his interests to keep you alive.

Suddenly you were set free from slavery into the infinite embrace of poverty. Now another game began. Money replaced the whip and the chain with necessity and the urge for survival. Emancipation provided the illusion of choice. Freedom now meant you could beg or borrow your way into oblivion. In effect, you borrowed against yourself and your projected labour. You became a sharecropper. Gandhi once said that poverty was the greatest violence. He was right. Whereas a slave in former days knew captivity, he now would learn poverty and a new modern concept: debt. Welcome to the brave new world.

Freedom meant that one could emigrate, providing you found the means to get far enough away to make more money. You left your family behind as collateral and you went off to larger islands in search of better. In the decades after Emancipation, Panama was the most accessible because of the availability of work on the canal. Construction work was the most dangerous and because of swamp disease and lack of inoculation, there was a constant search for fresh workers. Over 27,500 "official" lives were sacrificed to build that happy canal so that America could end up with a 99-year lease. It was, by the way, the fact that the 99-year lease was expiring that led directly to Reagan's invasion of Panama (which you might remember was led so ably by our very own Caribbean-born and native son, General Colin Powell, the beloved).

Other ports of call after emancipation were Cuba and Venezuela. Later it would be the Dutch islands of Aruba and Curaçao and eventually the three sisters – Britain, the USA and Canada – that would claim us. Each place held its promise and its danger. In the early days, it was the physical danger of racist attack that was greatest to us. Later it would be the psychic danger of exile in places like Great Britain where you were reminded daily that you were despised and perceived as a threat to their way of life: *The Other*.

The point of emigration is, of course, to make a better way for ourselves and our families. It is through the remittance of funds from the diaspora that small islands like Montserrat have survived. Those who go abroad keep in touch with those who stay behind. Return is the bond which binds us; it has kept us healthy despite the volcanic eruption.

If emigration is one means of survival, tourism is the other. But here in particular economics shows that it is, at best, an imprecise science. Although the theory look very impressive on blackboards at universities, it has very little to do with the real world because it fails to deal with either biology or ecology. Economists love the concept of tourism because they love revenue incentives. They never stop to ask the questions: "At what cost to people, and what exactly will this mean for the environment?"

One would think that these would be the first questions an economist asks, but they never are. There is never enough room on a blackboard for people.

It's naïve to think that we can have the benefits of a tourist economy without paying the penalty of a tourist economy. It would be good to have the tourist dollars without the tourist madness, the wealth without the penalty of private beaches and gated communities with ourselves under surveillance. Tourists are best when they don't become delusional and start demanding ownership of our islands. We must be careful what we pray for. It would be frightening to see Montserrat become like St. Maarten and others that have become lost to themselves. Do we want to find ourselves costumed and packaged like artifacts and labelled the official art of the island, to be trotted out for amusement like wind-up dolls when leviathan-like tourist ships arrive?

The problem of history is that it never leaves us. The dream for those of us who have been away from home has always been to return. The nightmare would be to wake and find ourselves: *The Other*.

MORE THAN CONQUERORS
(Montserrat's 50th – A Modest Proposal to the Tourist Board)
(For Justin Hero Cassell)

The other day I heard a foolish man say that everything of interest on Montserrat can be seen in two days. I kept my own counsel and did not talk of either his mother or his lineage. But the truth is this, friend: it takes a week at least to penetrate *one* individual person on Montserrat, never mind all its pathways.

Richard Samuel alone is worthy of study: a modest rum-shop owner and farmer. Now I have to say, in the interest of transparency, that there have been many occasions when I have wanted to cut Richard Samuel's throat, and the only reason that I haven't done so is because he was a dear friend of my father (Toomer Dyer of Kinsale). This, coupled with the fact that he is the best baker of bread on the island, has made me forbear. Richard Samuel is a complex character who in his very being encompasses many facets of Montserrat life. It's often said that those on Montserrat who are not cunning are sly. Richard Samuel, in addition to being an entrepreneur, is also a vast historian of Montserrat masquerade. This alone should qualify him for sainthood.

Richard is one of the few people on the island who you can turn to if you are about to be imprisoned. You can leave your musical instruments with him and be secure in the knowledge that whenever you emerge, your property will be secure. (You see why he can't be killed?)

Then there are other colourful characters like Murphy "Root's Man" of Carr's Bay. You can ask Murphy anything about the fauna and flora of Montserrat and if you catch him at a time of sun and not moon, he may even answer you.

Then there is Jackie Fire, a genius who has long had a mad love affair with Montserrat stone and is our greatest sculptor on island. He has, in fact, carved a five storey house that he lives in. His entire life is a work of art. (Sadly, Jackie Fire died in 2014 when his house collapsed.)

Then there is Pupa, another sculptor, but he tends to favour wood, especially bitter ash which is medicinal and from which he makes cups to cleanse the body.

Then, when it comes to the visual arts and music, we have Pops Morris who, together with 'Bigs' Fergus, can give you the whole history of masquerade in Montserrat. Bigs started off as a "mischief", which is what they call the small boys who apprentice in a masquerade troupe. Bigs says that something happens when drum and fife meet in the sun. What that something is he doesn't know but he knows it's mystical. And then there's Lord Cecil Lake (Cepeke) who arranges all Montserrat's music by sun and by moon. These men and others are our priceless resources, but they require more than two days on island.

In order to comprehend Montserrat you must first understand the complex network of family connections. In Montserrat everything begins and ends with family. Not that we necessarily love each other ("Go find family, find famine instead"), but we do acknowledge family and this complex network of cousins, godparents, half-brothers and sisters was how we survived the dehumanization that was slavery. When I was camping out at Carr's Bay, somehow a plate of food would always arrive mysteriously, and usually wrapped in a towel. This breaking of bread, together with emigration and deliverance into other family hands, more than government, is the reason Montserratians survive and will continue to do so. This complex network of family and affiliations is as mystifying as fibre-optic cable placed underground and crisscrossing the island, and certainly more binding. You never quite know who is related to whom until you make the fatal error of voicing an opinion about someone. It is only then you find out who they are related to.

Montserratians have a very philosophical approach to life and usually apply "the yes but…" clause. For example, listen to any conversation and it will go something like:

> "Isn't that Delroy, the one they say try cut he father throat?"
> "Yes but… he very good to he mother."

Or

> "They say that Euston molesting that young girl."
> "Yes, but he stop beat he wife now. So you see things not so bad after all."

Now you can pretty much bet your life that this is a cousin speaking.

I've often said that in Montserrat all wounds are fresh and never forgotten. Along with the network of family there is also the fact that everyone has two names. Many are given names by friends and enemies that haunt them a lifetime – the majority trying to outlive their nicknames. Names like "Bassy" (Bossy), "Twisty" and "Gas-bag" are given from grade school on and are more binding than the circumcision rituals of African tribes. The reason that they are given these nicknames is that as early as childhood, these individuals have already developed their strategies for living. One would certainly need more than two days to fully appreciate them.

It should be clear to even the dimmest among us that Montserrat cannot attempt to surpass Antigua, Nassau or even Montego Bay in terms of nightlife. We couldn't possibly. We have neither the casino culture of these Babylonian islands nor their resources. We don't have 365 beaches to play with at the moment. The question then should be: what are Montserrat's resources?

The answer should be: its people.

The Tourist Board, which has for so long been ably led by our Premier, who like the Holy Trinity wears three separate hats, has somehow missed this fact.

Montserrat's asset is that we do not have the gruelling schedules of most resort locales, which almost ensure that at the end of a holiday you need a next holiday just to recover. Here, you do not feel like you're on treadmill. The pace is relaxed because the people are.

It must be refreshing for tourists to come at last to somewhere where they can walk anywhere on island, by night or by day, without having either their throat slit, jewels snatched or their wife raped. This is the main reason why those who visit the island once tend to return again and again.

One of the greatest resources of Montserrat is its children – children, not street gangs. These are children who actually make eye contact with you and say good morning and their faces aren't taut and tense like urban youth; children minus the madness. That alone is worth a visit to the island. This doesn't mean that the children here should be exploited and made to don madras costumes and prance around like dolls. Simply be themselves. And on St. Patrick's Day, the performers should not have to appear as black leprechauns in some minstrel show.

Now I know that the marketing strategy of the past has been to sell Montserrat and its colourful history. This goes along with native costumes and the national bird (the Oriole) etc., and the poor tired mountain chicken who just wants to rest. He is as tired of these unimaginative marketing strategies as we are.

Since, as I say, Montserrat doesn't have 365 beaches to play with, we have to make do with what we have and turn hardship into virtue. Don't forget that we are the same people who, for centuries, by emigration, have saved Montserrat from sinking into the sea. We've learned well from Ireland, that other Emerald Isle. Another form of emigration is madness. People who leave their minds behind. This is called emigration of the soul and is a difficult exile. Classic example is the calypsonian, Rhaydio who penned "Sword Man".

THE LONG AND CHEERFUL ROAD TO SLAVERY TOUR
EXPERIENCE THE CARIBBEAN THE WAY IT USED TO BE!

What is necessary is a bold new approach. We must learn to think outside the box. What Montserrat has in abundance is rough terrain. Whereas Antigua is flat, much like Barbados, Montserrat is steep and goes up forever. The terrain is ideal for extreme sports. Montserrat should champion long-distance racing. Its hills welcome challenge. For those who are in search of such obstacles, Montserrat presents a novel opportunity to truly test themselves. It offers all the difficulties of Kenya and Somalia without the added hassle of armed pirates and guerrilla gangs.

Next, I think that we should put on offer "extreme" holiday packages such as THE LONG AND CHEERFUL ROAD TO SLAVERY TOUR – ten-day holidays that would offer intensive workshops in slavery. How this would work is that, immediately upon arrival, the tourists would be stripped of their clothing and given work clothes made of burlap from crocus-sacks. This would be a much more immediate experience than enjoying the locals dressed in our period pieces.

This would be a labour-intensive, hands-on course that would allow the guest to take full advantage of the Montserrat sun, which is especially spectacular at noon time. The object of this exercise is to get a full understanding of just what life on an estate was like for the young up-and-coming slave. Loads carried on the head, machete in hand, the participant would be asked "to clear bush" – a very invigorating enterprise – and then climb one of our more challenging roads such as Baker Hill. Slave shacks will be provided complete with outside privy. Some leeway will be given, however, in that shoes will be offered – sandals made from discarded truck tires.

In the spirit of authenticity, whipping will be liberally administered. Again, in the spirit of authenticity, rapes will be available in the Davy Hill area for a modest fee. And for any offence such as back-talking, arrogance or suspicion of theft or sabotage, the stocks will be set up by the Cannon Artillery Battery at Carr's Bay. This is the fourteen day package and will include escape attempts at Runaway Ghaut. The participant will be given a fifteen minute window of opportunity to escape before being pursued by plantation dogs. This tends to focus the mind.

This Slavery Tour could be set up in collaboration with the University of the West Indies and could culminate with a certificate in slavery, a genuine manumission document permitting freedom. An exchange student programme in concert with the History Department of the City College of New York and the University of Manchester in England is a distinct possibility. And of course, it is absolutely crucial that we launch the Slavery Tour to coincide with Her Majesty's Jubilee Year. Her Majesty could confer the certificates. Who would know more about the long and cheerful road to slavery than Her Majesty and Her Government?

A second and more modest package, which is sure to be a crowd-pleaser, and is certain to be popular with parents from the Diaspora, if not their offspring, would be THE WELCOME TO REALITY TOUR. A number of us have children who are totally spoiled rotten, having been the recipients of either American, British or Canadian education – parents who find that their college-age youths use their homes as convenient hotel rest-stops. The only contact we really have with them is through credit card collection agencies. To top it all, any mention you make of Montserrat results in yawns and hasty exits. What is especially heartwarming is when the son looks you in the eye and says boldly: "There's not a snowball's chance in hell of me even visiting Montserrat, never mind living there."

Or when your Boston-raised daughter (who has been taught from childhood that all men are good for is to be used conveniently) sits before you on her abundant ass (gift of her mother), thumbing through her copy of *Essence* magazine and saying: "Daddy, why can't you send me on a real holiday to Jamaica or the Virgin Islands?"

This is not the time to remind her of the $50,000 dollars owed for her school student loans, which has somehow miraculously landed in your lap. Instead, take a deep breath and offer the TEN DAY REALITY TOUR TO MONTSERRAT. You can get them to bite, especially if you offer to send them later to the dream holiday they really wanted. But they have to sign a contract to complete the course.

Immediately upon arrival on Montserrat, all credit cards and cell phones and i-Pads would be confiscated. They are allowed EC$10 dollars a day for spending. They are provided with a coal pot and provisions. No transport. They are made to wear a T-shirt that states clearly: *Children of Diaspora (Do not feed!)*. Now, Montserrat people are notoriously giving when it comes to visitors and will probably offer a fish or a breadfruit or green banana. This will be allowed with the proviso that they are uncooked.

This tour is especially good for obese youth, the Kentucky Fried generation. On the 7th day of the tour the youth will be taken by "Scriber", the Montserrat Forestry specialist, to the Mountain at Blake's estate and abandoned there overnight, thus giving them the opportunity to appreciate the difference between sun and moon, knowledge of which they will be forever grateful.

After completion of the ten-day tour without the use of credit cards or electronic devices I think a marked change will be noticed in attitude.

I sincerely believe that this more imaginative approach to tourism will reap great benefits for Montserrat's 50th. I think that the perfect person to be the Voice of Extreme Tours is Radio JZB's morning host, Basil

Chambers. He projects the sincere and caring attitude that Montserrat wants to foster. Basil, together with our diva, Rose Willock, will have special appeal for families. As I said, in Montserrat everything begins and ends with family.

We in Montserrat are more than conquerors with no fear in us, because we have experienced and survived every natural and economic disaster – hurricanes, volcanic eruption and even our governments. We survive not because of government or parties. We survive because in Montserrat who not cunning, sly.

The Caribbean, the way it used to be.

Fife Man
(Montserrat)

OF INCEST

(OR GOOD MR. BROWNE AND NICE UNCLE BENJI)

(For Núria Casado I Gual)

Montserrat is much more than Montserrat because we spread everywhere, like blood or the sea, over all parts of the world and we take our fears with us. We like to pretend that what we come from doesn't matter but it does because things stay in the heart until you deal with them.

Part of us went to America and part went to darker places like England and Canada, but, always, Montserrat lurked inside us like ring games or masquerade. We can't help it. When I reached America, I didn't know much, but I wasn't afraid. People said they couldn't understand me so I learned to speak slower. I learned to control this gush of life that was pouring out of me. So much I wanted to say and no one to tell it to.

There were buildings that stood tall without falling and for no reason I could understand. Trains that could travel under the earth like iguana, and planes that could fly like birds. But above all, there were people; more people than I ever knew could live on earth at the same time. This was New York where things moved and never stopped.

Now it makes a difference how you first reach New York. To come by air is not the same as to come by sea because if you reach by air it doesn't seem real and you haven't really done a damn thing but sit down. But when you come by sea, as I did, then you feel the journey of two waters. You ride the waves, you smell the tanker oil and you see it stain the water with rainbows. That's real.

We were a week out of Montserrat when I came down with measles and I had to stay hidden in my cabin because if they found you diseased they wouldn't let you enter New York. So I hid like a stowaway and my Aunt, who was bringing me, was terrified. The story is that I was the one who suggested rubbing me down with lime. How the hell I knew to do that is one of the many mysteries which make up my life. The best I could figure is that it was something I overheard some fisherman say one day while I was hiding under some table somewhere. (I was always good for that.) Anyway, it worked. By the time we reached New York, the sores had cleared up and I didn't feel like a leper anymore. Now that's an entrance!

One of the warmest memories I have of New York and the South Bronx where I grew up was my discovery of the mysterious and wondrous geography that is a woman's body. When you're poor, space and lack of privacy create interesting situations. The thing you crave most is your own room and it takes forever to obtain. Even if that room is nothing more than a closet without a door and just a curtain hung across a wire, it's yours. Migration works like this: the newest arrivals from "back home" don't get a room; they get the couch if they're lucky (and damn glad for it!)

So it was that I got my geography lesson when Lena, the newest arrival, came and slept on the couch opposite my drawn curtain. She was my first glimpse of woman – woman, as opposed to breastless girls in bathrooms, bathing by candle light. Believe me, at age twelve you take what you can get and are thankful. This was not a child; this was a big complete woman and I would nightly feast my eyes. I couldn't wait for night to come.

But the rule in life is to take time and not overdo. I never learned that one. The more I saw, the more I had to get closer. So one night, close around two a.m., what did I discover on the way back from the bathroom? Her partly uncovered body, it being summer. (In the Bronx at that time people would sleep outside on the fire-escapes because it was so hot – who could afford air-conditioning? Some even slept in Crotona Park and not from homelessness either, but to avoid the heat.)

Anyway, I'm returning from the bathroom and see this vision. She was sleeping soundly, a good safe snore coming from her. I bent over to get a good look and, of course, couldn't help myself. I had to have one kiss on those nipples. You know how some things stay locked in your memory forever? Her eyes suddenly flew open and she bust me one good slap across my face. I saw stars. Thank God she never screamed.

"Is what the hell you think you doing? Boy, go to you bed before me do fe you!"

That was the end of sightseeing. But to her credit, she never told on me. Bless her. It was well worth any slap. Which brings me at last to my subject: not slapping but incest, which I treat here not just as the breaching of forbidden consanguineal boundaries, but the abuse of the young by those with trusted family connections.

Thinking about sex almost always involves an attempt either to recapture a memory or have a memory force itself on you, sometimes from far back in childhood. It can either be good or terrifying. In either case it's forever. I suspect that in large families most boys learn about sex from spying on some member of their family (usually a sister or a cousin). I had no sister (I never met my sister until I was in my twenties). As far as I knew, I was an only child. People have often times accused me of cynicism, but I can assure them that I'm but a child when it comes to what people really experience in the journey of their lives. I could never be a cynic because I still have hope and only children hope.

The kind of curiosity I have described has a degree of innocence, the cauldron of incest is about the abuse of power.

Girls are more vulnerable to incidence of incest than boys. Not that it doesn't happen to boys, too (just ask your priest or rabbi, both of whom are notorious). And while girls may be more reluctant to speak up, they also get inconveniently and undeniably pregnant. And then the great hush-hush happens.

We are talking about Montserrat and Montserratians at home and abroad. In Montserrat, every village has its stories. The main reason for acceptance is the fact that each village believes itself to be less notorious than the other. Call it mutually acceptable denial.

In the olden days it was Molyneux that pretty much held the record. Incest became so prevalent that it was railed against in churches. If it was actually spoken of from the pulpit it must really have been widespread, because the church is famous for its silence on any subject other than sodomy. If it happens behind the closed doors of the family, it is glossed over. But what about the other villages, like the peaceful fishing village of Banks? People kept to themselves and yet everyone knew of someone who was sexing his daughter – quiet Banks where The Shoes of The Fisherman are buried. And what of Long Ground and Baker Hill? I have no reason to believe that, behind closed doors, things there were any different.

Here's where it gets interesting and why I say that Montserrat is much more than the island. What happens when, say, a husband leaves his family to seek work abroad and returns to find his wife has a child that he is certain is not his and refuses to accept? What if he then refuses to support that child, which is a daughter by the way? She grows up ostracized, but it is soon made clear to her that if she "accommodates" him, he will be willing to help her (i.e. give money for school uniforms, books and maybe even passage to the States). Which leads to the next question: how many mothers have given tacit approval to daughters getting involved in incest? How many swear that they never knew anything, while at the same time directing their charges in the general direction of uncles, and grandfathers even, especially in "white-water time" (times of need)? If the man is reported (which seldom happens) and there is a possibility of a trial and time in prison, it is usually the mother who persuades the daughter to drop all charges.

"Can't go with the scandal. Anyway, is you fault."

The offender might even take a quick flight to England, which is a good place to hide and reinvent yourself. Blessed is he whose sins are covered. The girl starts to believe that it was her fault for growing breasts and tempting him to commit incest and driving her mother's man away. Montserrat sometimes seems like a house of mirrors. It's impossible to ever really know what is real and what distortion. People choose a story and defend it, regardless.

Which brings me to Good Mister Browne, a Montserrat gentleman I met in London. He worked for London Transport and supplemented his income by making souse and black-pudding on weekends. I was glad to know him because we could talk about back home and you could always get a good glass of rum when you went by his house in Hackney, a hive of Antiguans and Montserratians in North London. He had a younger wife and was stepfather to her two daughters (twelve and fourteen years of age). So imagine my shock when I found that Nice Mister Browne was not only sleeping with his stepdaughters but selling them as well, to friends in the rooms upstairs. When I dropped by, he would have my package waiting for me. I couldn't wait to get home to eat some while it was still warm (no easy trick in grim, cold London). I often heard noises from upstairs but accepted his story about a card game going on. I never once suspected. Talk about innocent. We weren't even living in the same universe.

How could he justify doing that to children in his charge? You see, it's not particularly what people do that fascinates me; it's what they tell themselves about what they do. What was the dialogue in his head?

(a) "Them not me children, really." (b) "Well, them go have fe learn fe earn them keep sometime, no true?"

And what of the mother? She feels that she has to pay him back for their passage.

"If me go police, them a go charge me too and take way me children dem from me, so what me fu do? This not me country."

Fear on top of fear equals silence.

Now let's talk about nice Uncle Benji. Who exactly is Uncle Benji? Every family has one. He might not even be an uncle, but from respect they teach the children to call him uncle. Uncle Benji is the one who always comes to the rescue. He always makes himself indispensable. Nice Uncle Benji is always around children. He even drives the school bus. Whenever he visits your home, he always brings sweeties for the children. He is never in a rush. He makes himself available and just waits for you to come to him. You turn to him with any paperwork you find a problem. He always has the answer. He is the one who can always get anything on discount.

"Gal, why you never ask me? You could a get that for half. Me have a cousin who own a shop."

Nice Uncle Benji. He has a long term agenda and never frightens children away by fondling them too quickly. He always turns his face to receive an affectionate kiss. Look, he's even involved in the church. He uses his bus to pick up the elderly and carry them back and forth for the service. Nice Uncle Benji. He never *quite* penetrates them right away. There's no rush. He's a master of timing. He may use one child to help him get

another. He shows them that he can keep a secret. Then he asks them to
show that they can keep one too. It's the more precocious ones that he
prefers, the ones who ask for presents (a clear indication that they've
studied their mother's behaviour). Sometimes, he'll use the mother just to
get the daughter. Sometimes he can get both at the same time.

> Both the mother and she daughter
> working for the Yankee dollar.

But sex within the family is often preferred because it's cheaper and
safer. What's more readily available than your own niece or daughter?
It's just a matter of opening a certain door. She's always on call. It
usually stops after puberty but not always.

Now we're ready to look at more complicated situations. What if you
find yourself involved with a girl who has slept with her own father and has
continued doing it for years? What if you find yourself married to one?
Please don't think it doesn't happen. There are always signs but they're very
easy to miss, especially if you don't want to look. Until one day, you have
no choice but to deal with it.

In a small community like Montserrat, usually everybody knows but
you. If the girl admits it, your first response is blind rage. You want to go
and attack him. You want to take a cutlass to him. But what will that achieve
except to put everyone in scandal? Your woman, her father, your children
(if you have some together). Everyone will be angry, not at the father but
at you.

What if you find out that it's been going on for generations? Her father
has only done what he's seen his father do and his father before him. How
many people can you punish? Can you dig up a grave? Not without getting
everyone to hate you. In Montserrat, ignorance is bliss. You love her and
she feels so good beneath your hand. What are you going to do? Not even
fundamentalist Muslims would stone a woman forced to sleep with her
father. So, what you do? Run?

I began by saying Montserrat is much more than Montserrat. Montserrat
is England and America too. When we travel, we take it with us. I've been
blessed and cursed with eyes that see and ears that hear. I've known family
who have lived for years with lies. Drink helps but not enough.

In England, you can always tell a West Indian home by the curtains; the
embroidered fabric is a giveaway. The homes are immaculate with plastic
seat covers on the sofa and photographs on the nice living room table with
the crochet mats, but the desperate silence sometimes tells another story.

Those who go away and stay away may do so for good reasons. We
pretend that we want to return and pretend joy when we find ourselves in
Ridley Market and encounter a friend from back home. But the reality is
that the last thing we want to encounter is someone who remembers us

from our beginnings; someone who rode the same school bus with us and knows us by our nickname and why and how we got that nickname. You want to "Cuss them stink" but you can't. Instead, you smile and count the minutes before you can escape their company.

"Bull-Bud, that you? You forget me… Mission, man. Mission. We go school. Remember?"

"Of course, I remember you."

"So, Bull-bud whatever happen to that gal you was friending with from Harris' – what she name was again?"

"Diana. Diana she name. I married her."

"For true? Who she father was again? Weekes, right?"

"Right, listen, have to go."

"Didn't they say…"

"Didn't *who* say?"

"Nothing. Listen, give me your number, we'll stay in touch."

"Don't have no phone right now. Next time."

"Yes, sure. All right, okay Bull-Bud, we catch up. You want mine? Oh, okay then."

And so you exit quickly and leave him there under the Green Bay Tree and pray that you won't catch sight of him again in this life. But you know you will.

For over twenty years I've been obsessed with the same character, Legion, a man-demon, a man possessed. Since my first novel, *The Rising,* he's been haunting me, even in plays. I think he came out of the sea or maybe the volcano. Twenty years of haunting and eruption. Montserratians have a habit of chasing phantoms at the expense of the living. We can never quite let things go. We keep it all inside. Every wound is fresh. We want to soar like eagles but we peck the ground like fowl.

> Lost my happiness a few months ago.
> Where did it go?
> Nobody know.
> Nobody never know
>
> Nobody know.
> Where did she go?
> Nobody know.

What do you do when you find that you've married one of Lot's daughters on this broken island? You surrender and love her. You love her so that you can love yourself. Only then do the demons fly and leave you, and you find yourself. Legion no more. Montserrat is more than Montserrat. Much more.

Fife Man

LIVING CLEAN:
BIG GEORGE, A MONTSERRAT PORTRAIT

Funny the way the world goes. You never know which stranger will become a friend and which friend a stranger. I first met the man they called Big George, not in the bright green sun of Montserrat, but in the dark night streets of Harlem. I was walking a hill toward City College – what they called "The Castle on the Hill" because of its mock medieval spires. Suddenly from behind me I hear this cloaked voice: "Excuse me…" Extremely polite. I later came to know that was George's trademark, politeness at all times. Then he'd crush you.

"I understand you've been seeing ——?" He called the girl's name; it sounded strange coming from his mouth.

"Okay," I said, looking up at this giant in a grey wool cap and realising that this was no random meeting. He had a face like one of the gargoyles on the frescoes at City College.

"So could you please tell me what is your intentions?"

"My intentions?" I had to laugh. "What are you, her father?"

He didn't laugh. His face took on a tired expression. "Me ask you what your intentions be?" He clearly thought of himself as her protector.

"Okay, here goes. My intentions are purely physical. Right? I'm not the least bit interested in her mind or her money. Pure pum-pum and good wood, that's it."

I like to keep things simple so that I don't confuse myself with lies. I had reached the point in my life where if I didn't know what it was I wanted, I at least knew well what I didn't want. I had just gone through a marriage that at best could be described as *interesting*. I knew that I would never trouble that particular institution again. As regards money, I've never been too impressed by it. It's been my experience that the richer the woman, the more she wants you to lie to her. Lying is something I've never been good at, except to myself.

Anyway, Big George didn't seem satisfied with what I had to say. I had one thing in my favour though. I looked at his big clodhopper feet and knew I could outrun him. Big men always have bad feet.

"So, me hear that you suppose to come from Montserrat? Who you people be?" He looked sceptical.

"My mother is Phyllis White from Cork Hill and my father is Toomer Dyer from Kinsale."

He looked me up and down and then started to talk to himself more than to me. "Toomer Dyer, Toomer Dyer? How me could shoot Toomer Dyer son? No man, you can't shoot Toomer son." And so it was that my father seemed to do more for me dead than he ever did alive.

Big George then took me to his home and proceeded to cook up some soup. He loved to cook soup because it relaxed him and he was good at it. Now here we were sitting in his kitchen and he's making dumplings and adding them to the pot along with vegetables like christophene (what he called chocho), then some pig tail or cow foot.

Now my mother had taught me to never eat from other people (especially Montserrat people). "They good to poison you or put something in you food." But the damn soup smelled so good that I couldn't resist. Besides, he was helping himself to a generous portion. In short, I ate, and had the nerve to ask for more.

"You know you father, Toomer, did bull-whip a man through the streets of Plymouth, all the way from George Street to Kinsale?"

I had heard the story several times before but I had never heard why he did it. You see, I had only met my father when I was twenty-three, which was a bit later, I guess, than most sons, although I was lucky to meet him at all. Most his sons didn't. It was Howard Fergus who pointed my father out to me, but it was Big George who *explained* my father to me. Whenever I tried to ask my father anything about himself he would immediately turn away and smoke a cigarette. The look he would give me told me everything.

"Look boy, no bother ask me no damn lawyer question." No information was coming from this man who had been bent from a stroke and life. But he still walked with a kind of dignity with his cane. Brendan Behan, the Irish writer and alcoholic, said no two cripples walked alike, and, man, was he right.

"So you know why my father bull-whip the man?"

"Of course me know," he said with his face in the soup bowl, which meant I had to wait until he surfaced again. "Did you know that you father had a gambling house in Antigua?"

"I had heard about him living in Antigua."

"You father had the best damn gambling house in Antigua. He was bright, he could use he head although he never learn to read or write."

"My father couldn't read or write?" I was in shock because even my mother never knew that. He was a master actor and hid it well.

"No, he could just sign his name. But he knew enough to open that gambling house down by the docks, the same place that Lester Bird started as union leader. They were big friends so he never had no trouble. He just stay open from Thursday to Saturday and he would make more than people who stay open all week. You know why?"

"No, tell me."

"Because he know what people want and he provide it: gambling, woman, liquor and food. Man, he had the best black-pudding in Antigua, and you know when the rum spirit a tek you, the only thing that bring you back is that black pudding. But the best thing he did (and this is why me say he smart), was have the first American jukebox in Antigua. He had singers like Fats Domino, Brook Benton, Ray Charles and Sam Cook. People them love it. The place always ram with people. Sometimes they don't even leave from Thursday until Saturday."

"Not even to change their clothes?"

"You don't know nothing about gamblers, do you?" He was right. Gambling is the only addiction God spared me.

"Believe me, when things going hot, no gambler going leave the table. They not going nowhere except to toilet and some not even doing that when money is passing hand. See you father did have one gal working there who would deal with the money and the cash register behind the bar. But now you father always love Antigua woman them because they does like back door." His face disappeared into the soup bowl again.

"Like *what*? I asked.

"They like back door. Let man do it from the back. It start because the young gal didn't want to get pregnant and make dem mother vex, because most time the mother did do the same thing themself. So they just let the boys do back door and after a time the gal find they prefer it. Antigua gal them good at it." I made sure to take note of that information for future reference.

"You see, Montserrat different to Antigua. In Montserrat is the men who prefer back door, not the women. And most of them is in the government; that's why they could get 'way." Big George laughed his wicked laugh and scratched his head and then patted his hair, which he was always proud of because he said it came from his Irish grandfather. When he laughed you could see his tongue.

"Anyhow, your father was making money hand over fist. Life sweet! He was the man everybody come to see first when they come from Montserrat. Is he you go to if you need help or anything, if you stranded and can't find a place to stay. Toomer Dyer would always hook you up and watch you back. He was kind of like John Bassy without the politics. But now, hear what happen. He come to find that this same gal who me tell you about, was tiefing money from he and sending it to a next man in Montserrat. When you father catch she, he put one lash 'pon she scunt. He tek one big stick that was hard wood from a guinep tree. Fishermen use that wood to make boats. Let me tell you, the thing hard. He bruk it cross she back and all she begging is: 'Please Toomer, no kill me, no kill me!'."

"Did he?"

"No man, but she would never forget that day long as she live. She lucky he never use cutlass 'pon she and tek she neck, because remember this is waterfront we talking. It would be nothing fu tek off she head and throw the body in the sea. Nobody would ask no question unless she come from some big people, you understand? Somebody daughter, and she was nobody daughter. The next thing now he tek the boat a go Monsrat. He buy one bull-whip in Antigua and go look for the man who the gal was sending his money to. This man did promise the gal that when they get enough money he would marry she, which was just story because he done marry long time. So now here come Toomer and he find he in a rum shop in George Street. The man try fu run. Where you could run to in Monsrat? Any place you try hide, somebody a watch you. So that is why you father bull-whip he all the way to Kinsale, and no police no trouble he, and people stay in them car and watch, glad it not them."

I think you could say my father had anger management issues.

"It wasn't the money, you know. It's the disrespect; double disrespect. You must always respect people. You hear what me tell you? Live clean."

Big George had five rules he lived by and he taught me all of them. First was respect. That was number one because he said that lack of respect would get you killed every time.

What I couldn't understand with Big George was how he could work with the Mafia for over twenty years. "The Mafia don't respect Black people!" I said, pouting.

"Why should they if we don't respect we-self? You want to know the real reason the mob don't respect us? It's because we love to beg. Yes we beg every damn thing, just like Monsrat. The Mob only respect people who take what they want. Use a gun if you have to, but don't beg. We rather beg and if we rob or shoot, it's only each other. If we steal, is eighty-year-old woman's pocket book we run with. How you could respect people like that? Just like we still begging for freedom. How the hell can anybody give you freedom? It can't be given, you have to take it. Otherwise, it's not freedom, is still bondage."

The next thing that Big George taught me on the road to living clean: "When you find youself with some money in your pocket because you get lucky – maybe you been playing the same number every day, like take 474 (one of my favourite) say you hit for twenty thousand, the first thing you make sure you do before you spend it all off on white women and liquor – make sure you give $5,000 to a good lawyer. Don't wait 'til you get your ass in trouble to go search for lawyer, because, believe me, sure as sun a go rise, police go come for you one night and arrest you. The only how lawyer going leave he bed to come look for you is if you pay him in advance."

Big George, for all the time he was in "The Life", never spent one day in jail for over twenty years of activity in New York. Not one day.

"Now the second thing you do when you have money is to make sure and send something home to Montserrat. Make certain you have a place to go to when you get old. Is no fun get old in the cold, trust me. You make sure you build a house and get some land so you could have place to cock up you foot. Never forget is not America you come from." And this was exactly what Big George did and had Galloway build the house for him. This was the very house in which the radio station ZJB was situated. It was also the place in which he allowed countless people to stay during the volcanic eruption. He did a thing no politician did. He let them stay rent free and never charged the government.

"Rule Three: When you find yourself having to raise hand to hit you woman, then it's time to leave. It never get better, only worse. And if she call police for you once, she will do it again."

"Amen to that!" I said.

"Next thing is when you leave, make sure you have you passport and everything with you. Never go back again to get you clothes. That is when murder does happen. Somebody must get stupid, either you or her, and the next thing you know, your life gone because you going jail, or dead. When you leave, leave. Hear me?"

"I hear you."

"You see Duke Ellington? I used to go see him and his band at the Renaissance Ball Room. When you see him up close you see where a razor sliced his face from ear to ear. It was what one woman do him when he try go back for his clothes. Understand?"

"I understand."

"Good, me done warn you. Now, for the last thing: You must know when to leave the party. Don't stay until the very end because there's still some food left in the pot. Don't be greedy. Leave while the party still nice and the women looking pretty. Don't let morning come catch you. Nothing look the same in the morning. Know when to leave. And always keep a hundred dollars fold inside you shoe. That's not spending money. That's exit and emergency money to make sure you could get to you house. Better to take a taxi than to let police catch you drunk on the road or run somebody over and can't remember. Don't make nobody have to heist you up! Maybe when police catch you drunk, they good to plant evidence so they could hold you for more than one thing. Know when to leave the party."

When Big George came home after the volcano, we found our way to each other. He had done just what he said. He had house and property and a place to "cock up" those big feet of his. But in the end it was those same big feet that betrayed him. He slipped and fell and when a big man falls, the ground shakes. He never fully recovered from that fall and had to confine himself to his house and brief walks close to his home in Sweeney's. I tried to get him to Carr's Bay to take a sea-bath to ease his pain, but he never bothered to listen to me. So I would go visit him with my woman and his eyes would start to shine, but I never knew why. Every time I had the same routine. I would stand outside his house and call out, even if the door was open, "Big George, you dead? You jumbie yet?" and then I would enter and find him vexed.

"Me tell you fu stop that rass, if me dead yet."

"Just joking, man."

"Me tell you what is joke to boy is death to crappo."

"Just fun," I said.

"Fun make fart!" Then he would greet my woman. "What's that you have there?"

"I bring you a big bottle of Wray and Nephew."

Then I'd take out the bottle of white rum.

"This not Wray; this is just the nephew. The real Wray and Nephew is 151 proof; this just 68."

"They don't sell it here," I said. "Anyhow, Montserrat gets into enough trouble with 68."

"Montserrat is a funny place; a man could tell you he come from Long Ground, but you can't tell him." I didn't understand what Big George meant until he died. Montserrat is indeed a complex place. Everything has to do with family and respect. Even the man who steals mountain chicken demands respect. Have you ever touched the hands of a man who deals with mountain chicken? His hands are rough yet soft and quick. To capture the mountain chicken you must travel to the Centre Hills where spirits hide and attack.

But let's get back to Big George. Now we came to the major part of the day and the ritual. First I would pour the new white rum into the huge bottle-keg in which Big George kept his bush rum. You have to understand that each man has his own way of making bush rum. Fred Warner, for example (who is the master of Bush Rum), his smells of the sea. You put in ram-goat bush and ganja with the white rum, but then you must wait until the precise moment of revelation and epiphany. Big George, however, added his own secret ingredients. There had to be fresh peanuts and then he would add his sadness and blessings. He was unique; no one could confuse his bush rum with any other because the final ingredient is *patience*, which Montserrat teaches only eventually.

Listen, there are some foolish people who still believe that bush rum is easy to make. Don't argue, just smile at them and wipe the dust from your feet as you leave them to it.

Once the rum was ready, Big George would start with his stories. How he got to meet all the top figures in the Mob. The one he respected most was John Gotti (who I also met while working in the garment industry pushing the Jewish chariots – think clothes racks – through 34th Street in New York City). Gotti looked like he was living a movie. He had movie-star looks and liked to walk about with his white cashmere coat draped over his shoulders. His only sorrow was that his son was an idiot and that the only child with his brain was his daughter who, unfortunately, was a girl as most daughters are.

Big George talked about the way Gotti described his son as "the little ass-hole".

"You see, everybody is the same, no matter if you have millions or only a dime and you kill a few people along the way. Everybody wants to see they children prosper."

As we drank the first glass of bush rum, Big George would play "riddle me riddle, guess me this riddle", with me.

"What's the difference between a New York policeman and a Montserrat lawyer?"

"I don't know. I give up," I'd say.

"A New York policeman would just rob you house. He'd say that he looking for evidence, but he would only take way what he could carry. A Montserrat lawyer now, he different. He go take *all* you land and you property with just a stroke of he pen."

I had to admit he was right. Every time an old person kick the bucket, a lawyer's eyes would light up because he knew that it was just a matter of time before the poor relations would come around seeking advice about what to do about the deceased's land. The lawyer would then come with his profound knowledge of this mystical thing called "The Law", knowledge of which he had spent considerable sums of money to obtain. That's why he feels justified in charging huge fees for just signing his name to any letter.

Best of all, though, are the lawyers who are sons of lawyers. They alone know just how much money their father (the pirate) actually stole from poor people. Remember that often those old people who were their clients could neither read nor write (like my father), so they signed away everything believing whatever Good-Lawyer-So-and-So told them. Law-yer-fathers had no mercy, whereas, the sons sometimes have a little conscience and wear their shame on their shoulders like biblical Joseph did his coat of many colours. They need the sad eyes of an Ingrid Buffonge to look into their soul.

Big George died on me and didn't give me any warning. Death comes like that, like a Wilson's ice cream commercial, unrehearsed and unsolic-ited. But the Kingdom of God is not a democracy, it's a dictatorship. The angels do not get to vote, nor, in fact, do you – although Big George had long said, "When a man gets so that he can't even wipe his own ass, is time to go, to leave the party." He was as clear on that as he was on most things in his life. If there were any regrets, he kept those to himself.

"Live clean, man, and then you don't have to keep looking over your shoulder. Don't be double-mind like a politician or a lawyer. Live clean and mean every word you say because, in the end, all you be is your word. Money goes and women go, but in the end all you own is your word. So keep you name from out of people mouth. Don't let them have to call you liar and scamp. Never threaten a man. Just promise him that if them a push you, then you a go push them back. Then do what you say you a go do. Take them out!"

I will never forget the story he told me about when he first came to England in the fifties. How he had to sell his cattle to get the passage. How, when he reach, he find racism that he never knew was there.

"They have this gang; they call themselves Teddy Boys. They try to comb they hair like Elvis Presley. They hate black people. Call us monkeys and tell a-we to go back to Africa. Me tell them is Montserrat me come from and them want to know what part of Jamaica that be. I don't bother with them. As long as them don't trouble me, then me no mind. But one night six of them try kill me. Attack me with chains and no police no come because them hate we too, maybe more. Anyhow, me tell them come try. First thing you must do when they attack is go for the one who have the most chat, because the leader is always the weakest one. All he have is mouth. Never forget that. Always go for the general, remember that!"

"I will," I said.

"The first thing me do is give him the coconut." He meant the head butt, which was a lethal weapon because Big George had a head that was like stone. He would break your nose and maybe give you a concussion at the same time. He knew that once he did that they wasn't coming back from that. Now the other five were confused without the leader giving orders, so they started swinging their bicycle chains. That's when Big George drew his razor from his pocket and started slicing. A razor isn't as good as cutlass, but in a skilled hand it would do.

As he said, "No sense me trying to run, me foot too big fu run. So me just stand there in the centre and when a next one fall, I pick up his chain and now me start swing with the chain in one hand and me razor in the next. By the time the police arrive they had was to call for ambulance. And would you believe is me they arrest for attacking them? They say that me one couldn't have do so much damage. Is then I decide is time to leave England and try America."

Now, the funeral of Big George was on this wise: they had a Vestal Virgin do the eulogy. It was a good choice. She kept it light and innocent. By the time she finished, Big George was a choirboy. I took the precaution of hiring a masquerade band so that things didn't get too boring. We all danced to the burial ground like real Montserratians do. Fittest Man led the procession with his saxophone and wearing a long black leather coat and a tri-corner soldier's hat from the 1732 battle. He looked good. I followed after with the band and my fife. People moved their bodies in time and I think I even saw the Anglican minister do a discrete dance. Big George's daughter looked sweeter than sin as she moved in her tragic black pant suit and high heels. I wanted her bad but I hadn't got Big George's permission before he died. He'd have to give me some sign that it was okay.

Then I remembered the revelation he had given me two month before he died. He admitted to me that he was in love with my woman's mother, who had died recently. Every time he saw my woman (who was the spitting image of her mother) he couldn't help but think of her mother. This was why his eyes lit up every time I brought her with me to see him. He liked to place her on his knee and give her avuncular advice while I went out to the store. So we had come full circle. We met over a woman twelve years before. Now he wanted mine and I wanted his daughter. That's the real Montserrat way and even the Bible says that fair exchange is no robbery.

Once thing I was glad of, I didn't have to carry Big George's coffin for it would certainly have ended in hernia. It was hard enough to lift the fife. I watched the drummer who put down his drum and helped bury the coffin. The ground was so hard the grave diggers had to soften it with their sweat.

There is a secret society of undertakers in Montserrat, all based on family. One undertaker will never go to the funeral of another man's work. (Just like rum-shop owners will never visit each other's shop.)

Everyone was genuinely sorry that Big George was dead, but not all for the same reason. Some were sorry that he was dead because it meant that they could no longer rob him. They would come into his house while he was sleeping from his medicine and steal money, rum or anything else they wanted. They knew they didn't have to worry about his cutlass anymore.

Then there were the politicians, the clever and Honourable men who lied to him constantly and kept promising to come by his house and visit. They never did. They would accelerate their cars as they passed in front of his house lest he might be sitting outside and spot them. Not one politician came to his funeral. There is in my Montserrat a little thing called class. They would never consider someone like Big George for an award. He was just what they called "a character".

At the end, Big George was being harassed by the government about back taxes they swore he owed them. No reduction for the time he housed all those people during the volcano. No reduction for the fact that Radio ZJB was housed upstairs. People are funny and governments are made up of people, mostly anyway.

Now there are those who are foolish enough to believe that Big George is gone and they won't have to give an account. But late that funeral night I saw a ball of fire come from Silver Hills, a ball of fire like a Jack-o-Lantern and I knew in my heart that he wasn't through with us yet. That was the sign I was waiting for. He liked the funeral we gave him.

"I shall turn my eyes unto the hills…"

Big George had one advantage over the world. They never thought a man so huge could have a brain. What people never knew was that he had a photographic memory and could memorize a hundred numbers in sequence and never get one wrong. (A useful skill to have if you ran a numbers racket.) This is why police could never catch him. He never wrote numbers down. He had a mind like a writer. He could spend a whole night concentrating on a single problem until he solved it. Then you were in trouble.

I know he'll be watching over his family and Montserrat. And one still night someone will hear a soft, polite voice saying, "Excuse me…"

Big George wasn't afraid to love or to punish. He gave me more than my father ever did, but then that's not saying much since my father never gave me anything but life itself.

Good night, Big George. And may flights of angels fly you to your rest. Until the next time.

IN THE GHAUT
(A PARABLE OF MONTSERRAT)

As we all know there is no such thing as poverty in our Montserrat (praise God). There are, however, two classes of people on island: the Men of Cars and the Men of Foot. The Men of Cars can be easily identified. They have big bellies that they follow behind. The Men of Foot have no belly. They are too poor for bellies. There's a certain arrogance to the Men of Cars. There is a clear understanding that all Montserrat roads belong to them and they have the right of way, always. And let's not forget the women. The same big belly rule applies. Women in Montserrat may even be more deadly behind the wheel than men. Not that they aren't good drivers. Every driver in Montserrat is a good driver. I say that because in Montserrat you are either good or dead. There is no middle state. The roads are so treacherous that the weak or the uncertain perish. The same rule applies to pedestrians. You cannot be double-minded in Montserrat. If you start to cross, then cross; don't change your mind in the middle of the street (like a politician) or you will lose your life.

The only time I've been struck by a car in Montserrat, it was a woman behind the wheel. Fortunately, she wasn't travelling at speed. The funny thing is that she paused long enough for me to cross, and then hit me. It was a slow, erotic and intimate strike. I must ask my favourite woman on Montserrat, Dr. Clarice Barnes – who is an expert on psychology and the trauma of displacement – I'll have to ask her what that driver was trying to communicate to me. It was Clarice who made the big breakthrough in recognising that post-traumatic pain still exists in Montserrat. It did not only affect those who left here so hurriedly with their cheap suitcases (all bought from Arrows Man's Shop). It remains with us still here.

Understand it was night, at the start of a workday week. Christmas was done and Montserrat had put away her dreams in a box and slept the sleep of the blessed. Not even the jumbies were out. I wanted to celebrate the eve of Don Romeo's birthday, but no one would join me. I cradled my shak-shak in my arms like a lover and walked with nothing at my side but my fife. I thought to myself what a peculiar place this Montserrat be.

It's a place where no rum-shop owner drinks. Not Fred Warner, who makes the best bush-rum in Montserrat and hasn't taken a drop in fifteen years. Not Richard Samuel who has the only rum-shop that stays open all night in Montserrat. Not Murphy (Roots-man). Not Silcott of The Rising Sun (now he'll take a drink, but never his own stock unless, of course, *you* pay for it). The two most profitable professions on Montserrat are rum-shop owner and undertaker. They always have work.

I was lonely so I thought of searching for the late Premier, Reuben (the only man in Montserrat whose mood matches mine when it comes to rum, an area of life where even a politician has to be honest). Unfortunately, he was off island and perhaps it was for the best because we two would agree on little else. I couldn't very well ask him to come and celebrate the eve of Don Romeo's birthday with me – that would have been too cruel – so instead I walked alone with my spirits and laughed because sometimes in Montserrat it's best to laugh than kill.

I walked to Carr's Bay, the one place in Montserrat that I feel safe, the Gun Battery. I kiss the cannon where I once made my bed. It never betrayed me. I bent and give it kisses three. Then I played my fife for the sea. If you catch her just right, then she gives you all her foam. The sea is the one woman in Montserrat who never lies or tries to hold you hostage if you make her come.

Now there's a constant dispute in Montserrat as to which village contains the most jumbies. Some argue for St. John's because masquerade started there. Some argue for Baker Hill because it's long and dark at night. The truth, though, is that Brades and Banks have the most. This is a fact. The record for accidents is the road leading to Carr's Bay – long, twisting and guileful. That road is filled with jumbies and jumbies in waiting. I see them always. The young boy on his bicycle who was run over by his own uncle. But there are worse things in life than death. The worse thing in life is life itself and having to live in guilt.

There is something about Brades that encourages cars to speed. Perhaps it's because it's the only bit of smooth road in Montserrat (because it crosses Government Headquarters). The men of cars feel safe and entitled to speed and so they're easy prey. As Fred Warner says: "You life long but you careless with um."

The jumbies I see in Brades all come from the ghaut where cars suddenly found themselves airborne. The jumbie faces all have the shocked expression of sheep. I saw the same expression on the faces of shop owners after the eruption as they fled the volcano, when men of cars had to suddenly become men of feet.

"Montserratians are resilient," people say. This is always said by people who now abide elsewhere. Like the farewell speeches of pastors as they try to explain to their bereft parishioners why God suddenly called them to seek residence elsewhere. They either plead their families or health as the reason for their hasty departure to England or America.

The really resilient ones, though, are the ones who stayed and watched as ash fell slowly and relentlessly on their houses. The women who tried to do laundry only to have to repeat the process hours later as the ash would wait them out. And men like Levon Watts with his Harbour Court Restaurant and his folded napkins and a towel over his shoulder trying to beat away the ash like Don Quixote and his windmills. Until even he realized it was hopeless and finally shut down his restaurant – which you had to enter with your shirt buttoned. Undefeated, he resurrected himself, selling ice cream from his car.

"People still eat ice cream, eruption or no eruption. Man must live."

That's resilience! The ice cream men of Montserrat – Johnnie Dublin, Chico, Watts, Wilson and Glenford Phillip, the Taekwondo expert who sold ice cream from his truck – warriors all!

But to get back to the jumbies. Only foot people see them. You can't see jumbies from a car. It's a foot thing. It's only when you walk slowly you can see them moving behind the dancing leaves of trees. First they try to frighten you, but when they hear the shak-shak, they dance. It's then they miss their bodies. You see, jumbies can't feel. Only the living can feel. That's why jumbies grudge us. They can want a woman but they can't feel her.

Speaking of not feeling, it came to me as I walked from Brades into Banks, what a good job the British have done on the Montserrat man and woman both. They emasculated the men and lobotomized the women, between the Church and the education system. There are women on this Montserrat who go through their entire lives without ever experiencing one orgasm; not one. Don't have a clue as to what it is, even those who have had babies. To tell you just how well Britain has done its job on us, there are still people on this island who have never seen their wives naked. Ever!

"I don't like to see me wife naked. A lady shouldn't do that."

"But you have five children!"

"And so? It's better to leave it to the imagination."

Montserratians have vivid imaginations and many children.

That good British job is why prostitution does so well here. This is a prostitute's Paradise. They arrive in droves here because the word has gone out that Montserratians are the most hypocritical and repressed people in the Caribbean. That is why both prostitution and the Church flourish. I mean, look, you can't tell your wife what you really want her to do to you (she is after all the mother of your little girls. We have no desire to tie up our wives), however, when it comes to tying up our neighbour's wife, we can become extremely creative. Sex with the wife is a duty (the women certainly treat it as such), whereas a prostitute pretends in earnest she really enjoys what you're doing to her, and with her there's no nonsense about not taking off all her clothes. There's the added benefit of being able to learn Spanish at the same time.

Some over-educated women can't move their backsides, even if their very lives depended on it. Only the masquerade can overcome this because its rhythm is rhumba. That rhythm takes us into trance. It originally came from Ghana, which is where most Montserratians came from as slaves (whether we want to admit it or not). When the real rhumba starts, women have to move their backside, PhD or not. Accountant or lawyer or not. There's no defence against the drum and fife. They must move what their mothers gave them. (For some, this is the only real gift their mother gave them!)

When number five quadrille starts:

> Swing high, swing low
> Even though you knock me to and fro.
> No matter still me go.

When I started to play fife for Masquerade, I thought the purpose of the fife was to make the dancers dance. Then I found that it's not the dancers you must play for, it's the drummers. If the drummer doesn't become possessed, then the dancers can't. So the fife-man must stand at the left side of the drummer (like the thief on the left side of Christ on the cross), then you bend close to the drummer's ear, low and close like a lover. It's the fife that keeps him in time. I prefer the women masquerade to the men. The movements are more erotic and it's the rhumba rhythm that finally frees them from themselves. The more educated the girl, the more she needs masquerade to help her heal.

Unless you understand masquerade you can't hope to understand Montserrat, because everything that is Montserrat comes from it. When you hear masquerade music you forgive Montserrat anything, even not loving you back. It's the one thing the British haven't managed to take from us.

So now here am I walking the road to Banks, my head full of quadrille and trance and I'm shaking my shak-shak and driving the dogs crazy (which I love to do because of all the animals in nature I hate dogs most, especially Montserrat dogs because they are cowards). Give me a cat any day. They, at least, are graceful and cunning. Only the wise know how to use cats as guard-dogs.

"Vicious Puss no easy. Trust me!"

One thing I love about Montserrat: there's no stupidity about letting pets in the house. Only ex-pats do this (and into their beds as well).

So here I am disturbing the dogs with my shak-shak and quadrille when all of sudden a thought came into my mind that once upon a time all of

Banks was owned by a single person. Nice days ago. Again I stopped and laughed. But then my foot began to slip on the gravel. The next thing I know I'm falling over the edge of the road and rolling into the ghaut. That's when I realize that I'm not Scriber! I try to regain my balance and at the same time hold on to everything: my cane and my bag with my fife, my shak-shak and my pride. The more I struggle to regain balance, the further I slide, until I tumble right into a cusha tree. Now I wonder, "What is this warm liquid I feel running down my face?" Blood! So I surrender, shut my body down and fall into this deep dream and see the face of Jackie Fire.

"Am I a jumbie too?" I asked him.

"No, you life still long, but you careless."

"I fall."

He laughed. "Me a see you. Pappyshow you be!"

"Tomorrow's Don Romeo birthday; I was just celebrating."

"You shouldn't try play at big people party. Didn't me teach you about ghaut?"

I felt ashamed then because he did teach me how to navigate the ghauts when we'd sneak into the Forbidden Zone. He warned me to always follow the tracks of the goat.

"Only follow the goats not the sheep. Sheep too foolish. They would stand in rain and drown theyself waiting for somebody to lead them. They like Montserrat man, dumb and dumber. Don't bother with them. Sheep them be when they live. Sheep they be when they dead. Check for the goat. Eat what them eat. When them nyam noni plant, you nyam it. Can't go wrong then."

"But goats could eat cusha; I can't," I said.

"Maybe you go come to have to eat cusha, too."

I remembered a poem:

> In Montserrat where not even cusha free
> I saw a man and I watched him cry.
> He had was to sell his donkey
> Just to buy an eye.
> You could tell me why?

I was glad to see Jackie Fire and to see him move the same way that he did in life. He could move quick-quick like lightning when he was ready. Even with the bullet in his leg where Montserrat police shot him.

"So what happen, you not getting up?" he asked me.

I didn't want to move. It felt nice inside this dream with Jackie. He had carved a house of dreams. But then it fell over on him. And now I wanted to join him. He just stood over me laughing.

"Montserrat man too foolish Them have diamonds beneath they feet and them too lazy to even bend pick it up. Slaves they be and them love it.

The Tourist Board should just advertise: *Come Montserrat. We love White People more than any island in the Caribbean, more even than Barbados*. (And that's saying something) Come Montserrat, let we love you."

I didn't want to argue with him about how Montserratians love their slavery. We'd had that same argument so many times before when he was alive.

"What you mean diamonds at they feet?" I asked.

"When the volcano blow it wasn't just ash it send down on we. It send down diamonds too and you let the Englishman take them away and say he going study it. You sheep, you let them take it and you never ask no question. How me could take people like you serious? You don't see is slavery still? And then you a look to these same people for help you. You don't see is madness that? Get up man, stop sleep! And look, make sure you tell these fools on Montserrat that they must never give way the secret to Montserrat bush rum. Sell off you hog and you goat if you have to, but never sell the secret. Now, come get up, man! "

But I didn't want to get up. I had to decide if I wanted to live or not. I tried to think of something I wanted to live for. My son Markhus? No he was alright. He had his own son now (Kairo). Now he could become the father I never was to him. I was too busy searching for my own father. I tried to find him everywhere in Montserrat. Tried to find him in the eyes of Richard Samuel.

Richard is damn scamp. But there is only one thing he loves more than money and property: music. "If music be the food of life, play on." When he hears the fife he goes into trance and he must find something to knock on. So I tried to find my father in him. I tried to find my father in Murphy of Carr's Bay, but Murphy had no time for sons; he has daughters enough. I even tried to find my father in Port (Black Sam's son). Black Sam was the best fife man in Montserrat. They called him Black Sam so as not to confuse him with Sam White (Vernon White's father who played saxophone and formed a group, Sam & Pam, which was the favourite group on Montserrat).

If anyone tells you he loves his father, he's a liar. No son can ever really love his father. There's too much contest. A father is either too much or too little to love. And fathers are so easy to hate. Only daughters can love a father (like my own sister (Rita Dyer) loved our father, Toomer Dyer). She needed someone to love, like my daughter, Nicole, needs me. Like I needed my mother, Phyllis White of Cork Hill, but my mother was never raised to be a mother. She was raised to be someone's daughter, eternally.

I found myself waking to the sound of barking dogs. In the darkness I heard a voice coming from somewhere above me:

"You alright down there?"

"I've been better," I said.

Wait there; me'll get a rope."

"Don't worry man, I'm not going nowhere. Trust me."

Then I saw the beam of a flashlight and this piece of yellow robe descending, a rope more beautiful than a sixteen year old girl at dawn with her nipples standing. I tried to gather up all my things, but it left no hand free to climb. Again I fell, embarrassed.

"Look, leave the damn things them, man, you could come back for them when morning come. Don't worry man, nobody a trouble them. Leave them, man, and come!"

I had to leave everything. Not even my fife could I take. I had only one good hand because the other (my left) was full of the thorns from the cusha. Slowly, so slowly I pulled myself up.

There I was sitting in my torn clothes and shame. Dawn came up so slowly, so slowly. I watched Montserrat reveal herself to me.

The farmer showed me the best passage around through the ghaut. I walked on bruised feet and picked my way through the cusha. I found my bag and one by one my instruments and there she was, hidden beneath the cusha: my fife. I plucked thorns from my hands and picked up my bamboo fife hoping against hope that she was not cracked, but still whole, still pure. There's no recovery for a cracked fife. She has only one life. If anything happened to her there was only one man in all of Montserrat who could make another for me, John Jones. But he's behind prison walls, which meant I would have to go and steal some wild bamboo from Blakes Estate and Roy Lee. It would take a year before it would turn from green and be ready for me, and only Jones could carve her to just the right pitch. I put it to my lips and my hands were shaking from the pain. Then I heard it play.

> Morning cock a crow, ko-ki-o-ko
> Morning cock a crow, ko-ki-o-ko.

I just stood there crying. Then I heard the voice of the Rasta boy who drive bus:

"Wha happen, 'e mash up?'

I felt violated, exposed. I don't like people sneaking up on me and catching me crying. That I do alone.

"No, is all right," I said.

"So wha you a cry for?"

"Just God, man, just God," I said, wanting him to go away. But then I remembered he didn't have to go away, he lived there. It was me who had to go.

A man only has two hands and one of them is full of cusha, which leaves you but one. So you have to leave everything behind if you want to crawl out from the ghaut. If you want life, you must leave everything – family, women, friends, even knighthoods behind. If you really want to climb out the ghaut, leave everything. Return back alone at dawn for them.

"Fife still sound sweet man, wha you a bawl so for?"
"It's Don Romeo's birthday," I said. A good excuse for tears.

> Morning cock a crow, my darling
> And morning comes too soon
> Morning cock a crow
> Much too soon
> Much too soon.

> Stay a while and have another drink
> Stay a while and have another drink
> Stay a while and have another drink
> Because morning a come too soon.

Jackie Fire said, never travel anywhere in Montserrat without a rope. Now, I'll listen. I once wanted to steal my father's hat. Now it's his cane I want to steal.

4. RIGHTS AND PASSAGES

OF ENGLAND

If a black man of a certain age talks to you of England, listen. If he speaks of the year 1955 you may be certain that he wasn't born there, because few Blacks were in England then who hadn't come from the sea. Watch his hands and his eyes. His hands will tell you things which his words can't and his eyes will mask tears that won't fall.

He's of that generation who came with nothing but God and rum in their bellies and a desire for more.

If you ask him he'll relive his first encounter with snow, ice and fog in London. Fog so thick that you couldn't find your own house even though you might be standing right before it.

"But everything look so alike then, you couldn't tell anyhow. That was England."

He'll remember forever his first winter, his first job and the first English child who followed behind him in the street and begged him: "Please mister, can we see your tail? Me dad says all you wogs have tails. Come on then, please mister."

And his look of disappointment when you didn't produce one.

He'll remember, too, his first pub and the piss taste of English beer and his experimenting with all the strange drinks that faced you behind the bar until at last the discovery and wonder of Guinness, which was dark and bitter like life itself and brought pleasure.

This was a time in Britain when even a banana was considered exotic because no one had ever eaten one (no one worth knowing anyway). No one travelled more than fifty miles from where they were born except to go to war, and the only Blacks ever seen were in movies from America where they either danced with Shirley Temple or ran from Tarzan in the jungle. Or else they came as soldiers during the long war and everybody hated them because the English women found them strange fruit and exciting.

You went to work in darkness and returned home in darkness and in between was the pub and the fish and chip shop, where they served the chips wrapped in newspaper; this was a great treat and the ink was rumoured to kill germs. What saved you during the day at the factory was the tea break. Workers lived for that, and would strike for that if for nothing else. It was the one thing that confirmed you were human after all. You had your "cuppa" and poured in as much sugar as possible for the energy boost it promised. For wasn't sugar the currency of our lives? Didn't King Sugar make Britain and bring us to the islands?

They'd ask you where you came from and if you answered Montserrat they would want to know what part of Jamaica that was. It didn't matter. Sugar made you royal. Sugar and Sea Island cotton – so that kings could eat from plates of gold and drink from crystal. Slaves died at the rate of up to 20% of their numbers each year. One historian has estimated that there was an almost complete turnover of the slave population every seven years. Montserrat was tiny in area of sugar acreage and slave numbers (6,400 in 1834), yet even after the slave trade ended and owners were expected to improve conditions out of self interest, there was a decline in numbers.

History formed us and maybe the very same firms of shipowners who landed us in the Caribbean now brought us to England, only now it was called immigration and we got to pay for that privilege – and to do those jobs that the English didn't want to do, because of danger, class pride or low pay. Those were the years when it went from: "Rooms to rent, no Coloureds, no Irish or dogs need apply", to harassment on the shop floor and no union to appeal to because they'd write the word "Troublemaker" on your work card and that would seal your fate. No one would hire you. You either kept your mouth shut or quit. No shop steward was going to take your side over an Englishman.

On the streets there were the Teddy Boys with their brothel creepers and bicycle chains (a generation later it was skinheads with their "bovver" boots) and they'd chase you into alleyways. There was Oswald Mosley, variously a Tory, independent and Labour M.P. who started the British Union of Fascists and supported Hitler during the war; he loved to stir things up. The Teddy Boys acted as his storm troopers. On Saturdays you had to stay off the streets because football meant you were in trouble, regardless of which side won the match. Drunk with anger or celebration it didn't matter, you were always a target of the mob.

It was in 1958 that things finally reached a breakpoint and the Notting Hill riots happened. The Teds came expecting an easy skirmish, the usual breaking of heads, followed by taunts of "Go back where you came from!" What they encountered instead was a major battle. They hadn't planned on Blacks who had served in the war as soldiers preparing their area for a siege. Blood ran in the streets and the Teddy Boys were soundly beaten. It was only then that the police acted and the wagons arrived to cart people away. The defence of Notting Hill had been well planned and caught the intruders totally unprepared. It was a major turning point for race relations; Britain would never be the same again. Now things were said out loud which before were only said in whispers. The Labour Party was forced to take a stand and promise that if it won the next elections it would put in place the first anti-discrimination act in Britain, although it would take another six years to arrive. By then, Blacks had stopped apologising for their existence.

The most baffling thing about Blacks in Britain is that, when they first came, for the most part, they had no intention of staying. Although many had been asked to come through recruitment campaigns in the islands – which said Britain needed workers after the war – most who came never planned to stay. Most had a five year plan. It was, I'm sure, the vicious prejudice they encountered that made them refuse to be beaten. The reflex response was fierce resistance. It was only later that you came to realize: "My God, it's here I live now."

And what was it that kept us whole during all those years of drought and wonder? Was it the family and friends sent for from back home, who arrived one by one and fragment by fragment? Was it the women who came and kneaded us like cassava bread? Yes. And the sanity that came – and which could only come – from the music that raised us up. You must keep it close no matter what the struggle outside. Keep the cadence and the cadence keeps you and holds the harm away.

> Bring me me food in a calabash, calabash
> Bring me me food in a calabash
> Bring me me food in a calabash, calabash
> Me no want no food in no bowl.

When a black man of a certain age talks to you of England, listen. Watch his hands and then his eyes for they'll pierce you and tell you the things his words never can. Hear him.

RITES OF PASSAGE AND WRONGS OF TIME
(Israel and Palestine)

If we in the Caribbean are guilty of anything it's our total lack of interest in matters beyond our borders and things wider than ourselves. Conflicts in the Middle East, for example, fail to concern us until they impact on our lives by way of higher oil prices, higher transport costs and less tourism. Now that gets our attention!

Other than that we choose blissful ignorance every time. We act only after things happen and seldom ask why. The world, however, is much like the Church – one body – and what affects the head affects the heel as well. Isolation is, therefore, more than ever a luxury, rare and scarce as clean water in the desert.

In his book, *Beyond a Boundary*, C.L.R. James, the black historian and cricket wizard, wrote of the calm continuity of rhythm and time that Caribbean cricket had come to represent: a culture of grace and style of stroke-play that has come to define us as a people. There was the blessed assurance that, regardless of the madness of the world outside, Caribbean cricket would always endure. As long as the sun rose, there would be the sound of bat and ball, footsteps and awe on the playing field where time and the timeless meet, whether it be on Queen's Park Oval in Trinidad or the Jim Allen Playing Field in little Montserrat.

This assurance is very necessary to us and our sense of self, because it is a very African concept, this way of being and reverence for the eternal. It has to do with respect for ancestors and the rites of passage, generation unto generation, as we, in turn, become our fathers – the way a batsman like George Headley transformed to Gary Sobers and he in turn to Vivian Richards and he in turn to Brian Lara. (Of the three, it was Richards who was the most important because, of the players of his period, he was one of the most politically conscious, who saw that cricket was about much more than itself.) This, then, is our sense of Caribbean time and represents what is best in us.

Now, thinking about our Caribbean sense of time in cricket, it occurs to me that for different peoples and places the sense of time is not the same, and that the failure to comprehend this might well be why people seem out of sync with each other and why, more than ever, they seem to be at each other's throats. We're witnessing more nations in conflict, more refugees in flight, and, on a global level, a pervasive mood of chaos. Or perhaps it's just me. Let's see.

The Greeks had two words for time. There was *Cronus* (what we call clock time; we can see the hands moving because it's temporal), and there was *Kairos* – internal, non-sequential and nonlinear time. We don't see anything move, but it moves in us. It is what we feel. For example, the time Christ spent hanging on the cross must have been quite different from, say, the time he spent being a guest at the wedding at Cana, where he spent time turning water into wine to please his mother and the newlyweds. We perceive time very differently under extreme circumstances.

Another sense of Kairos is the "timeliness of time". For example, a very skilful lawyer will, in addressing the court during his summation, take into account not just the choice of words for his closing argument but, sensing the mood of hearers , will use just the right word at the right time, delivered at the right tempo. That moment is the Kairos moment, a moment of grace, opportunity and danger. It seems to me that the reason that we are witnessing so much displacement and bloodshed is the fact that we're living in different time zones of existence.

For many Israeli Jews, for example, the calendar year is not 2014 but 5775, and they mean that seriously. They see Israel with an unbroken history. They may have taken a brief holiday of two thousand years but they are back now and they were in – and remain in – an urgent need of a homeland. They've hypnotized themselves with the mantra: "A land without people for a people without land." With this different perception of time they seem to have willed themselves into a tunnel vision that justifies any action regardless of how inhumane. And so, because they returned from Europe where they'd been persecuted, they felt justified in the genocide of anyone who got in their way. They have the biggest bombs, the greatest weaponry and the world's sole superpower backing them, plus a few pages from the Bible that state they have permission because they have been chosen.

I know an Israeli girl, Naomi, who has green eyes. She could pass for Palestinian. Her hair is thick and nappy like a Puerto Rican's. She opens her lips to me but not her mind. She can speak reasonably on any subject – except Israel. The door closes. The mind closes and she gets lost in time.

The Palestinians, on the other hand, see fifty years of living under occupation and apartheid. That's the only calendar they see. Long enough for two generations to come into being and experience nothing but displacement and bob-wire fences.

Try this for a history. The British, during World War I, needed the Arabs to fight the Turks, who were on the side of the Germans, so they promised the Palestinians that, if they fought, they would have freedom from the Ottoman Empire, have their own homeland again. At the same time, they promised the Jews the same thing, and took as much money as possible from the Rothschild banks for the sale of land. At the same time, they made a pact with the French that included Palestine as part of an agreement to divide the spoils of the Ottoman Empire. Only the British could manage to make three promises for the same land and describe it as "regrettable misunderstanding." (Think Lawrence of Arabia on his white horse in the desert in search of truth and the *Seven Pillars of Wisdom*. The British kept him in the dark, too, thinking him some fool who'd smoked too much hashish and gone native. He was of use only because he could speak Arabic.)

The solution was to keep everything secret from the Palestinians until after the war was won. The Palestinians were the most expendable after all, having nothing to offer other than their blood. Lord Rothschild, on the contrary, was actively pursued by Lloyd George (the British Chancellor) for his support for the war effort, because he had the financial resources and access to international influence (i.e. the ability to draw America into the war as well as to ensure the overthrow of Tsar Nicholas of Russia, who was at the time the richest man in the world). Imagine the shock of the Palestinians when, at the end of the war, they were informed of the secret treaty, which came to be known as the Balfour Declaration, that Britain had signed. The outcome, thirty years later, was to drive people from their homes and land, many in a single day. Some Palestinians have passed on the key to their houses, generation to generation, in the hope of return.

Oppression leads to resistance, which leads to more suppression, which in turn leads to yet more resistance. How can any rational person believe that this can result in anything other than perpetual war? You might even suspect that the greater the feeling of guilt, the more rabid the cruelty exacted. You would think that those most acquainted with suffering would be the most merciful, but this is not the way of the world. I think that only Blacks, in both the US, post-slavery, and those in South Africa, post-apartheid, have managed to escape the cycle of becoming in turn oppressors. We Blacks, in general, tend to internalize our anger and turn it on ourselves and each other instead, but that's another matter.

And even if, instead of identifying what makes us different, I search for what all people have in common, I still find conflict. We share a desire to win at something, regardless, be it in sports, music or even food. You'd think that food could bring us together, but it's not easy. Kitchens are intimate spaces that encompass time and memory. The taste of a certain dish takes us back to a time and place of safety. In times of uncertainty, we always seek the calming comfort of food. To open our kitchens is to open our hearts, and even in Montserrat it may take fifteen or more years to move from casual conversations on the doorstep, to being invited inside someone's kitchen.

So it is not surprising that in the Middle East even food can divide. There is competition as to who created falafel and who makes it the best. It actually originated in Egypt but has now been claimed by Israel. It is a favourite everywhere in Palestine. Even this simple dish made from chickpeas and oil has been ammunition in the culture wars. The truth is that people who exist side by side for centuries will share the same food and share the same lies about exclusive ownership.

Music is another common denominator: the greater the oppression, the stronger the music. This is why Black music is popular everywhere in the world and why totalitarian governments once tried to ban their citizens from listening to Black American jazz. Can we open our music and allow our artists to play together? This, too, can be dangerous. Hence the potency, in image at least, of Daniel Barenboim's and Edward Said's the West-Eastern Divan Orchestra. But the West-Eastern Divan Orchestra has not ended the war, and all repressive governments continue to love national anthems but fear the people's music, particularly the music of youth.

The youth are always courted and feared at the same time. They are a necessary evil to every government, because it is they who are sent to die, either as legitimate soldiers on the frontline, or else coaxed into strapping on a suicide vest and travelling halfway around the world in response to some cause or situation that they find unjust. Only youths sacrifice themselves so willingly. Leaders of countries tend not to do this but instead make those accommodations with reality that allow them to live long and comfortable lives and make many speeches.

The danger of youth is their different sense of personal time, and hence their volatility. Failure to capture them may result in either their marching in the streets or even taking up arms against you. Again, timing is delicate. Great care must be taken that repression is not so total that you give the victim the feeling that they have nothing to lose. I think that this is the mistake that Israel is making. The odds are so obviously in their favour and the slaughter so overwhelmingly unbalanced, with the US as their ally and chief monetary funder, that they don't allow for that glimmer of hope that allows a subject people to accept colonization.

I would have thought that Israel would have learned from South Africa that you can only squeeze people so far. But then again, South Africa didn't have a holocaust to justify the need for absolute security, although they (the Boers) did claim that they were the original inhabitants of South Africa, and they, like the Jews, were the chosen of God. Perhaps this is why Bishop

Desmond Tutu finds it so amazing that the world doesn't see the similarity of the situation between Israel and apartheid South Africa and rise up in outrage.

Lastly, in thinking about time, we have to deal with the whole business of what is called history. My suspicion is that history is a commodity that can be bought and sold, and, for those with power, history is of no value unless it sells the present. The past, as we know it, is owned by the present and truth belongs to those who control the lighting. He who conquers gets to name things, be it a territory or a star. This commodification has swallowed everything from religion to Shakespeare. Unless someone somewhere is making a profit from the knowledge of "its" existence, that "it" will remain unheard of. Only when Christianity became the official religion of Rome did worship move suddenly from stables to cathedrals.

This illustrates the movement of how something becomes a faith and not merely a cult. Only when a set of beliefs and ritual practices attach themselves to a state, a homeland, a nation, is it taken seriously. This is why many vulnerable youths are willing to sacrifice themselves to bring into existence the Caliphate of the Islamic State, and the exact same reason why Israel was and is willing to sacrifice whoever or whatever stands in the way of the establishment of the theocracy of Israel. The frightening thing is that there are those who are willing to sacrifice not only themselves but other nations as well, whether by means of war, environmental destruction or by wrecking economies. The new currency has moved from gold and oil to water as well.

Those who control the World Bank control the IMF and Wall Street too. Destruction on the one hand leads to acquisition on the other. Likewise, war is always followed by philanthropy, for pennies on the dollar. It's interesting to see how often the legend "Gift of Rothschild" appears on every other street corner in Israel, as if the entire country were a private fiefdom.

What then is time? Is it only a series of cycles that must endlessly repeat themselves?

Some ask me what my work is about. I say: the rites of passage and the wrongs of time. Better the ink of scholars than the blood of martyrs, for if none remembers, what then?

TRANCE (LANGSTON HUGHES: IN TRANSLATION)
(for Hafiz)

There are many ways to kill a man. Gun and knife will work, but to make a man irrelevant will also do, and what better way to ignore an artist than to place him in a high school or even college textbook for generations of students to ignore? This can be called death by anthology. This is when you take a vital and radical giant like Langston Hughes, who was global before there was the word global, and place him in a box marked "Poetry of the Negro".

Langston Hughes had many contradictions, an enigma disguised as a poet. His sadness he kept to himself and his laughter he gave to the world. In his whole life he was searching for Pushkin even before he knew who Pushkin was. Born in Missouri of a black father who almost instantly abandoned both him and America for Mexico, and a mother who came from privilege and no money (can you get a better crucible for the making of a poet?). Add one grandmother who could actually remember John Brown and Harpers Ferry where she saw her husband die. Given all this, wasn't it inevitable that Langston would ask: "What becomes of a dream deferred?"?

The answer is that the dream goes to Broadway and becomes a *Raisin in the Sun*. But what becomes of the poet who asks the question? Well, he must travel the world like the Flying Dutchman. He visits every port but will never really fit in anywhere. He will wander and wonder but fortunately for him, he will wear exile well.

It was a good thing that Langston's father, James Hughes, chose Mexico to hide in. As a result of this accident (though in an artist's life there are really no accidents), Langston had a lifelong love of Spanish that served him well when he later met Garcia Lorca in Harlem. Langston would translate Lorca's *Poeta en Nueva York* (*A Poet in New York*) but that was later in the odyssey. First we have to get the sixteen-year-old Langston out of Mexico, where he can't decide who to kill first – his father or himself.

Nobody loves a genius child.

Kill him – and let his soul run wild!

Fortunately, he didn't kill his father because it would have brought him bad luck and he had enough of that already. The irony, of course, was that his father, whom Langston referred to as "Our father who art in Mexico", may have left America, but in his mind and values he would always be essentially American, which is to say, obsessed with money greed and success. He was a total capitalist and despite his own experience of exploitation and poverty, had no moral dilemma whatsoever about exploiting the poor of Mexico and becoming quite the black "jefe" or the landlord of a slum housing estate. Langston couldn't stand him. When he asked Langston what it was he intended to do and Langston replied, "Be a writer", his father immediately gave him an account book and told him: "Here, you want to write, write this. Go collect my rent, boy."

In all the years that Langston was apart from his father he always wondered and fantasized about him – this man who had dared to take a chance and leave America. When he met him, he found the dream of the father was better than the father himself. As for his mother, what did she want? She wanted him back home where he could go out and work to support her, but he had a dream, a secret dream, to come to New York and go to school, see Harlem and become a writer.

But you have to be very careful with dreams because the minute you put them into words you lose the trance. People wake you. They wake you and step on your dreams. So now he's very careful when he asks for a year of tuition at Columbia University, which he wants his father to finance, and if he's not successful then he'll come back to Mexico and be the accountant son his father wants him to be. His father agrees to this, so perhaps it was a good thing he didn't commit suicide after all.

A year later, you land in New York, wired with wonder. You've never seen people move so fast but you pretend that you're not in awe, that you're not a stranger, that you're not overwhelmed. Now enrolled at Columbia University, people make clear that they are less than thrilled to have you. (You see, when you sent your application from Mexico, they were expecting you to be Spanish not Black). Columbia doesn't like Blacks or Jews, but they're willing to make an exception if you agree not to publicize the fact. In other words, keep a low profile, especially while living in the dorm. They even allow you to write for the school newspaper, *The Spectator*. (Langston hated the racism at Columbia so much that he wrote under the pseudonym LANG HSU, taking a Chinese alter-ego much the same way the jazz musician, Charlie "Yardbird" Parker, would later record under the name Charlie Chan when he was banned from the studios).

There's compensation for attending Columbia. It's Harlem – although Columbia denies it – Harlem, with all its possibility; Harlem, the fertile crescent, that crossroads where the South and the Caribbean meet and ideas germinate and explode into renaissance.

Timing is everything and it is important if you're an artist to be born on time. Although Langston caught a lot of hell, he had the good sense to be born in the age of W.E.B. Du Bois, who had a significant magazine, *The Crisis*, that dealt with issues of race and class and also published poetry. That tiny magazine became the fulcrum that influenced the thinking of many Caribbean, African, and even Asian activists to come (among them a quiet cook and sometime longshoreman named Ho Chi Minh, who was at the time visiting Harlem).

Another student who hated his time at Columbia University was a Spanish poet in hiding, named Federico Garcia Lorca. He hated not only Columbia but New York as well. At the time he was studying the work of the sixteenth-century mystic Spanish poet, Gongora, whose poetry, together with that of Walt Whitman, was to have a major influence on his writing. But it was only when Langston introduced Lorca to Harlem that Lorca really found his stride. His best poem in the volume *A Poet in New York* takes place in Harlem where he goes in search of the King of Harlem.

> Con una cuchara
> arrancaba los ojos a los cocodrilos
> y golpeaba el trasero de los monos.
> Con una cuchara.

> With a spoon
> he gouged out the eyes of crocodiles
> and beat on the backsides of monkeys.
> With a spoon.

And the final image:

> iba al sitio donde lloraban los negros…
> sordomuda en la penumbra,
> a tu gran rey prisionero, con un traje de conserje.

> Went to that place where the blacks were weeping…
> deaf and dumb in the shadows
> for your great king imprisoned in a janitor's uniform.

There are many images as well of the workers who must: "lick the wounds of their diseased masters." Lorca would never write like this again. Those who knew his previous work kept asking the question, what in the world happened to him? The answer was Harlem.

Langston lasted one year at Columbia, but instead of returning to his father and Mexico he went to sea and started a lifelong love affair with travel. He threw away his books but not his pen. The sea brought him to Africa where he worked as a merchant marine, cabin boy, whatever was available, and found more questions than answers. For example, why was it that the richest continent had the poorest people? Everyone had come and carved themselves a slice: placed flags at will; renamed mountains, rivers, and countries after themselves, their families, or their monarchs; and brought bibles, schools – and language enough to explain why. Langston wondered where God stood in this great trance-dance of history. One thing was certain. *He* wasn't speaking and therefore the foreign governments who were there felt the need to interpret for Him. They saw to it that God justified empire.

The same sea that took Langston to Africa took him to Europe, and there he jumped ship. He spent time in Paris writing and sending poems to *The Crisis* magazine. Although jobs were scarce, one thing that was on his side was timing. Jazz had just reached Europe in the Twenties and many musicians and artists were part of the mix and the excitement. It was as if Harlem had suddenly been exported overseas. What had been despised or taken for granted in America was much celebrated and prized, in France especially.

France, between the wars, was a good place to be and being twenty-one, Langston was able to live without sleep and his work was beginning to appear with regularity. Some, like Samuel Beckett, were translating Langston's poetry into French (later Borges would translate some of Langston's poems into Spanish). Returning to America is always good if you return in triumph, especially from Europe. He had collected enough poems now for his first book, *The Weary Blues* (1926).

But what was good was that Langston didn't, as the majority of the literati were doing in Harlem, go in for endless parties, gossip and being seen in the company of the socialites and celebrities who were now flocking to Harlem for the nightlife: the Cole Porters, the Noel Cowards and the Orson Welleses. Langston never let them drain him. Instead, after a few months he was back at sea and this was how he generally lived his life, always getting fresh material from the day-to-day struggles.

Sometime later Langston found himself in Cuba and saw first-hand how invisible forces were still at work controlling labour and making certain that racism stayed firmly in place. He was arrested for sitting in a hotel lobby – he'd made the error of thinking he was no longer in America. He forgot that the same rules of segregation applied wherever an American hotel happens to be. As the manager explained, it was not the policy of Cuba that denied him entrance, it was the fact that American tourists objected to having Blacks in the dining room in any capacity other than servants.

The truth of the matter was that Langston was on the government's radar the moment he landed in the country. A Harlem poet who was travelling steerage class along with cane-cutters and the labouring classes was sure to draw attention. The biggest fear even then was Communism and labour organization. His poems in *New Masses* had certainly come to their attention.

It was in Cuba that he met the poet, Nicolás Guillén, and developed a lifelong friendship. Guillén would go on to become Cuba's greatest poet and it was Langston who was a major influence, causing Guillén to turn his eyes away from French Baudelaire and Rimbaud to the street rhythms of the musicians of Cuba (the form known as *son*) just as Langston had done with jazz and the blues.

> Búcate plata,
> búcate plata,
> poqque me boy a corré.

> Go find some money
> find some money
> or else I'm gone.

Can you get more basically street than this injunction by a woman to her man?

> Yo bien sé cómo etá to,
> pero biejo, hay que comé:
> búcate plata,
> búcate plata,
> poqque me hoy a corré.

> Look, I know how things stand
> but listen man, you have to survive,
> so find me some money or I'm gone.

Now, would Guillen have found his way to this earthy street style of the *son* without Langston? Perhaps, but we will never know. As I said there are no accidents in an artist's life. Langston continued to translate many of Guillén's poems. The two would next meet up in Spain during the Spanish Civil War in 1936. Langston had gone over with the Abraham Lincoln Brigade. He functioned mainly as a correspondent. In Madrid, the two were reunited but he couldn't do anything to save the life of Garcia Lorca who was assassinated by Franco's police/guarda. Langston translated Lorca's "Lament for Ignazio Sanchez". Many feel that in this poem Lorca was foreshadowing his own death, but, in truth, Lorca had been rehearsing his own death since his days in Harlem.

> At five in the afternoon
> At exactly five in the afternoon
> A boy brought in the white sheet
> At five in the afternoon.

This is a perfect poem. The repetition of the phrase, "At five in the afternoon" ("A Las Cinco de la Tardes"), pierces the heart. This is the poem for which Lorca is best remembered. There are no accidents in a poet's life.

Langston's next port of call was Haiti. It was his lifelong dream to visit the first Black republic to achieve independence. (He always said this was an act for which it would never be forgiven in this world or the next.) Never forget that Haiti's revolution can be considered more amazing than the American Revolution because the odds against its success were even greater and, irony of ironies, the American Revolution was only finally achieved because of the decision of France to become an ally. Haiti, on the other hand, had no major power to call on for assistance because they all wanted to own Haiti, not help her.

When Langston came to Haiti it was in fact the completion of a circle. His great uncle, Langston (for whom he was named) had been the first American ambassador to Haiti. Now the Haiti that Langston entered was under US occupation, where US marines had been sent in to protect US corporate interests and banks. It was on Langston's first visit that he met Jacques Roumain, a writer and social activist who came from Haiti's elite class. Race and class are very important in Haiti. When the two writers met it must have been like looking in a mirror. They could have been twins, both fair complexioned and both products of privilege. They could, either of them, so easily have stepped off into the secure and corrupt middle class. Haiti was divided between those with shoes and those without. Both Jacques Roumain and Langston chose to cast their lot with the "sans souliers".

Later, Langston would translate Roumain's greatest novel, *The Masters of the Dew*, and he was heavily involved in the campaign to have Roumain released from prison when he was arrested for socialist activities in Haiti. Langston would also go on to write a powerful children's book on Haiti called *Popo and Fifina*, which gave a beautiful and accurate portrait of life in a Haitian village.

Back in America, Langston fought with publishers who had little interest in Cuba, Spain, or Haiti, other than as travelogues, who were extremely reluctant even to allow translation by a black writer of a Spanish or French work. Langston soon learned that there was apartheid even in translation.

Perhaps in response, he then wrote one of my favourite poems.

I'm looking for a house
In the world
Where the white shadows
Will not fall.

There is no such house,
Dark brothers,
No such house
At all.

But if Langston thought he had trouble with getting his Caribbean translations published, it was nothing compared to the response in the USA to his translations from Russian of Pushkin, Yesenin, and Mayakovsky. The response in Russia was very different. When Langston visited Russia, they hailed him in the streets. His work was published and known. Together with Claude McKay, he was a celebrity. The Russians tended to want to touch him and call out, "Pushkin, Pushkin." It was a source of pride that Russia's greatest poet was a black man, and they accepted the fact that Pushkin had single-handedly changed the perception of Russian as a barbaric language not worthy of poetry. (Before Pushkin, the intelligentsia barely spoke Russian except to their servants; the thought of actually writing poetry in anything but French was inconceivable). Then God sent Pushkin. So to be called Pushkin was quite an honour, even if they did want to rub your head like a Buddha.

No, I'm not Pushkin
So please don't rub my head
In the Russian way (Po-Rooski) for luck.
I'm not going to die in a duel over some woman
Once loved
Then twice regretted.
Although I've died many times already
It was always for freedom
Mostly my own and seldom forgiven.
No, I'm not Pushkin although
Like him I've worried words unto a page and waited.
Not that I fear dying
It's the dead I fear
The dead among the living who won't let you pass
Pass to joy
Pass to art.
The dead among the living, who always try to block the way.
Yet I've worried words unto a page
And prayed.

Later, Langston Hughes would be made to appear before HUAC (the House Un-American Activities Committee). The experience was as frightening as being summoned to Rome by Caesar. Some committed suicide, some betrayed friends and family. Most betrayed themselves. In effect, what he was asked was: "Mr. Hughes, who gave you permission to travel to these places?"

He answered quietly: "My youth gave me the permission."

They wanted him to recant many of the statements he'd made and promise never to do it again. He said, "I promise only never to be so young again in this life."

After HUAC, Langston would let his character, Simple, the everyman, speak for him. They say that Galileo, when asked to recant for saying that the sun was the centre of the universe and not the earth, replied, "And yet it still moves."

The stillest fall of all is that fall from grace. There's no sound to it. Like a feather falling in some forest. And yet the sun still rises.

SPREADING OUR GARDENS, SPREADING OUR HOPE

If ever there was a time for gardens that time is now. In this time of global melt-down and anxiety there can be no finer remedy than that of returning to the earth. Gardening provides a hands-on therapy because it is one of the few remaining outlets for those of us who feel increasingly powerless in the face of corporate forces that threaten to overwhelm us by trying to convince us that unless we buy their products and messages we do not exist.

Just the act of entering a supermarket can be soul-destroying. The atmosphere is more like entering a casino than a food store. While we are being bombarded with advertisements encouraging us to buy-buy-buy at ever increasing prices, we have less and less knowledge of where the various items on these shelves have been shipped from and when.

The only area of the supermarket that has anything that is in anyway good for us is the area of fruits and vegetables. Anything in a can or frozen is suspect to me. Colours have probably been artificially added and the expiration dates are often barely legible. Most of the chickens have never seen natural sunlight and have spent their entire brief lives in factories as much controlled by light bulbs as the workers who mind them. Too many of the cows have never eaten grass and may even, until the disaster of "mad cow" disease, have been fed on each other in some form. And even when we buy "fresh" fruits and vegetables we have no idea either what pesticides have been sprayed on them or how long they have been preserved for us.

Even in the Southern USA, the number of farmers has been reduced to only one third of what it was fifty years ago. Agri-businesses have swallowed up small farmers with such heavy costs to the environment as deforestation and loss of habitat for many species. In the Caribbean, there has long been a flight from the land and a desperate shortage of farmers, because few governments provide any incentives for agriculture and seem happy to rely on imports mainly from the USA. Inevitably, farming has little appeal for youth.

In our cities we see a tremendous increase in obesity and diabetes. Fifty years ago, type 2 childhood diabetes was almost unheard of; now it's reaching alarming levels, even in the Caribbean. It is not just the quantity of food that we eat, but the quality, and in particular how much fat and sugar-heavy, ready-made, convenience food we consume.

For African Americans especially, the garden has had a particular significance. It provided the provisions that might well have meant the difference between life and death for a family – during enslavement and even after emancipation. During the slavery period, even the most benign slave owners did all they could to economise when it came to providing food for their slaves. (George Washington, for example, was always frugal when it came to feeding and clothing his slaves at Mt. Vernon; he allowed them a garden and a few chickens but limited their poultry lest they were able to sell their produce and earn enough money to eventually buy their freedom.) After emancipation, the problem was the Jim Crow laws that taxed small farmers out of existence.

Only when you grow your own and follow the process from earth to table are you really safe. And then there is the incredible feeling of pride to know that what you are eating is the product of your own labour.

The last time that Victory Gardens were planted was Eleanor Roosevelt's time; it was an excellent affirmation of her husband, President Franklin Roosevelt's sense of optimism for the country after the depression. Now Michelle Obama is growing organic green gardens on the White House lawn. She should be commended for her example. To see her and her children actually go out and dig a garden is a tremendous example for the country. It is an activity that can bring a family together, and it is amazing how few urban children have ever seen vegetables or fruit in any form other than either canned or on a shelf.

Gardening encourages a sense of hope. You put seeds into the earth in the belief that you'll see some result from this effort – it is not, of course, absolute certainty, but at least there's the hope, the expectation that something will come of it. The very act of planting is therefore life-affirming. A garden can become not only a source of nutrition but of identity. The quality of your produce defines you.

One segment of society that is especially in need of both nutrition and identity are the incarcerated. Prisoners are woefully neglected when it comes to diet. Prisons are a haven for junk food and, of course, the junk food industry. You would not believe the amount of money made from coin-operated vending machines in these facilities. The prison diet at best is a massive overload of carbohydrates augmented with sweets and pow-dered substitutes. The most difficult things for the incarcerated to obtain are any fresh vegetables. They cannot be gotten from the canteen at any price. A family member may send a candy bar or the latest sneakers in a package, but not an onion or a carrot. I find it interesting that they may send nothing of any nutritional value to an inmate.

Why don't the prison authorities encourage gardens? Provision would allow much needed healthy and rewarding exercise as well as a remedy for the malnutrition that so often results in dental agony, which is usually the first sign of incarceration. Making a green garden would instill a much needed sense of responsibility. This is not wishful thinking. Many prisoners take up food collections (that is to say that they contribute to food pantries by way of the churches). I have seen this at Sing-Sing Prison as well as Green Haven in Connecticut at the time of the Hurricane Katrina crisis.

Every culture has a creation story as part of its mythology, and this nearly always involves reference to a garden to signify some perfect time. In this garden there was no death and no hunger. These stories can be found in Africa, Asia and the Middle East. Then there follows some act of violation, either a refusal to obey some law or a betrayal of trust that results in expulsion from this garden, be it Eden or wherever. This story is not just Biblical but universal.

After the expulsion from the garden, man is forced to struggle and attempt to fend off death and all the elements that threaten to annihilate him. In other words, he is forced to try and transcend himself and his circumstances. While we were in the garden, we were still in the womb and now we are in the womb no longer. We have, all of us, become aliens because we've been cast out, but who is more cast out and dispossessed than the incarcerated?

To enter prison is to lose the right even to your name. A number is assigned and the individual is made to relinquish all rights to identity and become, in effect, "a package" that may be shifted about at will, moved arbitrarily from facility to facility without any advance warning. How, therefore, can a package transcend itself and become human? I think the answer may be found in the garden.

What can give a person a greater sense of worth than to know that they are actually still able to contribute something to society despite being incarcerated? Learning to tend a garden provides not only a form of release but an inspiration and a useable skill for the future. Indeed, to tend a garden is to know that there is still such a thing as a future.

To paraphrase Voltaire, the French philosopher and satirist, all we can do in the end is tend our garden, for even a slave, while he tends his garden, is not a slave but a gardener. Every garden is therefore a victory.

WE PRISONERS ON BOTH SIDES OF THE WALL

> We who live like prisoners
> on both sides of the wall
> We who live like vultures
> yet cry like humans

People are always eager to accuse the prison population of having prison mentalities and being incapable of change, yet we fail to see ourselves, Western, oil-addicted consumers, in the same light.

We're so used to plundering the world and its resources that we never think in terms of giving anything back. As a result, the relationship of man to nature is always that of master to slave, the exploiter and the exploited. Our first thought upon encountering new land is always, "How can I own this?" Followed by: "And what's the cheapest way to get those who live here to work for me?"

We can't help it. Even the simple farmer thinks in terms of reaping as much from the land for as long as he can, regardless of the biblical injunction of alternating seven years of harvest with seven years of leaving fallow. Good luck, by the way, in finding a simple farmer, since more and more of them have been swallowed up by agri-business.

The thought that the earth and its resources may have a limit, and that we can cut, burn and dig for only so long before we exhaust it, never occurs to us until disasters happen: torrential flooding or crop devastation such as during the famous "dust bowl" of the Midwest during the last century, for example. The same relationship we have with the earth is the one we have with each other: domination and exploitation. In a class-conscious economy, people are just as disposable as land. We use them for only so long as it's feasible and then we cast them aside and move on. There are even those who have gone so far as to suggest moving on to other planets once we've exhausted the earth's resources.

The problem with this system of endless exploitation is that it will destroy both mankind and the planet itself, not only by exhausting the resources we depend on, but by creating endless toxic waste. The result is that we are always living (call it existing) in a constant state of war.

Now what would it be like to live a life in harmony with the earth and not in constant strife, conflict, and urge for domination and ownership of the land? I don't know, because the only people who lived this way were the original inhabitants of this land, those they call the American Indians or indigenous people. We who came after had different ideas.

The American colonists were mainly concerned with securing freedom, that is to say, their own freedom, and that could only be obtained by wealth. To this end they set about confining the so-called Indians on reservations and the new means of production (i.e. African slaves) on plantations. Although it might seem as a contradiction that freedom could only be achieved by genocide and slavery, it nevertheless made perfect sense to the founding fathers. The most radical concept they followed was "the pursuit of happiness." This concept was first conceived by John Locke, the British philosopher who placed property in lieu of happiness. The thought that one was inconceivable without the other was very pragmatic and very British.

The exchange of the word "happiness" for property was also very Jeffersonian and very American: particularly the pursuit of happiness at the expense of those who were and are too weak to matter. The American Indians were the first POWs. They were placed in containment on those reservations where many still remain. As for the formerly enslaved, we have managed to make the transformation from plantations to ghettoes. We may now have choice of movement since there are no longer any signs pro-claiming boldly: *Whites only*. But there is, nevertheless, the silent apartheid of wealth that speaks far more loudly than words. You don't need to be told you don't belong where you can't afford.

The government's response to Hurricane Katrina speaks volumes about who is considered expendable in this society. Those who didn't have the funds to secure their own exit strategies were abandoned. Among the first to be sacrificed were the elderly in hospitals and nursing homes, prisoners awaiting trial, and poor Whites as well as Blacks. The bridges were secured, manned by armed deputies made up of private soldiers. Their mandate was containment not rescue. Two years later and many have still not been able to return to their neighbourhoods. Women and children were treated with the same indifferent cruelty as men and, unbelievable as it sounds, even the evacuation of animals received greater attention as planes were actually found for them. Meanwhile, families were left to suffer, trapped in the Coliseum without food or water.

There was a time when it was possible to travel halfway across the world, make war on an enemy and then return home without consequence. The enemy and the consequence stayed where you left it. This is no longer the case. Now our wars return with us. It is part of the air we breathe. Now the disposable people include the veterans of foreign wars. We have no use for them because they've now become toxic. The radiation we designed to destroy the enemy has annoyingly returned to us with our soldiers. Those who returned from Iraq find it difficult to fit into a world that is quite different from the one they left. The scars veterans carry are both mental and physical. Worst of all is that there are no jobs waiting for them. The economy is in a state of free fall. They leave one conflict and return to another. There is a statistic that shows that more vets from the Vietnam War die in prison than died in the war itself, the majority from homelessness and addiction. The same will be true for Iraq and Afghanistan.

We use prisons as the dustbins for the toxic waste of society. The prison-industrial complex and the military-industrial complex are family to each other. The economy that limits job opportunities is the same one that determines the number and make-up of the military and determines the make-up and maintenance of our prisons. It's no accident that the United States has the highest number of people incarcerated in the free world and that over sixty percent of these are Black and Latino. At least ten percent of inmates were veterans of the armed services.

The common thread is that there is an actual limitation of choice. Equally important is its perception. If you are told constantly that there is no place for you in the workforce, other than as a minimum wage worker at McDonalds, you are far more likely to offer yourself as cannon fodder, especially when they throw in sweeteners such as the promise of free education and owning your own home at the end of service. The truth of the matter is that now, with the economy in recession, even these offers have had to be cut back. So much for the pursuit of happiness.

What is needed is a whole new approach to living and caring for ourselves and the earth. What if care of the environment could itself provide jobs, work that is neither soul-destroying nor toxic? What would it cost to provide prisons with gardens that, as I have argued already, would provide a source of fresh vegetables and also teach a trade that could contribute to the economy? This is only a first step towards transforming society. If the incarcerated were also taught how to recycle items such as computers and televisions it could provide a lucrative form of employment and contribute to clearing the toxic dumping grounds that are the ghettos of the South Bronx, Detroit, Philadelphia and elsewhere. How many new jobs could be created? How much potential has been wasted because we've excluded so many from the creative mix and denied voice because of race or because they've had a record?

So intent are we on punishment that we deny the possibility of reform and rehabilitation. Incarceration does little except create future generations of felons. A never-ending spiral develops in which society itself becomes incarcerated, trapped by its own inability to change.

We pay a heavy price for stagnation and decay, a drain not only on our fiscal economy but our spiritual economy as well. The result is the kind of spiritual bankruptcy represented by the CEOs of Wall Street, privileged and just hidden enough behind their hedge funds to (mostly) avoid conviction. What message does this send to the youth?

Do we really believe that no one is watching what one small section of the society is able to get away with at the expense of the majority? Note well that the machinations of this small elite has negative worldwide repercussions, including starvation in the poorest countries and, but for foodbanks, in the affluent West.

This generation of vipers has caused global warming. The attempt now is to put a friendly face on the gas-guzzling car manufacturers and the oil companies that have polluted so much of the earth. The problem with greed is that it makes us greedy. The highest rates of obesity and pollution are right here. They go together.

I remember walking in the South Bronx one day, when a thought came into my head: *Wouldn't it be wonderful if a bomb fell and cleared all this away?* Now, I know that I'm strange, but I'm not so unique and if it came to me, then it must have come to others in parts of Jersey, Philadelphia, Detroit and Baltimore, places that they euphemistically call the inner cities. Perhaps we just want to change the lighting from desolation to hope.

You have to be careful what you ask for, though, for no sooner do you clear up a few vacant lots and make a garden or two, the next thing you know is that you're being asked to leave. Gentrification happens and you suddenly find yourself excluded. Which makes you wonder: are the walls of prisons for keeping out as well as keeping in? A simple observation: when we build and maintain prisons we ourselves become prisoners. All through upstate New York, whenever a factory or an industry closes, the first thing to replace it is a prison. It has become an important source of income, yet it offers no hope to the youth in terms of job prospects. What does it say when the most a family can strive for is employment at some correctional facility? Many are made to choose between custodial employment and incarceration, though in effect they are so alike.

I have to give much praise, therefore, to people like Majora Carter who started a green zone in the midst of the South Bronx Hunt's Point area. She has managed not only to transform a significant section from urban blight but has set about the task of creating jobs through recycling and green panelled rooftops that utilize solar energy for heating. Whereas Robert Moses and others saw the Bronx as nothing more than a bridge between Westchester and Manhattan, a wasteland to be sacrificed for the greater good of those who really matter, Majora Carter reminded the world that there are people here, not just fish and meat markets. People and potential.

Not only are we what we eat, we are also the means and method by which we obtain what we eat, what we see about us, and what we hope to become.

America is a unique place. It has the greatest inequality, highest rate of incarceration and yet the greatest opportunity for change. No nation on earth is a greater paradox. Never before in history has a debtor nation had the ability to bankrupt the world, and at the same time the potential to free the world. Every move we make is copied by the world. If it happens here, it will happen everywhere. The liberation of America means the liberation of the world. It must, therefore, for the first time be a true liberation, one that is not in name only. Can we accept our hope, the pursuit not merely of property but of total possibility? We have the challenge, the gift and the responsibility for change, because finally we are how we live.

We can't live vulture yet cry human. We must choose.

THE BIRDS OF BAGHDAD

There are still birds in Baghdad. I know, because they wake me without warning before the stillness and the dawn when God pours away the darkness with light.

From my window I see the young boys come out from the stone of the streets, barefoot and ready to conquer another day in the risen jungle of the city.

Don't look for camels in Baghdad, you won't find any. What you'll find instead is only yourself and whatever you've come with. Be it New York or London, Johannesburg or Paris, all are the City of Man. The only thing about Baghdad that is different from your city is that it has the most powerful army on earth poised and waiting at its gates to annihilate it, assist it to freedom and then remake it in its own image.

There are still birds in Baghdad, and trees too – despite the strange air and water that taste of war and the strategies of night – trees with branches that bend low and straight like white women's hair.

Today is the first of the ten most sacred days of the city, *Ashor*. Within the space of these ten days, four miracles are said to have taken place. First, the prophet Abraham (revered by Muslims, Christians and Jews) survived his trial by fire, walking free from the fiery furnace, protected and cleansed by God. This was in the *Quran*. Next was the sparing of Abraham's son, Isaac, offered to God as a sacrifice in a test of faith as recorded in the Bible. Then Moses parted the Red Sea and led the Jews from their captivity in Egypt – Egypt, that peculiar place people are either fleeing from (like the Jews), or fleeing to (like the family of the infant Jesus escaping Herod). Another miraculous event was the martyrdom of Hussein and his family at Karbala in 680 AD. Hussein was the grandson of the Prophet and father of the Shia form of Islam.

The last miracle of all is that I'm here in Baghdad. Here at their New Year when the very ground of Iraq trembles and the walls cry out. Why have I come? I've come because, like people everywhere, I hunger and thirst after miracles. And, also like you, I would like to see little David win against Goliath, even though, like you, I have all my Wall Street money on Goliath.

The real miracle, though, is that Iraq is still standing after all it's been

through, and that they're not afraid, though there's still dust flying everywhere, the dust of past invasions.

"Tell me something, my friend." The old cab driver turns to me.

"Yes?"

"Why did God curse us with oil?"

"My friend, God didn't really curse Iraq. If he wanted to really curse you
he would have given you gold and diamonds too, like Africa. Then everyone
in the world would make absolutely certain that you stayed poor forever. If
he wanted to, he'd curse you like the Congo [Zaire] or like Liberia. No, he
doesn't really want to curse you, just kiss you with a little pain."

I kiss him twice in the Iraqi way. He laughs. He's never met a black man
before who wasn't a soldier come to kill him and his children for freedom.
When God wants to bless you he gives you things. When he curses you he
gives you more.

Iraq still looks good, though like a woman in hiding. She waits. This is
nothing new to her. People have been invading Iraq from the beginning of
civilization. Five thousand years of Persians and Greeks, Turkomans and
the most devastating of all, the Mongols. They destroyed the land so
thoroughly that it took three hundred years to bear fruit again. One of the
recent invaders was the British. From 1920- 1932, Britain had a mandate
over Iraq (which meant you on your knees, we above). It's for this reason
and others that Britain has a special desire to return and assist Iraq, assist her
back to her knees and give her more of the blessings of freedom.

The area between the Tigris and Euphrates is just too good not to lust after.
It could make even a prophet sin and most men are not prophets. First it was
the oil, not in the ground, but oil made from dates (of which there are over
three hundred varieties in Iraq). Oil was always especially important in
biblical times because it cleansed the skin and hair (guarding against lice):

> Thou anointeth my head with oil
> my very cup runneth over.

Also as oil for lamps to keep away the terrors of night:

> ...as a lamp unto my feet.

Almost every army known to man has come to Iraq. If they could make
their way, they came. The only difference now is that they come by night
and bomb by computer. There is no Darius. No young Alexander the Great
who would die at thirty-three after having conquered the world. No, these
now are faceless men playing at video games who will never see the effects
of the 600 bombs an hour they intend to test on the people of Iraq. They
want what the Mongols wanted: to break the spirit of the people with
"Shock and Awe".

So why am I here? I'm here because I lived through a volcano and, as I have described in other essays, seen how it changed everything. I had also, like other West Indians and Africans, on a return to New York, gravitated to the job of guarding, of security. It's all that British training in a love and awe of uniforms. The Africans may come in a close second. They, too, love a good uniform. So it was that I found myself on that day they call *Nine-Eleven*, guarding the thing Americans love most: money, on Wall Street. The day the high towers fell, I was there guarding their property. Not Pharaoh or his army, but a keeper at his gate.

Then everywhere, and at once, the smell of ash and flesh, and because my eyes had already been washed with the ash of the volcano, I wasn't frightened. I saw the same ash fall from the sky like sand, such that you couldn't tell black skin from white or night from day. Those who died first were the guards, who weren't firemen, but foreign, West Indians and Africans who died unnoticed – some at six dollars an hour.

So now, why am I here in Baghdad? Because I needed to witness that situation, too, first-hand. Plus travelling from New York to Baghdad takes only a minute, relatively speaking. Pain is pain; once you see it you know it, but only if you let yourself see.

So, as I began, there are still birds in Baghdad. Birds and palm trees, where the birds love to hide. The trees reminded me so much of my island, I tried to claim them as my own.

"Excuse me, but are those my trees? Did they take them from the Caribbean?"

"No my friend, those are our palm trees. They've been here in Iraq for over three thousand years."

"Well then, fair enough; I guess you can keep them. It's not palm trees I've come for anyway."

Today is the second of the ten holy days. Today, I walk the wards of the children's hospital, the Al-Mansour. You asked to come here and yet you don't want to come. Still, you find yourself walking from ward to ward. The doctor is explaining things to you and you nod in agreement. Why not? The head isn't so heavy; it can move by itself in agreement. Yes, they desperately need medicine and there's none. Yes, it's unfortunate – something about uranium from the bombs that were dropped causing cancer, especially in the Iraqi children. Nod and nod again. Turn, and then you see what you've been trying so hard not to see, the shadow in the corner of your eye.

You have to look down now, having no choice, at the *something-like-a-baby-but-more-like-a–Rhesus-monkey* in an incubator. But as you try to turn away, you end up looking right into the face of the Shiite woman who you know – without any language – is the mother. Now, there are three women clad in black, but you know, without any doubt, that this one is the mother.

You suddenly become very interested in the walls and the alms-house green paint of the ceiling, anything to get away from her eyes. But damn, she's so young. You want to ask her, "Who dropped the bomb that is killing your child?" Dropped it years ago and waited – uranium in the water. Was it an American or an Iranian airman? Doesn't matter, we made them both. First we used Iraq to get Iran and then we used Iran to get... The smell of ash, like Montserrat. You want to ask her something, but as they say in the islands: *You done know already*.

The Shiite women dress in black. They needn't go far for death. They're always ready. They can close the headcloth they wear like a curtain and grieve in private. You bear witness whether you want to or not. You reach in your pocket to find some money to turn her away. But all you find is bits of paper: paper worthless as words, notes that you used years before in some class you taught at City College somewhere else in the world. What is conflict? Conflict is tension between two or more forces or when two or more people desire goals obtainable by one only. Notes found in the pocket of a dead jacket, worthless now as Iraqi money. Not even enough to fill the small hand of a woman.

> Wars are nice
> When you're fed with rice
>   Not so nice when they simmer
>   But men look good in uniform
> And the young girls
> They always linger.

Now there's a thing in Iraq called wind. It moves not only across the desert but through the city as well. It comes out of Basra, in the South. It's Basra I want to get to, but they're already bombing there, although no referee has blown a whistle and the war hasn't started officially. The wind blows as it always has because in Iraq only people change. They change from Adam to Abraham and Eve to Sarah, but land, it stays the same, unless of course you bomb it with uranium. They say the women in Basra are the most beautiful in Iraq, when they're not crying.

Suddenly, the wind from Basra comes through the hospital. It comes like the trade winds of the afternoon in Jamaica or Montserrat. If you don't expect it, then it carries you, like a woman, way out into the ocean. But now it's the child this wind wants. It flies across the room and slams shut a door. Glass shatters everywhere, impolitely. We drop to our knees because we think the invasion has started. Only the doctor maintains his dignity, priest-like, and doesn't duck. "It's only the wind." He gestures with his hand and we rise slowly. It's only the woman's child the Basra wind wants.

You finally get outside in the street. Your lungs are tight. In Iraq everyone smokes. You need not wonder why. From the nice government SUV that awaits you, Bob Marley is playing:

> There's a natural Mystic blowing in the air.
> Listen carefully now and you will hear.

Marley's music sounds even stronger in Iraq.

I'm glad to escape from the children's hospital. It pierced me too much. I think I need a church to hide in. A church is always good for hiding. You can shut your eyes, pray and not have to look. It's the only time you don't have to see the face of the leader on every wall.

The Eastern Orthodox Church of Iraq: the chalice and the dream. The church is already full. The Christians in Iraq pray, shamed by the fervour of Islam. Everywhere in Iraq is prayer. People pray while they murder or die. Here the mass is performed in Aramaic, the language of Christ.

> "Eli, Eli Lamah Sabathani."
> "My Lord, my Lord, why has thou forsaken me?"

What I love most about the ceremony of the mass here is that the priest, having lifted the secret and sacred host of Christ, now gives the touch of grace. But he gives it not to the congregation but instead to the altar boys, the acolytes, robed in the blue of Mary. They bring the touch of grace to the congregation. "Likewise after the supper he took wine and when he had blessed it..." But there is no wine here because we're in Iraq. I'm anointed with the oil – not the oil which America is coming for but the oil of vineyards, for which others once came.

Later, I sit with his Holiness the Archbishop of the Eastern Chaldean Orthodox Church. He gestures toward me with his ringed hand. The divine purple of privilege rests easy on his shoulders but he doesn't trust it. The Eastern Church believes God can enter anywhere or anyone. And they trust the laity more than the clergy.

"Tea?"

"Thank you."

"Could you follow the mass?"

"It's the same mass, only in Aramaic. He still dies for us in the end."

"Yes. But would we die for him?"

"Well, we shall soon see, won't we?"

On the walls are icons over a thousand years old; their faces are dark. I think of the Black Madonna of Poland – Poland, who agreed to join Napoleon's invasion of Haiti. She was hungry then. Now Poland will join with America. She is still hungry.

"You come to my house, I give you my eyes. But if like the wolf you try and take my house, I will eat you. My English, not good."

"Good enough. I got that. The Pope, will he come here to Iraq?"

"He wants to but he's too old."

He knows that it's not just Iraq; it's the whole state of Christ's church which is on trial here.

A young priest enters and bends just low enough not to call attention to himself and gathers up the cups. Slantwise a shadow falls. The pain of the cancer ward of the hospital is starting to lift from me. I still can't forget the mother's face. The mass helped but not everything leaves.

"What do you tell your parishioners? Those you know will probably die."

"I tell them to pray without ceasing."

"You don't tell them to leave?"

"Why would they leave? They're Iraqi."

He looks at me and then remembers that I'm a stranger here. The Eastern Church hasn't changed in a thousand years. They say, "Alone we are damned, together redeemed." And they mean it.

"Of course, why should they leave?"

I remembered the Cathedral of St. John in New York – the time that the Word came alive for me after the towers fell and the fire. For close to Christmas that year, the Cathedral itself caught fire. After that, the priest couldn't give the same sermon because he saw the waiting eyes of the parishioners and knew they wanted more. It frightened him to truth or at least frightened him awake.

But fear is a funny thing in man. We do things to get as far away from it as possible. Fear I mean. It's only when you know yourself and the terrorism of your own heart that you can speak truth to power. For instance, I know I fear the Shiite woman's eyes. I fear them more than Montserrat's sea. Let me tell you how. It was a day like so. The volcano had erupted and because I was lonely in a time of storm, and the waves broke fierce across an open sea, I decided to test God and swim out past the silent eyes of the fishermen who took bets as to whether I'd live or die. I was already known as strange. Who else would live alone on an open beach under a volcano without even a tent?

Now the Montserrat water is a dark, brackish thing, and not the pretty coral of Antigua or the waters of St. Thomas. Montserrat water is not welcoming. It's sudden and cross, like the lash of a bull-whip. They say you never turn your back on Montserrat water or Montserrat women twice.

I swam far out that day. The thinking – if madness can be called thinking – was that I would wait until the first huge wave broke and then dive beneath it and come up. Usually, the further out you go, the smoother the water becomes, but not this day. This day was white-water time. (On the island that's an expression we have for times of trouble.) When all you see is white foam, you *know*.

That day there would be no easing off. The first wave hit. I went beneath, but when I came up there was a second wave higher and rougher than the first, and if that wasn't enough, a third came behind it, leaving me no time to take a breath, hitting me like a wall. It was then I knew I was dead. It was then I knew Islam. If Islam means submission, then I submitted. There was no further struggle. I surrendered and thought: *So then this is what death is like.* Tonight the fishermen would collect their money. To expect them to come out after me and possibly lose their boats would be ridiculous. I wasn't worth that much to any of them. Any fool could tell you: don't swim in a storm, not when you see waves breaking against rocks.

The strange thing, though, was that once I ceased to struggle and went diagonal – not against the current but across it – the salt of the water held me up. I didn't know if the current would take me to the island of Redonda, which was uninhabited – at least by people – or maybe across as far as Antigua. I knew I would never make it to Antigua. A shark would finish me long before. But God wasn't done with me yet. He spilled me like seed against the rocks and I knew that I only had one chance because the rocks are sharp there and if I didn't grab on I would be pitched out again. So I braced myself and when I was slammed in, I held on even though I was bleeding. I crawled up on the shore, lay on my back because I could move no further and as I looked up at the sky, the volcano chose that moment to explode again. I had to laugh. This must be the true meaning of between a rock and a hard place. There I was spilled out upon a stone. And then, somewhere above me, hidden in the trees, I could hear the piercing cry of the oriole, the Montserrat bird, seldom seen, much given to hiding. But this meant that it too had survived.

The day after you have to go back out again, only further. Otherwise you'll fear the sea, become a fisherman and never swim again.

There are still birds in Baghdad. I know this because today they came early to me singing. Today, the tenth day of the New Year, *Ashor*. They say that when the Prophet comes again, he'll come disguised as a bird. It's for this reason that in Iraq they play the singing of birds before the morning call to prayer.

St. Francis knew. He moved calmly among birds, and always spoke with them. They confessed to him. Told him what trees they hid in. I wanted to tell them, the birds of Baghdad, about the oriole bird of Montserrat, a yellow bird, sometimes orange with its mood. I had wanted to confess to this bird. As I lay on the beach, I had known that close by were the birds of Barbuda where the slaves hid.

I want to go to Basra, but they might not let me. The birds can go there, though, even though they're from Baghdad. Even the soldiers let them pass. I wanted to tell the birds about Audubon, the man who painted birds, a black man from Haiti who came to America and painted the dreams of birds – birds dreaming birds. They never say he's a black man, though. Only the birds and his family know. America is good at this. She doesn't so much lie as doesn't say.

Tonight, we eat fish together, fish cooked in the Iraqi way, two hours before a blazing fire of cedar wood.

"Don't rush; here we take our time. This isn't microwave, my friend. And if they should invade before we finish, well then, we'll eat our fish in heaven. Insha'Allah."

"Insha'Allah."

The music plays as we watch the fire blaze and the fish is seasoned. The children come out and laugh at you and disappear again into stone. Suddenly you hear a voice so piercing you have to look up.

"Who is that singing?"

"That? Nadhem, Nadhem Al-Ghazali. He was our greatest singer. They say when he died he was so poor he had to beg bread to cut his beard."

The Iraqis love the expression, *so poor he had to beg bread to cut his beard*. He died and left nothing except his music to ambush my heart and cloud my eyes with tears. Through Iraq, God gives us a chance to find out who we are, who we really were all along.

"*Shukran*."

And if by some fluke there is a God who listens, tell him I want to go to Basra. They say that the women there are the most beautiful in Iraq except when they cry for their children. I want to go and dry their tears but first I have to dry my own. Yes, there are birds in Baghdad, but there are those, too, who love not birds but cages.

The stillest fall of all is the fall from grace. There's no sound to it, only a falling and awakening.

OF SADDAM (OR SCHEHERAZADE REVISITED)

I have suggested some of my reasons for going to Baghdad on the eve of the American invasion, though I don't know exactly when the desire came to me. In life, the things you don't know are always more than things you do.

Maybe it was one grey morning on my way to prison (to teach; not stay). There's a certain early morning train that takes you from Harlem to Ossining, New York. White people didn't like passing through Harlem then, even in a train. It reminded them of how easy it was to fall and why they'd better keep their jobs and their asses in gear. Call it a cautionary tale. As for the Blacks, you could tell instantly who was on their way to work as domestics in rich people's homes and gardens, or else on their way to visit some son, husband or boyfriend in prison. They sat with their pocket books in their laps and Victoria's Secret bags with their lunches beside them on the seat.

I learned a lot from my time working in prison. I went there to teach but got an education instead. One of the things I learnt was that there are three things that no prison can ever stop: First is sex (love and lust will find a way). Second is music. Third is religion. An inmate will find a way to pray and not just alone. He will find others to pray with him (witness the power of Islam in prisons). It was the Muslim students in my class who took up a collection for me to help me make my visit to Iraq. I couldn't believe that prisoners who were earning pennies a day would sacrifice their canteen money and cigarettes in order to get me there. When I asked them why, they said that they wanted me to see what they couldn't. Their love shamed me. There was nothing I could say but thank you. I didn't want to cry in front of them. It was no big money but it was enough to make me determined to get there, whatever it took.

Now to get to Iraq you first have to get to Jordon. Jordon has a lot of history and a lot of people trying to sell you sand in bottles. Thousands of people, too, walking around looking like Jesus (only darker than the ones we see in paintings by da Vinci); dark mysterious women with hennaed hands and secrets. I would have liked to spend more time there, but Jordan is expensive because it is the escape route out of Iraq and Jordanians knew they could get whatever they asked for. Jordan's nice as long as the money lasts, then people change quickly, like lawyers who no longer know you.

People take your bags long before you ask them to and then they open their hands and say: "Bakshish" meaning, "Pay me my tip, motherf…" To which you're supposed to reply: "Ali Baba" meaning thief. Now you have entered the world of Scheherazade.

Once you get bundled into an Iraqi plane, you are searched yet again. You know it is an Iraqi plane because everyone in charge looks like a clone of Saddam. They all sport the same Saddam moustache (which, by the way, Saddam stole from Stalin, his hero). They also wear expensive black leather jackets over their black open-collar shirts and trousers. They always wear black and are easily identifiable. When the plane lands in Baghdad the first thing you are told is to surrender your cell phone. Cell phones are "Haram" (banned) in Iraq. You want to make a phone call, use one of theirs, on which you can hear the heavy breathing of a government spy.

I was driven to the hotel with a several other clergy. (Did I mention that I went as a minister? It was the only way I was allowed to travel.) We were supposed to pray for Iraq and peace in our time, and just in case we failed, America was waiting right outside with the heaviest fire power known to man.

I slept soundly that first night and woke at sunrise to the sound of birds. Iraqi radio always opened with the sound of birds. Then you hear the call to prayer. Then I knew for certain I was no longer in New York.

When you go out into the Iraqi morning, the first thing you notice is the face of Saddam. Hard to miss since it's ten feet tall and plastered on every wall. I later played a game with myself. I would try and go five minutes without seeing the face of Saddam, an impossible thing to do. (I once made three minutes, but that was because we were stuck in traffic and couldn't move.) Another thing was that his eyes seem to be following you. The man knew well how to stay in the consciousness of his people. In the hotel I was told quickly, in whispers, never to say anything inside your room that you didn't want recorded.

One funny thing. A spy-waiter just happened to be passing when someone's cell phone suddenly went off. The entire place went silent. Everyone turned their head in the direction of the chimes of the luckless culprit as it played Beethoven's Fifth. Three men suddenly appeared. The senior man in charge, who looked like a caricature of a merchant, stared in disbelief at this malevolent device:

"What's this? Didn't we tell you no cell-phone? NO CELL-PHONE!" They snatched it away from the man and led him away.

"But my wife, she's having a baby!"

"Would you like to live to see it? Then shut-up and come, fool!"

Then there were the "Minders" who were assigned to drive us around, who never let us out of their sight except to pee, and I'm certain that was videoed too. Fortunately, I was used to being watched. In Montserrat, someone is always watching you, and you're never more watched than when you see no one there. I'm also used to ex-police becoming taxi drivers (this is what most retired police do). Of course, there is no such thing as ex-police – that's like an ex-priest. Not that some police aren't nice people, I just don't trust them. It's in my DNA. I even have some police friends. I don't trust them either. If there is a choice between betraying friendship and betraying the Law, the Law wins every time. Snakes bite. They can't help it, they are snakes.

There was a lot of poverty in Iraq and a lot of children get slapped for begging. The minders didn't like beggars. "They make the country look bad." When I looked at the eyes of the children after they'd been viciously slapped, I knew one thing for certain: if Saddam ever fell, all these minders would be dead in a week unless they vanished into the ether. There's a Haitian proverb: "*Bay kou Bliye Pote Mak Sonje.*" ("He who slaps may forget, but he who is slapped never forgets.")

Perhaps I also went to Iraq because of Paul Robeson. I had met him only once. It was at his funeral so we didn't talk much, but I was moved to write this poem called "The Death of Robeson":

> Rainwater made pools in the children's eyes.
> I didn't know the way to Benta's Funeral Home
> So the junkies and winos showed me the way
> Their bodies bent like trees.
>
> Like a Jacob Lawrence painting
> Each in their jagged silence separate
> Like leaves
> Bowing.

Robeson was the greatest football player America ever produced, but he was the wrong colour, so his own team (Princeton University) hated him, so he had to play against both sides. He became a lawyer, then an actor (the first Black in modern times to play Othello). The last great thing he did was sing. It was his voice that made the hairs on my head rise. He could sing in twelve languages including Russian, Chinese, Spanish and German. Everything he ever did in his life was to honour his father, who was a Baptist minister who died way too soon. When I found Paul Robeson, I found myself: Black without apology. America pulled his passport because he asked the wrong question:

"Why should Blacks fight in foreign wars against people we don't know when we are made to live like slaves right here at home?"

Mohammed Ali asked the same question twenty years later and he got licks too.

So that was another reason why I came to be in Iraq, looking at Saddam's face looking down from ten feet above me on some wall. I took out my flute and started playing, not the Communist "Internationale" as in a different time Robeson might have sung, but instead, "I Can See Clearly Now the Rain Has Gone," Johnny Nash's reggae tune. The children began to come out from inside the concrete walls. The minders weren't happy with me but the children were. Music is one thing they can't stop.

Saddam had done a good job of cleaning up the streets. Women were safe to walk any hour of the day or night in Baghdad. No one would dare attack them for fear of Saddam, no one except Saddam's son, Uday, that is. Uday was a problem. When he was drunk, he would take any woman he wanted, and if he was awake he was drunk. He would race around the city in any one of his hundred or more select sports cars and cruise for women. Not many dared refuse because to refuse was to end not only your own life but that of your family as well.

Uday was Saddam's first born and his mother's favourite. He had a voracious appetite and his taste in women went from Paris Hilton look-alikes (slutty but expensive) to private schoolgirls in uniform with white cotton panties and white socks. As a matter of fact, he once argued for the return to white gloves as well, as part of the school uniform. He, after all, owned all the newspapers and media, so he could afford to argue for anything he wanted. All the crazy things he did (including running the Iraqi National Football Team) was just amusement for him while waiting to become the next Khan. As for the people of Iraq, they knew that they were dealing with a Caligula who was five times more cruel than his father. There is an Arab expression that the poor use when asked how things are going. "Kif-Kif" is usually the answer, which means *not too bad*, or *it could be worse*. You usually use this expression after being shat upon from a great height, but you can't do a damn thing about it.

I wondered when Saddam realised that his son was crazy, crazier even than he. He is reputed once to have said of him: "Me, I never enjoyed torture. I did it from necessity, to keep enemies in check. Uday, he enjoys it. He even films it. I should have killed him at birth but I waited too long. I let him get tall and his mother, Sajida, loves him."

Uday had a gap-toothed smile even when he wasn't smiling. Many got fooled that way and relaxed in his presence – always a mistake. He had zero patience and even had a timetable for his father. He gave Saddam three more years. At the end of this time if he hadn't retired, he (Uday) would assist him into the next life: "INSHALLAH, he will depart by then!"

Another little thorn in Saddam's family tree was his eldest daughter, Raghad. He hadn't asked very much of her, merely that she keep herself quiet long enough to make a good marriage. What more could you ask of a daughter but "Keep both your legs and your mouth closed, and marry well." She married her father's second cousin, a lieutenant general who ought to have been useful for Saddam's defence plans. Unfortunately, they had some doctrinal differences and son-in-law chose to betray Saddam to the Americans in exchange for asylum. Not good.

The daughter could be excused for having made the wrong choice in joining her husband in Jordan after his hasty departure. The poor girl had grown up all her life believing she was a fairy princess, an easy thing to believe if you live in a palace and have North African slaves wiping your ass for you every day because it's too much work wiping your own. You develop a certain way of seeing the world. It didn't help knowing that you had the power of life and death over your teachers and everybody else you come in contact with. Then there's your brother Uday who is a heroin addict and coke fiend who, you suspect, might be sleeping with your mother (with your father's knowledge, if not approval).

No doubt the mother, Sajida, had the same expression on her face as my pastor's wife concerning her delinquent son. First Ladies are all alike: "My son is a good boy, he's just misunderstood."

So one can see how the little princess might have had a great deal on her mind when her husband suddenly came to her one night and announced – at least this is how I imagined it:

"We have to get the hell out of here, now, before your father has me killed. I have a driver waiting!"

"Now? But what will I take?"

"Nothing! You want to let them know we're running? Don't worry, I have money waiting in Jordan. Just come!"

"But I have to tell Mother goodbye!"

"Why? She never liked me anyway, or you either for that matter. And as drunk as she stays, she might just betray us. Call her later if you want to. But come now while the roads are clear, or I'm leaving!"

Having fled successfully, they made the fatal mistake of being enticed back to Iraq for what Mommy swore was a family meeting and healing session when they would all reason together. Once across the border the fairy princess daughter was forced to sign a divorce statement and the lovers were parted. That particular ceremony was attended to personally by Uday who took many pictures of the execution for Saddam's private viewing.

Families can be tricky things. I think in some ways Saddam welcomed the war. It was safer to deal with than his own family. Many people ask why Saddam didn't flee the country on the eve of the war. The simple truth was that he loved Iraq and had no desire to live anywhere else. He always stayed close to Tikrit where he was born. He didn't trust anywhere else. As for the war, I think he found peace in war. For his own fate I think he had no complaints. He had come from nothing and ended up one of the most powerful men in the world. You can tell by the bounty on his head. He had respect for only two people in his life: Stalin of Russia and Nasser of Egypt. He learned a lot from both.

Now on the eve of the invasion, there was a strange phone call from Colin Powell. The call wasn't made to me but to Congressman Fauntroy who was part of the Congressional Black Caucus and leading the peace mission. He was a minister as well, which allowed him certain perks. Although Colin Powell and I had grown up together in the South Bronx (he in exile from Jamaica), we never spoke. We both went to the same college and still managed not to speak because he chose the military and I chose philosophy (the college was City College and the Castle on the Hill). But where he saw ROTC and a career, I saw nothing but pum-pum, so I guess we had doctrinal differences.

What General Powell had said on the phone was vague but immediate:

"I would suggest that you take the first plane out tomorrow because I suspect that after that it will be impossible."

Translation: *We're coming in now*. This started a lively debate because I had no intention of leaving. I was going to die in Baghdad.

They informed me that I couldn't die in Baghdad.

"Why," I asked.

"Because we will be held responsible. You used us to get here under false pretences. You planned on being a martyr all along. And you lied!"

They went on to explain how my presence would only get a lot of people killed trying to shelter me. They certainly knew how to use guilt. In the end, they persuaded me.

In the opening salvo of the war, Saddam lost two sons. Bush thought that he had gotten Saddam too and started celebrating prematurely. Bush had already bought all of Saddam's generals for ten million a pop, so he knew exactly where Saddam's bunker was. Give Israeli intelligence a little credit too. (I once had a girl who worked for the Mossad.) The only error was that Saddam wasn't in it at the time. Bush had planned on an Israeli-like war, over in a few hours, but it would prove a bit more complicated.

Saddam undoubtedly qualified as wicked, card-carrying monster. But before I start pointing fingers, I have to stop and consider what and where Saddam came from. He came from Tikrit, which can best be described as "The ass hole of the world." To emerge from there and end up as leader of Iraq was a major accomplishment, not to say a miracle. Add to this a mother who tried to kill him before he was born and ignored him thereafter. As to his son, the mad Uday, I've seen what power can do to a man even on a little kiss-me-ass island in the Caribbean like Montserrat, with its five thousand souls. And if they could do this in a dry time, what would they do in the wet?

I can only thank God that he didn't see fit to bedazzle me with power. I've seen men transform to monsters who use, abuse and share the women who had the misfortune to serve beneath them (literally). I've seen how mothers have settled out of court when their daughters ended up in hospital after attacks that would have made even the Marquis De

Sade blush. So let's stop the hypocrisy. Power corrupts (thank you, Lord Acton).

In Iraq, I wondered to myself what made a man, who knew that Uday was capable of anything, parade "his" woman in Caligula's court knowing that she would most likely be raped. Why do people accept anything in the hope that they will make enough from a bribe to be able to flee forever? What do they say? Hope springs eternal. Once you start bending over it's not long before you assume the position. Let's make it simple: If you ask your woman to take it up the ass for you, it's only a matter of time before Caligula will ask you to take it up yours too. That's the nature of power. Simple truth, if there's nothing you're willing to die for, you are already dead.

I was willing to die for Iraq but they persuaded me not to. They were right. There was nothing I could have done to save Iraq. Better I go home, not to America, but to Montserrat where I was born. I decided I might as well die in Montserrat where God and a volcano lived than go back to America and wait for the repercussions of this glorious adventure of shock and awe.

There once was a writer named Terence. He came to Rome as a slave from Africa. His writing won him his freedom. He penned one of the most important lines in Roman literature:

"I am man; therefore, nothing human is foreign to me."

This line determined how I live my life.

Both Uday and Saddam regarded people as sheep. They failed to realise that not all sheep are sheep. Some are ram-sheep and you really don't want to get between two of them having a discussion about a young ewe. You'll learn much more than you want to. This is why Uday just missed assassination and ended up paralysed well before the invasion.

When Saddam was captured his only disappointment was that his son never achieved the destiny he had planned for him. It would be good if we could buy the sons we want, but we can't. In the end it's a lottery and we have to take what we get. More often than not we get the ones we deserve.

One final thing. Despite all my good intentions, I failed to realize that, a mere ten feet from the hotel where I was staying, there was a torture chamber in the sewer, beneath the ground, where men and maybe women had suffered electric shocks and flayed skin. Like the rest of the world, I knew nothing about it. Just like General Pinochet of Chile and Mobutu of the Congo. Where do screams go? And did America really think that they could fix Iraq by breaking it? Sunni, Kurds and Shiite – all hating and waiting.

In the end I couldn't do anything for Iraq except leave it. Paul Robeson said, "Make them sing your song." I couldn't do that in Iraq. If it's martyrdom you want, we have our own volcano and politics waiting. In life what you don't know is always more than what you do. Be at peace. Kif-Kif.

THE CARIBBEAN AFTER CHAVEZ

It's ridiculously easy to remove a man from the earth. What is not so easy is to remove his memory. Chavez is dead. That much at least is clear.

I neither believe nor disbelieve that the US may have had some role in his death, but the fact that the allegation is even made and considered in the realm of possibility itself speaks volumes about the age and the world we live in. Given the amount of time, effort and money that the CIA spent in recent years to dislodge Chavez from power, as well as the general euphoria in Miami on the announcement of his death, foul play (on the evidence of the CIA's efforts to assassinate Fidel Castro) must be a distinct possibility. No clear evidence is likely to come to light in less than fifty years, by which time, the world will have moved on to much more horrific and contemporary outrages.

What is of more interest to me is how the passing of Hugo Chavez will affect the Caribbean in general and, in particular, the three most dependent of Venezuela's allies: Haiti, Cuba and Jamaica.

Haiti, especially, will be hit by the absence of Chavez because Haiti is the most vulnerable of the three. Haiti has never been allowed to recover from the devastation of the earthquake of 2010. This incredible occurrence took an estimated 300,000 lives and left a homeless population of over 350,000. Add to this catastrophe a sudden cholera epidemic that thus far has claimed 8,000 lives and over 640,000 stricken ill.

The irony of all this, of course, is that the cause of cholera has been traced back to the very UN Peacekeepers who came to bring aid and relieve the suffering. (It was St. Bernard of Clairvaux who said: "Hell is full of good wishes and desires." How right he was.) What is interesting is the fact that the UN can't be sued because of its immunity from prosecution, as stated in its 1946 convention, a very useful clause to have in your constitution. All of this, despite the fact that cholera has a very clear finger print and can be easily traced. This particular strain of cholera was unknown in Haiti until the UN Peacekeepers arrived from Nepal in 2010 and carelessly deposited the waste from their campsite into the Artibonite (Haiti's largest river) and polluted the drinking water. Yet they cannot be held accountable.

Haiti's response to the epidemic has been a campaign of posting signs in creole stating: "*Lave ak men ou ak savon,*" which means wash your hands with soap, wonderful advice except for one thing: there's no available free clean water. The only clean water is bottled and sold privately by international or local NGOs for profit. The poor have to travel some fifteen or twenty miles to find a stream and pray that it hasn't been contaminated, and this is the reason why the cholera has spread so quickly.

The UN doesn't feel that they are responsible for water management and so the private firms are free to do as they like in the midst of this devastation. The UN is there only to erect tents and maintain order, and no one seems concerned with the fact that three years after the earthquake adequate housing has still not been provided.

Now, where does Venezuela come into all this? It is only the fact that Hugo Chavez provided oil through the Petrocaribe Accord – which effectively eliminates the middleman and offers generous deferred repayment plans – that Haiti has been able to function at all. The people have to pay for water and sanitation trucks. The more expensive the oil prices become, the more expensive will water become and therefore the less accessible. Privatization will kill more and more of the poor and effectively leave all goods and services in the hands of the Creole middle class who don't give a damn about the diseased tent-dwellers in their midst.

The sad thing about cholera is that it is not the bacteria that kills you, but the dehydration. The body is starved for water, clean water. That's the simple cure. A combination of saline solution and fresh water could save countless lives. In Haiti, poverty is a death sentence. The more rain that falls, the quicker the cholera spreads. Now is the rainy season.

The question is: how long will it take right wing Venezuelans to dismantle every positive programme Chavez bequeathed? Maduro, Chavez's successor, knows well what a fight he has awaiting him. Many have vowed not to allow Venezuela to a step back into the dark ages. But the first thing to be sacrificed will be the foreign aid programmes, and certainly Haiti will suffer. What we will witness is "petrocide", murder by (lack of) oil.

The second country in the Caribbean under threat is, of course, Cuba. Venezuela has long been Cuba's lifeline since the USSR's collapse and America's relentless embargo [lifted only as this book is being prepared for press], which was constantly renewed under pressure from those ever busy boys in Miami, the Cuban lobby, who are always about the Lord's work. It has been estimated that if all the money that has been spent in the last fifty years on assassination attempts against Castro was collected, it would be enough to put ten men on the moon and maintain a colony there. Suffice to say that there were those who've not wished Fidel well.

It is because of the US embargo that Cuba has had to purchase all goods in cash, leading to many shortages. Likewise, it's only because of Venezuela and its generous subsidies that Cuba has somehow been able to withstand the many difficult seasons of drought and hurricane and has still been able to maintain the highest literacy rate in Latin America, as well as the best medical schools. In exchange, Cuba has exported doctors around the entire Caribbean, has always been there in times of crisis and has certainly been a saviour, especially to Haiti and others in the region. No one else has done this except Médecins Sans Frontières, which operates out of France.

With Chavez gone, Cuba might have to depend solely on tourism to keep itself afloat, at present mainly people from Canada and Russia who are very attracted to the island and are unaffected by the US Embargo. There is also the Cuban diaspora who faithfully send remittances. Even so, Cuba knows that life will become much more difficult without Chavez.

Next door to Cuba is Jamaica, which has been experiencing crushing inflation due to the collapse of tourism and the world economic slump. Fewer people are filling the beaches these days and a rise in oil prices would certainly spell further catastrophe. Venezuelan oil has made the difference. Even so, Jamaicans have been experiencing power cuts because of the rise in electricity prices.

People have taken to the streets. The police are regularly called upon to maintain order because people are stealing electricity. If the Petrocaribe subsidies cease, the next stop will be oil theft and arson. I hope that the pressure doesn't reach to that point. Yet the degree of poverty is still nowhere that of Haiti.

I don't know how long the Maduro government will survive, but it is certain, if it falls, that the right wing in Venezuela will dismantle the foundations of Hugo Chavez's social policies. One can only hope that if that happens, another country will have stepped forward in the region. Will it be Brazil, which is at present experiencing a booming economy because of its discovery of oil, billions of barrels of oil? Will Brazil be generous and do as Chavez, or will it continue its policy of supporting relentless agribusiness that has destroyed its rain forests and indigenous peoples, all to the greater good of McDonalds? Just how important is the ozone level when compared to a big Mac? Only time will tell.

Then there's Mexico, surprisingly wealthy because of its auto and telecommunication industries and vast supply of resources (especially gold and silver mining) as well as boasting the world's richest man, Carlos Slim. Mexico, however, has shown no signs of sharing the sort of Bolivarian vision that inspired Hugo Chavez. The Caribbean will surely miss Chavez, but his spirit will be a constant source of inspiration that can never be totally destroyed, regardless of attempts to do so. Chavez's ghost may yet prove to be more of a problem to topple than his existence.

ON STANDING GROUND

Stand Your Ground is the new expression for the right to kill Blacks with legislative approval. It has just received legal sanction in Florida with the Zimmerman case and his acquittal in the shooting of Trayvon Martin, a seventeen-year-old unarmed black youth. The shooting was justified on the grounds that Zimmerman felt threatened and had no way of knowing that the youth was unarmed. The case was further complicated by the fact that it took the authorities some forty-four days to even consider arresting the shooter.

Zimmerman, who was a member of neighbourhood watch, pursued and confronted the youth despite being instructed not to do so by police radio. The worrying thing about this case is that no matter what action Martin might have taken, he would have ended shot. Had he run, had he been armed, the result would have been the same. We have no way of knowing exactly what words were exchanged. All we have is the sworn statement of Zimmerman that he felt that his life was threatened after he confronted this youth, who was on foot while he, Zimmerman, (in his car) had pursued the youth who, he felt, was acting in a suspicious manner.

This case calls to account two fundamental principles of American justice. One is the right to bear arms and the second is the right to life, liberty and the pursuit of happiness. Clearly, in the case of black youth the right to life and liberty is seriously curtailed.

Had young Martin been in the company of a white person, he would probably have reached home alive. Little has changed in that regard since emancipation. It is hypocrisy to pretend any different. Straying too far from the plantation without written permission still results in corporal punishment and, more often than not, death: the greatest corporal punishment of all.

Still, the most frightening thing about the Zimmerman decision is that it gives *carte blanche* to any white vigilante to act on impulse and be assured that they can walk free from the most flagrant act of gun violence, as long as there are no witnesses present who could be classed as credible.

The incident took place in the racially charged state of Florida. There was a general reluctance to even bring the case to trial. The shooter, George Zimmerman, took it upon himself to leave his car and confront Martin who was returning home from a grocery store and had nothing more lethal on his person than a bag of candy. What could he have done to defend himself from a handgun?

Although the solution of the NRA and the other gun lobbyists to every problem in America is yet more guns, I don't think in this instance even they would have advocated that young Martin be armed. The question then is: What was it (other than the boy's race) that made George Zimmerman feel that he was under threat, even when advised to stay in his car unless he witnessed actual criminal activity?

There were two people present but only one survived to give their version of the tale. But in actuality there were a host of other characters who took part in that tragedy. When you have a society that is privatized and prison oriented; a society ruled by scarcity and greed; an atmosphere of fear and violence with talk-show hosts daily stirring up racial tension (in fact, instructed to do so by managers and sponsors); where you are constantly encouraged never to travel anywhere unarmed, even when taking your children to school or church, what other result could there be but a shooting murder?

From young Trayvon Martin's standpoint, what must it have been like to know that if you dared to venture beyond your home or neighbourhood, there was always the possibility that you'd be gunned down with impunity. Florida is filled with Latinos and Haitians and Blacks from the South. It has a toxic mix of anger and resentment over years of racial abuse and discrimination at the hands of police and those who control business and housing. It is ridiculous to even attempt to claim that race was not a factor in this trial.

It is money that determines politics in America (and in much of the world). Florida has spent a great deal of money to ensure the success of legislation and this *Stand your ground* is a result of action by powerful Republican lobbyists.

It was the then Governor, Jeb Bush, (brother of George, and the one who was so very instrumental in getting him elected president) who, in 2005, signed into law Statute 776 that states: "A person has no duty to retreat and has the right to stand his or her ground if they think deadly force necessary to prevent death, great bodily harm or commission of a forcible felony like robbery." And so the law only requires law enforcement and the justice system to ask three questions:

(a) Did the defendant have the right to be there? Yes.

(b) Was he engaged in lawful activity at the time? Yes.

(c) Could he reasonably have been in fear of his death or great bodily harm? Possibly.

And so, his attorney having very cleverly restricted the area of the trial to these three questions, George Zimmerman was able to leave court a free man. His attorney made certain that the issue of profiling never entered the discussion. Even more cleverly, he never allowed his client to take the stand.

America is a place of paradox and irony. One would think that having a black president would be clear evidence of a more liberal attitude in America regarding Blacks and the justice system. Not only have things not improved, they have gotten significantly worse. Young Blacks are now more at risk than ever. What is evident is a general feeling of resentment that has resulted in a backlash.

The atmosphere is very much like post-Reconstruction when whatever small gains Blacks had made were quickly abolished and more and more draconian laws enacted. Now you get only as much justice as you can buy. Money determines justice if not right. Lobbyists determine legislation all the way to the Supreme Court because lobbyists determine appointments. Corporations have achieved human status and the right to be regarded as people, whereas the individual has lost any right to be heard. Talk about irony.

The situation becomes so absurd that it is as if the victim, Trayvon Martin, should be made to apologize for forcing Zimmerman, the shooter, the inconvenience of having to kill him.

Once we take the stand-your-ground ruling as acceptable, we condone the lawful murder of unarmed black youth in any circumstance where the defendant can claim intimidation or threat as a defence.

What is really on trial is history. What we're asking is that our youth don't pay the price for all the guilt and fear of America. If we simply accept this verdict, we may as well paint bull's-eyes on their chests and send them out to be slaughtered. We can never call this state of affairs acceptable.

We all of us need illusions. We pretend and allow things to happen. I, for example, need to believe that it is the state of Florida that is responsible for young Trayvon's death, when I know in my heart of hearts that it could happen with equal ease up North in cosmopolitan New York or Boston. It could happen just as quickly at the hands of uniformed officers or plain-clothes men with an agenda, and the case would vanish without trace or murmur. But I can't accept that. I need my illusions.

The president has appealed for calm. But when does calm mean comatose?

PASSING THE BAR
(The death of Margaret Thatcher and Black Britain, 2013)

The death of Margaret Thatcher may be the passing of an age but not the end of an attitude. Thatcherism is a way of viewing the world and a stubborn refusal to compromise on radical right-wing neo-liberal economics and reactionary Conservative social policies, regardless of harm or sacrifice of country.

What effect did Margaret Thatcher's leadership have on Blacks in Britain? Having lived in London throughout that period I know several things with certainty. Firstly, her social policies led to a great deal of unrest and anger.

She loved to provoke and exploit the issue of immigration whenever possible and found a great ally in the National Front with their cry of "Take Back Britain". The result was the Brixton riots of 1981. This was brought to a boil by the police tactic of harassing young Blacks. This was justified by the newly implemented "Sus" Law. Sus, which is short for "suspected" person, was constantly utilized to give the police the right to arrest black people at will. Margaret Thatcher had a perfect enforcer in her Home Secretary, William Whitelaw. The prisons swelled.

Note how similar the technique of the Sus Law in Britain is to the "Stop and Frisk" policy of New York's finest. The Brixton riots were bloody and sold many newspapers. The constant theme of Thatcher and her administration was that Britain was under threat. This threat justified everything from false arrest to the planting of drugs and weapons on alleged offenders. In short, entrapment was the order of the day.

In 1985 came riots in Birmingham and then to the Broadwater Farm Estate in North London. The Broadwater estate is like a large American project. The atmosphere was claustrophobic and grim and the uprising followed the shooting by the police of a black woman, Cherry Groce, in Brixton, and then the death of Mrs Cynthia Jarrett when the police searched her house, mob-handed. The police occupied the estate and I· remember the feeling of being entombed whenever I entered. The police set up cameras and paddy wagons at each entrance.

Along with these attacks on black people came the assaults on the labour unions, the National Health Service and social welfare programmes, even cutting free milk in schools for children over the age of seven. Everything was justified by the same rhetoric: help the poor by easing the burden on the rich and thus create an incentive to private wealth.

Margaret Thatcher used a similar argument to explain why she refused to back sanctions against apartheid South Africa. She justified doing business with this regime because she said she thought it the best way to help the Blacks. Her main concern, she claimed, was humanitarian and had nothing to do with filthy lucre.

At the same time, she refused to have anything to do with Nelson Mandela and the ANC because, as she said, she would never negotiate with terrorists (at least not until they were free and it made good business sense). Meantime, she was always a great friend of the Chilean dictator General Pinochet, a fellow neo-liberal in economics, who came to power through a murderous military coup and ruled through terror.

The greatest success for Thatcher was the Falklands War. Quick and painless, (a war of months, not years – three months, in fact) this was war the way it should be. It was a source of pride and a great boost to the economy and her previously low popularity ratings. Having seen what having the country on war footing could do in terms of allowing her *carte blanche*, she then tried to implement a state of war on the inner cities whereby the police did not have to give account to anyone but herself. This, however, proved to be more problematic.

The appeal of the Britain under siege attitude has not died with Margaret Thatcher. It is still very much alive and well and is used whenever it is necessary to explain unemployment or justify increasing economic in-equality. It's ironic that there are even members of the immigrant commu-nity who respect her Iron Lady image and the fact that she supposedly never backed down. They were particularly impressed that after her attempted assassination by the IRA in Brighton, she refused to leave the site of the bombing and went on to deliver her address to much applause (even grudging admiration from the IRA themselves).

Many immigrants would love to identify with her and her Tory values – once they are allowed through the gate. The problem is that gate. Narrow is the gate.

Margaret Thatcher unleashed a number of demons during her reign as Britain's longest serving prime minister in the Twentieth century. It wasn't that she invented corporate greed, but she presented it with an acceptable face. She set the stage for the looting carried out by British banking and it hasn't stopped since. Best of all was her technique of blaming the poor for poverty. Having shut the mines, she then accused the miners of idleness, which was epic in cruelty. As for anti-immigration, she didn't invent that either, but she used it to a frightening effect. She stirred fear and anger and the result was riot and bloodshed. In truth, for most Blacks she destroyed far more than she inspired. There are wounds from her period in office, both physical and psychic, that still haven't begun to be addressed.

In Britain, when a lawyer dies they say that "He passed the Bar." Well, Margaret Thatcher, who started as a lawyer, has certainly passed the bar. The question is to whom.

TERRORISM AND PANDORA'S BOX

Terrorism is an emotive word and like holocaust and racism, its meaning seems to change constantly depending on who uses it. For example, I feel an almost parental love and ownership of the word *slavery* and have to be constantly reminded that it's not mine to keep, since, in fact, it's still being busily practised in a good portion of the world. That gives others the right to use it too. So feel free. It's hard to keep possession of words once they slip from your mouth, because words, once they leave you, are as difficult to redeem as your soul.

Recently in London, a soldier was killed in the street, hacked to death by two men. This brutal incident was labelled an act of "terrorism". Politicians and the media were quick to respond. Some tried to manipulate the situation by appealing to hysteria and panic, while others called for calm. Likewise, some clergymen were fast to label this the end time and the last days before Armageddon.

But before we go leaping into the abyss, a few questions should at least be asked. Firstly, is a soldier still a soldier even if not in uniform? Is a soldier a legitimate target in a time of war? What and who exactly are we at war against? However you answer these questions they lead only, like a Socratic discourse, to yet further questions.

For me, the larger question is this: why is there no outrage and outcry when drone missiles fall daily on innocent civilians, killing women and children in Pakistan, Afghanistan, Palestine and countless other places? Why is it permissible to merely shrug a shoulder and use words like *regrettable* and *collateral damage*?

It is amazing that someone tosses a rock up into the air and is shocked if it falls and hits them on the head – as if for some reason they think the law of gravity doesn't apply to them.

To unleash violence, whether by the state or non-state organisations, is to open Pandora's box. Once we let free the demons we can never lock them back in again. We can't be random or selective. We can't say this death is acceptable because it's not face-to-face but through some glass, darkly, as when a button is pushed from a faraway vantage point in some bunker. Whether it is the release of a napalm bomb or drone missile or a meat cleaver in a street, it's all the same.

Of course, the really disturbing fact about this action in London was that, as opposed to the clinical distance of a suicide video mailed to a television station, people were made to witness the calm interaction of the perpetrators with onlookers there on the street. Explanation was given for exactly what was being done and why. People actually recorded it on their cell phones.

The whole situation was surreal and yet the faces of the attackers were the familiar, common, everyday black faces that can be encountered anywhere in London, even in the most gated communities, where they might be, if not neighbours, at least workers. With bloody hands, they were engaging others in calm and polite conversation before returning to continue to deal with their selected target.

There has been an attempt to label this incident as a racist rather than a terrorist attack. Racist attack is a category that has hitherto almost always been the exclusive domain of whites of the host community unleashing venom on Blacks or Jews or Muslims. Now the hope is that by labelling this incident as merely being racist, the oxygen of publicity will somehow be avoided. At the same time, there is a desire to highlight the incendiary nature of the crime. It's a very tricky tightrope to have to walk between racism and terrorism.

So, before we set off on our vigilante campaigns and start to attack every Muslim man, woman and child we come upon, it might be as well to pause just long enough to think: Where will this lust for vengeance lead us? The answer is never-ending war. This was something that was hinted at on the outset of the Iraq war. How eager everyone was to set upon the enemy with a "Shock and Awe" strategy that would guarantee victory. Once the enemy was subdued (remember Mission Accomplished?) we would then set out for our next target.

We never foresaw that instead of waving a white flag above their heads, the enemy would simply morph into countless other forms, slipping back and forth easily between borders, toppling whole countries and turning those who were once considered safe allies into unrecognisable failed states riven by competing factions. We never thought they might spring up in our own communities and perhaps even our own families. And most important of all, none of the experts and so called pundits had even an inkling of the domino sequence of the "Arab Spring".

Why did no one tell us that people might one day tire of injustice or even get bored with fear? The answer is because it was unthinkable.

The strategy of the West, especially the US and Britain, has always been to prop up and support cruel dictatorships with the proviso that they remain stable. Why? Because such regimes have proven to be very profitable. So we had the Shah of Iran, Marcos in the Philippines, Mobutu in the

Congo, Papa Doc Duvalier in Haiti, Mubarak in Egypt, et al. The list is almost endless. As a matter of fact, a good test of corruption in a leader is whether or not the US embraced them and allowed them to remain in power for at least twenty years. There's a lot to be said for consistency – at least until it fails and you find yourself on the wrong side of history.

So now, before we go rushing off on the crusade of vengeance and skin-head rallies in support of the lone slain soldier, it might be well to ask just how much support does Britain actually give to its soldiers once they return from war? The answer is not-a-hell-of-a-lot.

There has been a record spike in the suicide of war vets recently. Even the Falklands, which rushed our recently fallen Margaret Thatcher to popularity, has resulted in some alarming figures. Whereas 255 British soldiers died in the Falklands conflict, a veterans association claimed that 264 have committed suicide in the twenty years since (the Ministry of Defence admitted to 95). I don't see people marching or Prime Minister Cameron going biblical about that. Truth be told, they were getting ready to cut veteran benefits even further.

I was shocked to learn these statistics and the cavalier attitude of the military, which states very simply: "Sadly, veterans are no longer soldiers; they are veterans and so not our priority."

Britain loves ceremonies and commemorative events. They'll make much of the twentieth anniversary of the Falkland victory (in fact the last victory Britain's had) and forget the rest. This is why I can't take too seriously this professed outrage at the death of a soldier. True, this attack was savage and meant to shock. There was a time when people went to battle and came home. Now all battles are brought home. We bring them with us on cell phones. There is no safe ground because the madness has been unleashed. The bloodier the outrage, the more scores yet to be settled. The result is perpetual war when we ought to be searching for perpetual peace. Why is it that the worse things we do to each other as human beings, the less we feel? Why the greater the cruelty, the more numb we become to cruelty?

If instead of trying to justify murder, we admit that we're wrong to kill any unarmed human being in the name of a cause – be it in the name of Islam or some abstract war against terrorism – then the use of drone missiles is wrong and the reckless killing of civilians anywhere in the world is wrong. Save all our sanctimonious statements about being on God's side.

When we kill we're on the wrong side, period. War leads only to endless war and the rape of the soul isn't any kind of rapture.

OF AFRICA
THE OTHER SIDE OF THE COVENANT

I'm not yet paranoid enough to believe that the Ebola virus was developed deliberately in some lab or other for the express purpose of destabilising and wreaking havoc in Africa. I'm not quite there yet, but what I do find puzzling is the casualness and the lack of urgency on the part of the news media when reporting this epidemic. In the early stages of the outbreak, it was relegated to one of the last items at the bottom of the news, somewhere before the sports and the weather. In other words, we open with the Middle East and conclude with Africa. Only when nurses and doctors from the USA or Britain caught the disease and were flown home for treatment did Ebola move up the news hierarchy.

And here is the paradox: We want more coverage and yet, at the same time, something within us cringes at the very mention of the word *Africa* on the news. In the pits of our stomachs, we anticipate some new horror. Will it be the abduction of children, draught, famine or a refugee crisis caused by war? "Oh hell, what now?" we wonder. We want to know and yet dread to know.

We've been so saturated by endless reports of atrocity that we expect nothing less. If we listen to the television evangelists like Pat Robinson *et al.*, Africa is simply being punished, like Haiti, for wickedness. God has cursed this continent. The myth of Ham's curse was used for centuries as the biblical excuse for justifying slavery, a very convenient and lucrative explanation for continued exploitation by the West.

If God is so in the business of punishing sin, why hasn't He visited His wrath on corporations such as Goldman Sachs and Lehman Brothers in America, who wilfully and knowingly caused global chaos by fraud and stock market manipulation, thereby ruining whole economies and causing countless millions to lose their homes and life savings? No one went to prison and more often than not executives were rewarded with huge pay-offs, with the proviso that they did not name their fellow conspirators.

So, I have to ask, what exactly is Africa's sin and who determines the sentence? When we look at Liberia and Sierra Leone, where the outbreaks of the Ebola virus were first reported, we notice some striking similarities. Both have natural resources in common: gold, diamonds and iron ore worth trillions of dollars and yet these countries are in dire poverty. A

further fact connects these countries. Both have suffered civil wars distin-
guished by horrific atrocities. Is it merely a coincidence that these places of
abundant resources, poor people and atrocities happen to be the first places
of the Ebola virus? Just happenstance, right?

To begin to understand the connections it is worth focusing on one
man: Charles Taylor, the former president of Liberia, who is now serving
a fifty-year prison sentence for crimes against humanity (courtesy of the
Hague Tribunal). He is a perfect template for how things are done in Africa.

First, we have to take a look at Liberia and how it came into being in 1821.
It was the answer to the question: "What the hell do you do with a bunch
of ex-slaves when you don't want them hanging around and maybe causing
revolution?" You ship them back to the old heartlands of the trade, back to
where they supposedly came from, i.e. Africa.

Now the fact that there is no postal address called Africa doesn't matter.
You just dump them on some shore, leave them some provisions and
money and wish them well. The money came from Quakers and Methodists intent on righting wrongs and doing some good thing to make up for
centuries of abuse. The only problem was that the indigenous population
who were already living there weren't consulted. The repatriated Americo-
Liberians were mostly mulatto (most of them having white fathers and
black mothers who had been raped), and who felt superior to the savages
who had never witnessed the blessings of Christianity and slavery. The
result was the establishment of an elite creole class who tried to lord it over
the native inhabitants. (Think Haiti and the mulatto elite who have been
in power from 1800 to the present – picture Baby Doc Duvalier who has
just died.)

What the Americo-Liberians did, with the blessing of the United States,
was set up a little Southern plantation system based on the principles of
Booker T. Washington and the Talented Tenth leadership elite promoted
by W. E. B. Du Bois. In other words, if you just pull up your pants and shine
your shoes, embrace Christianity and get an education you will prosper.

The Americo-Liberians thought: we may live in Africa but that doesn't
mean we have to be African. "Don't keep company with those no 'count
boys from bush." Eyes should be firmly on America and Europe. In this, I
find that Liberia has a lot in common with Montserrat. From the beginning,
certain prominent Liberian families stayed in power, the King, Tubman,
and Tolbert families. The main party was the Whig Party (the name says it
all) and they made absolutely certain that the top 5% (Americo–Liberians)
owned everything and were never out of office because the indigenous
people lacked the right to vote, even though they had to pay for the comforts
of those in power.

Add to this the presence of Firestone Rubber, the American company,
which was pretty much the sole employer. They were synonymous with

the United States government and they determined state policy. It was Firestone Rubber who, at the behest of W.E.B. Du Bois, demanded that Marcus Garvey not be allowed entry into Liberia. There was also the threat of the loss of a five million dollar loan to the Liberian government from the American government. Firestone ruled supreme with a ninety-nine year lease of a million acres of land at rock-bottom rent.

Everything went along peacefully for over 150 years of what was effectively one party rule until one day an army sergeant decided on a different approach. Rather than waiting to be born again and returning as an American, in 1980, Sergeant Samuel Doe chose instead the more direct route of a Stalin, entered the mansion of the then president Tolbert and put a bullet in his head. This involved little dialogue but made an immediate impression on the long disgruntled Liberian populace, angry that the price of rice had risen.

Sergeant Doe's communication skills were not great, but he did make himself understood. What he couldn't do was to calm foreign investors or to locate the funds that the former president (like most African leaders) had hidden away in Swiss accounts. For help, Samuel Doe had to turn to another Liberian, one who was more familiar with the habits of the West. Enter one Charles Taylor. Taylor had studied abroad and spent much time in Washington and New York, two locations where there are sizable exiled Liberian communities. He had also attended school in Boston, which would prove very useful to him.

Charles Taylor had all the charm and guile of a calypsonian. As a matter of fact, his father was a Trinidadian – his mother was Americo-Liberian. He grew up enjoying privilege, knowing he was a son of expectations. He was not from the bush. He got his degree from Bentley College in Massachusetts. What he learned from an early age was the gift of making himself useful to those in power. Since Samuel Doe was almost illiterate he needed someone to transcribe his thoughts and arrange meetings and accounts. Taylor was a master of logistics. He was minister in charge of commerce and he could produce when called upon. He was famous for his "can-do" attitude. He always knew he was the cleverest man in the room.

The problem with ambition is that it always draws attention to itself. Eventually, Samuel Doe began to notice that Taylor had a facility for making money disappear from accounts. This state of affairs came to a crisis when Taylor vanished to the U.S. where he thought he was safe, but was arrested in Massachusetts. However, even while awaiting extradition back to a certain firing squad, Taylor was able to call in a few favours. He was able to buy his way out of prison and put into play a new game plan.

Charles Taylor had some things going for him. Chief among them was his ability to appear totally confident and reasonable. He knew that the powers involved (the United States and Britain), did not like dealing with what they term: "a loose cannon". They prefer doing business with a known quantity. In other words, when doing theft and plunder, they prefer their puppets submissive and reasonable. They did not know what to make of Sergeant Samuel Doe with his machine gun and army fatigues. They preferred Charles Taylor in his Brooks Brother's suits and Rolex watches (which he got into the habit of giving away as gifts to Bill Clinton and the televangelist Pat Robertson, together with Arabian race horses and real estate).

Taylor did return to Liberia eventually, but not in handcuffs. He returned leading his own forces. With a little help from friends like Muammar Gaddafi and others he was able to arm and maintain a liberation army. Drawing on the general dissatisfaction of rival tribes in the North (The Mano and Gio, especially, who weren't getting any of the goodies that Sergeant Doe was dispensing to his own Krahn tribe in particular), he soon had a brisk civil war going and Doe was captured and killed. Charles Taylor then became president. This was quite acceptable to Washington.

Now the question often asked is why Charles Taylor employed the tactics of mutilating the young? Did he just wake up one day and say: "Time for some atrocities!" No. Charles Taylor was a very keen student of history and he merely followed the example of King Leopold of Belgium who mutilated and killed some 10 million in the Belgian Congo to teach them fear of disobedience. He demanded a certain daily quota of work and failure to deliver resulted in loss of limb. Leopold never once visited the Congo but his genocidal policies led to him becoming the richest man in the world at the time. I don't think God got around to cursing him or Belgium, although He ought to have done. As the Haitians say: *"Bay kou bliye pote mak sonje."* (He who whips forgets, but he who is whipped never forgets.)

Charles Taylor, as I said, is the template for what happens with power in Africa. He went on to do a brisk business in arms and diamond smuggling. He was also just as at home in Sierra Leone as he was in Liberia. They have a very similar history; instead of an American sphere of influence, write British. Sierra Leone, too, was started by repatriated ex-slaves, mostly Black Loyalists who had fought on the side of the British in the war of American Independence, who did exactly the same thing to the indigenous tribes as the Liberians had. In the 1980s it was just as ready for explosion and change as Liberia. Charles Taylor took advantage of his opportunity and exchanged arms for diamonds and was able to move freely from border to border. When he faced pressure and sanctions in one place, he merely moved to another.

To add to the feast there was also Guinea, which was ripe for his special skills in diplomacy, not to mention Narco dollars from pure Colombian cocaine. He had endless funds to finance his civil war. He also perfected the art of the Liberian sailing flag, by which, for a certain fee, any rig still afloat could obtain a licence to sail and pollute anywhere on the high seas. (Remember the Exxon Valdez, anyone?) Charles Taylor made enough to conduct a war on three fronts and keep a flock of lawyers busy at the same time. (For what is war but diplomacy by other means, as Von Clausewitz wrote.)

But here, then, is the country as takeaway. Generation after generation, fresh exploiters come to Africa and take. When will it cease? The answer is never – unless Africa overthrows its class of political middlemen. It would be nice to pretend otherwise, but the truth is that Africa's curse is its endless resources. No other continent on earth has such an inexhaustible supply. Every time an exploiter thinks that there is no more to be found, a fresh discovery happens. The result is that foreign exploiters come and go but never quite leave. China is taking its turn. There is always something new in Africa to steal. This was a saying at the time of the Egyptians and it hasn't changed. Men will always look on Africa the way King David looked at Bathsheba when he saw her sunning herself on the rooftop – with lust. The sin of Africa is poverty. It is a crime punishable by death. *Not* having can be fatal to your health.

But despite all this disaster-talk of wars financed by foreign corporations, and countries like China, which will happily sell arms to both sides of any conflict, knowing full well that they'll do business with whoever wins, yet I don't feel despair because I see a new and unapologetic energy in the youth of Africa. They are ready to do business and find a way out. They keep finding new uses for the cell phone – including banking and rescue services in rural areas where there are neither banks nor police). Wherever there is a need they come up with a solution. This is why they say there is always something new coming out of Africa.

As to Ebola, now that it has spread beyond Africa to the West, a miraculous cure will suddenly be found. Capitalism is more resilient than even Ebola. There is too much money to be made for a cure not to be found, and this might have a little something to do with why America is suddenly sending humanitarian aid (to Liberia though not to Sierra Leone). Britain is suddenly sending humanitarian aid to Sierra Leone (but not to Liberia). And France is suddenly sending humanitarian aid to Guinea alone.

Governments do not have friends; they have interests. Still, be at peace my friend. Success has many parents but failure is an orphan. When Africa dies, then the earth dies, and not until.

5. EPILOGUE

ONCE UPON A TIME IN PARADISE

Once, and just once upon a time in Paradise, a man fell from grace and lost all words, all speech and language, so all that was left to him, there in the shadow of a volcano, was a dream. The words had slipped from his head and he couldn't remember how, only the slipping. He remembered a dream but not the meaning of the dream. But since all he had was the dream, he thought he'd better keep it.

He was mad, that much he knew. Mad with God but he couldn't remember why. He didn't know if he'd been promised something and then lost it or what. All of that went away with the words and once he'd lost them he couldn't remember the incident. All he knew was that others were speaking and he wasn't. Even the goats and the sheep seemed to have their voices and he not. They'd wake in the morning and go off and cleave together in herds and he couldn't. He just wandered the island, watched the sky watch him and tried to figure out why things had gone so wrong. Back and forth he walked, back and forth like a lion. Roaring. There'd been a change; that much he knew, an eruption. But was it just in his head?

"There was a time I didn't feel like this." He remembered that much, a time when he had a different feeling. Many had left the island and gone. Some stayed. They all had their reasons. He had some too, but he'd lost them. He lost his reasons and he couldn't remember where. Were they buried in the ghaut or washed away with the sea? There were other mad people on the island, for sure, but they didn't know it. He, at least, knew he was mad, although just knowing didn't make him feel any better.

"I should feel better because I know," a voice told him. "If I can hear a voice, then I must be thinking. Yes, a voice must mean thinking. I couldn't hear it otherwise."

He was still a stranger to himself, though, and had to get used to it. Sleep left him, too, like a thief. It came in the night but then it left, and still he hadn't slept. All he remembered was a song:

> I lost my happiness a short time ago
> Where did it go nobody know.
> Lost my happiness some time ago
> Where did it go nobody know.

Since he'd lost words he couldn't work. Well, he could work but since he couldn't ask permission, nobody paid him for it. He would just do a deed only to find that no one wanted it done in the first place. At least, they didn't want to have to pay for it, so all his labour was in vain. He'd cut grass or fix a road only to be told, "Is who ask you do that?"

He moved rocks from one side of the road to the other. People murmured. Then he moved big stones from the top of hills so that they wouldn't roll down in a storm and kill people, but still no one thanked him.

"No harm done, I'll just put things back the way I found them," he thought. But they wouldn't let him do that either and even the rocks cried out. One rock became jealous of the other. He tried to hush them but it was no good. They gave him away. Not so easy to fix things back to just how they were.

Sweat bathed his skin because it's harder to lift things up than to push them down and harder to rise than to fall. People called him a vandal. Said he must be up to wickedness and trying to cause accident. He couldn't make them understand him so he stopped coming out by day and only travelled by night. He lived quiet and did his goodness unpaid.

A man tried to remember when it was he went mad exactly. "Was it after the eruption or before?" But he couldn't.

"I should have tied a string around my finger that day. It would have help remind me. But how you could know that today is the day you go mad? Now, no one can tell me, because they're too busy going mad themselves. Well, well, well!"

The more he walked the island, the more he knew that things had gone before. Things that mattered and were written, but he couldn't remember any of it. Couldn't remember why. Somewhere a big man had lived on an estate and in a big house. Somewhere someone had raised a flag, fired a cannon. It was part of history but he couldn't remember history because he didn't make it. He never made history so why should he remember?

He couldn't even remember why things were named what they were. Then an idea came to him. It fell out the sky and struck him right on the head: "I'll hang myself. Then I'll make history."

This was a big decision. He immediately felt better because he'd thought of it all on his own. It was a good day, different from the others.

Then he realized, "But wait, I don't even have a rope. What a thing, eh? All that work to think of something and not even a rope to pull it off. Advantage never done!"

Needing a rope he decided to venture out, even though it was day time and he had promised himself to stay away from people. He went to the hardware store to buy rope, but when he got there he couldn't call for what it was he wanted. He looked and he looked until he found some rope, but then he realized that he had no money to pay for it. Could he ask for it on trust?

"Just how much rope does a man need to hang himself? Can't be much," he thought. This day was getting complicated and it wasn't even noon yet.

"Maybe if I smile," he thought, "they'll let me go with it." He smiled his nicest smile and wrote one word in the book, TRUST, then walked toward the door holding the rope in his hand.

The store owner looked at him: "Is where you think you going with that rope?" The owner was big, A man was small.

"Look here, hope you not thinking you just walking out of here with that?"

A man nodded his head, still smiling.

"Since the volcano you've been acting very peculiar. Going around moving stones and walking the roads back and forth like jumbie. Man, people laugh after you and say they think you gone funny. Like you go England and come back with snow in you head. You alright?"

Now at last he knew for certain that it was since the volcano that he'd gone mad. Well that was good, any way. Now he knew for sure when it started, although when people ask you if you alright they usually mean you're not.

"What you want rope for? You don't have animals no more. Anyway, how you going pay for it?"

A man just kept smiling. He knew he wouldn't need the rope long since this very day he would be making history.

"You know what I think? I think we just put this rope back, yes." The storeowner took the rope from his hand. "You getting on very peculiar. Give you a rope, you might do yourself a hurt. Not to say you *would*, mind you, but you just *might*. Too much rope could be a dangerous thing for a man. Here, have this piece of string instead. You take this; yes, I take that, okay?"

He tied the string around A man's wrist, patted him on the back and shook his hand as if he'd just given him the keys to the kingdom. Then he walked him to the door and smiled him out.

"You go in love, my brother, okay. Walk good." Then he shut the door and turn the sign to closed, very quickly.

A man found himself standing there in the road. He looked at the string around his wrist and tried to make sense of everything.

"So, it's since the volcano," he thought. "Well if it's the volcano that send me mad, then it can fix me too, because what no kill, must cure." He started to laugh but he couldn't remember why.

He climbed and climbed and walked and walked the twisted hills toward the light. He laughed at things along the road, the cusha and the cactus. Walked until he heard a rhythm in his head:

> DE DA DE DA DAH
> DE DA DE DA DAH
> DA DA DA DEH DEH
> DAH DAH DAH
> DEYO DEY
> DEYO DEY

"But is not your father's fault."

"Is not your father's fault." Over and over it kept repeating. After a time, he found himself running, for part of the mountain was in sunshine and part was in rain, part in darkness and part in shimmering light. Just when his lungs felt like they were going to burst and that he could go no more, he found he'd reached the base of the Soufrière volcano. He cried out and hoped that he was speaking words:

"Whatever I did wrong, I'm sorry for. Whoever I hurt, whatever I stepped on or killed, I'm sorry. I once was glad when morning come. Make me glad again. Make it the way it was."

The volcano just stood silent; no sound came from it, quiet as government; only the smell of sulphur. He fell on his knees and shut his eyes. He didn't know what to expect and he started to remember the day of the fire in the mountain. He remembered the sound of the explosion. The flying stones. The day turning black like night because ash swallowed the sun.

Now he could remember and all the voices in his head fell, tumbling out like spirits.

Somebody screamed: "Oh Lord, we dead this time."

He heard the sounds of the cars as people began to flee the town. The honking of horns. The screeching of engines. The screams of animals as their hooves sank in burning ash. He knelt there waiting for the sounds to leave his ears and then he found it was night. He'd relived everything. It had all come back to him. The watching and the waiting and the losing of his house and land. His goats and cattle. The cleaning up and the clearing away again and again until finally the ash won and he had just walked away. Walked away from everything. Even the eclipse of the sun. Now he remembered.

> Lost my happiness a short time ago
> Where it go nobody know.
> Lost my very happiness a short time ago
> Where it go nobody know.

He stayed there on his knees and when he came to himself he found that he was cold there in the mountain in the dark. He wrapped himself inside a giant frond. The leaf of a philodendron. He passed into something that must have been sleep because there were stars at first and then only trance. Sleep had come to him for the first time in a year. It had come and stayed and not run like a thief. When he opened his eyes again it was first light. Had one day passed or was it three?

There were footprints of animals that had come during the night. Could have been a wild boar. He was lucky this time. Maybe it was himself who had come as an animal. He got up and began to descend the mountain. The volcano had said nothing to him, promised him nothing.

He explained to the trees what had happened to him. They listened with patience but they didn't answer either. He talked to the sea, which made promises but wouldn't say when. He didn't know if he had the strength to begin again, but then he knew he would. And there in the woods he came on some tall bamboo growing wild. He kept searching until he found just the right one for his hands. Weeks went by until it dried.

Slowly, because he cared, he carved the bamboo and made six holes. He played close to the sea and the waves called back to him. Music from the fife. Over and over, he tried to play what he heard in his head, until finally he played sweet enough to lose his anger and for God to forgive him. Sweet enough for a girl to trust him and share a coconut.

Words came slowly. He began to remember his dream. In his dream he wasn't alone. "Lila," she said before he asked her. They walked together. At first he walked too quickly and then more slow. She showed him a place where the sun woke out of the sea. He was glad now that he never got to use that rope.

How can you make history by yourself? Always we try again for a tomorrow and the sly Montserrat sky, where A man lost his mind to a volcano and found it again. Once, and only once upon a time in Paradise.

ABOUT THE AUTHOR

Edgar Nkosi White is a playwright and novelist. His work has been performed throughout the world from New York to New Zealand. His published work includes: *The Rising, The Crucificado, Underground, Lament for Rastafari, Redemption Song, The Nine Night, Omar at Christmas* and *The Children of Night*. He has also been a frequent contributor to *Monthly Review* as well as Writer in Residence at New York City College where he also taught Creative Writing.

His writing career began with the poet and writer, Langston Hughes, who was the first to herald his work and was instrumental in the publication of his first book, *Underground*, with William and Morrow publishers. The theatre began for him with Joseph Papp at the New York Public Theater where five of his plays were performed. The first production of "The Mummers Play" led to tours with Shakespeare Public Theater productions in Central Park. A performance of his play, *Lament for Rastafari* at Ellen Stewart's world famous Café La Mama Theatre led to productions in England both on stage and radio drama with the BBC. He also contributed to the BBC television series "Black Silk". Upon returning to the United States, the author received a Rockefeller award and became a member of the New Dramatist. Productions of two of his plays, "Trance" and "I Marcus Garvey" toured Canada in 2012.

He attended City College of New York, New York University and the Yale School of Drama. The author also attended New York Theological Seminary and has had a very close association with the Cathedral of St. John the Divine in New York. He is an ordained minister and has made prison ministry a major factor in his life. He has performed frequent theatre workshops at Sing Sing Correctional Facility.

Howard Fergus
Lara Rains & Colonial Rites
ISBN: 9780948833953; pp. 88; pub. 1998; price £7.99

These poems explore the nature of living on Montserrat, a 'two-be-three island/hard like rock', vulnerable to the forces of nature (Hurricane Hugo and the erupting Soufriere) and still 'this British corridor'. He writes honestly and observantly about these contingencies, finding in them metaphors for experiences which are universal. Nature's force strips life to its bare essentials ('Soufriere opened a new bible/in her pulpit in the hills/ to teach us the arithmetic of days') and reveals creation and destruction as one ('We celebrate Hugo child of God/ he killed and made alive for a season').

In a small island society, individual lives take on an enhanced significance as its one true resource and the sequence of obituary poems brings home forcefully how irreplaceable they are. Beyond Montserrat, Fergus looks for a wider Caribbean unity, but finds it only in cricket (and crime). Cricket, indeed, provides a major focus for his sense of the ironies of Caribbean history: that through a white-flannelled colonial rite with its roots in an imperial sense of Englishness, the West Indies has found its only true political framework and the means, explored in the sequence of poems celebrating Brian Lara's feats of 1994, to overturn symbolically the centuries of enslavement and colonialism.

Howard Fergus
Volcano Verses
ISBN: 9781900715799; pp. 84; pub. 2003; price: £7.99

Howard Fergus is amongst a very small minority of Montserratians. He lives in Montserrat. Emigration has taken generations away and the 1997 eruption of Soufrière destroyed two-thirds of its habitable space, its economy and drove the majority of its inhabitants into exile. The poems in *Volcano Verses* express the confidence that island life and folk will outlast volcanic tantrums, that though 'Tonight Chances pique still grows/...But cattle low and egrets ride/ Inspite of fire from mountain tides'.

But what Fergus does in the book is write against the absences, write into being again the people who have gone, the landscape utterly transformed, the society fragmented. The eruption has instigated the sternest truth-telling, the sense of a world purified, but it has also prompted a hugely heightened consciousness of the importance of the seemingly trivial, the myriad social interactions, the sounds, the smells of a literally vanished world. It is the very absences, the restriction of current possibility that drives Fergus to greater abundance of creation, in the conversational, muscular rhythms, the serious word-play that characterise his most mature and distinctive collection yet.

E.A. Markham
Marking Time
ISBN: 9781900715294; pp. 262; pub. 1999; price: £8.99

Pewter Stapleton is drowning under a pile of marking. He teaches creative writing at a university in Sheffield, a campus peopled with malign cost-cutting accountants, baffled security staff and colleagues cloning themselves.

Pewter is a brilliant comic creation, an endless lister of tasks which are never quite completed, who is strung forever between seriousness and send-up, a commitment to his writing and boundless cynicism about writers and the arts industry.

From Pewter's desk and his marking, the novel radiates backwards and forwards in time, to his childhood in the small volcanic Caribbean island of St. Caesare (Montserrat's alter-ego) and memories of his headmaster, the libidinous Professeur Croissant and Horace his half-mad cousin, and to his relationships with Carrington, a highly successful Caribbean writer whose plays Pewter is editing, to Balham, a professional of the race industry (where Pewter is a self-admitted slow learner in blackness) and to Lee, the woman he loves, but who despairs of him as 'sporadic'.

As a novel about life and writing, factuality and invention rub shoulders to hilarious effect as Pewter is incessantly driven to turn his experiences, his friends and their experiences into works of drama and fiction. Yet we note the awkward questions he asks about the Academy...

E.A. Markham
Taking the Drawing Room Through Customs: Selected Stories 1972-2002
ISBN: 9781900715690; pp. 332; pub. 2002; price: £9.99

When E.A. Markham writes a story about the Other World Cup (Montserrat loses 4-0 to Bhutan – the volcanic eruption has destroyed all the football pitches in Montserrat) and a few months later is actually invited to a literature festival in Bhutan, this chimes in with his fiction. In 1972, his alter ego, Pewter Stapleton, invented the island of St Caesare (next door to Montserrat, but more independent-minded) as part of an elaborate scam to enjoy the rich perks of a UN conference. Since then, the island has been pencilled in on a couple of maps; and a handful of people claim to have been there.

Nothing is straightforward in Markham's fictive world. His stories constantly deny conventional expectations and make us rethink both how we interpret experience and what we expect of fiction.

Conventional narrative could never convey the complexities of the recurrent and entertaining cast of mainly Caribbean characters as they make sense of their remembered and reinvented lives. Digression becomes an art form both in Pewter Stapleton's narration and in their stories. It is the rich web of words they weave that leads Markham to his image of the drawing room as a repository of the talk of family and friends as perhaps the most valuable possession taken by Caribbean people through Customs.

This collection brings together new and uncollected stories and selections from E.A. Markham's two previous collections, *Something Unusual* (1984) and *Ten Stories* (1992). Each of the stories has its own crafted completeness, whether in the observant humour of "The Pig Was Mine", the bleakness of "Skeletons", the audacious mythologizing of "A Short History of St. Cesaire", or the absurdist magical realism of "Digging". They confirm him as one of the most original users of the short story form in both British and Caribbean fiction.

Boyd Tonkin writes in *The Independent*: "Markham's deadpan wit and self-protective irony never desert him. He's never less than funny, and never less than moving. The English-speaking Caribbean has bred some wonderful wanderers from his generation, but none (certainly not Walcott or Naipaul) can boast a literary voice as wryly companionable as this. Read the poetry and prose back-to-back, and you'll feel you have made a friend: learned, intimate, sometimes angry at injustice, delighted by his wayward family amazed by how far this clan has come but always sensitive to 'that vague threat in the air' posed by racial bigotry, illness or misfortune."

E.A. Markham
Against the Grain: A 1950s Memoir
ISBN: 9781845230302; pp. 192; pub. 2008; price: £10.99

When E.A. (Archie) Markham came to London in 1956 from his native Montserrat, his ambitions were to make it as a writer or pop singer, and at the same time, fulfil family expectations to become a scholar and academic. Unfortunately the young Archie's attempts to combine elements of Little Richard and the now forgotten Jim Dale never found the success he was convinced they deserved and it has been in less lucrative fields that Markham established his reputation as a 'nimble-footed, silver-tongued' poet, critic and fiction writer.

His memoirs begin with a return to post-volcanic Montserrat to rediscover the now abandoned village of Harris' and his grandmother's old house and his meticulous and moving reconstruction of his boyhood in that house – a grand house that made the family feel that settling in the Harrow Road end of Maida Vale was a distinctly 'downwards' move for a cultivated Caribbean family.

And it is Markham's wryly humorous navigation between the poles of his family's confident sense of their worth and the racial attitudes of those times that makes his account of his travails in the rag-trade, his pop-singer ambitions, the discovery that they were living next door to a leading member of the British Union of Fascists, and his involvement with the 'angry-young-men' shifts in 1950s British culture such a rewarding and human document.

Yvonne Weekes
Volcano
ISBN: 9781845230371; pp. 120; pub. 2006; price: £7.99

Yvonne Weekes' memoir of eight years dominated by the awakening, eruption and still grumbling aftermath of Montserrat's Soufriere is a remarkable document at many levels. It is an acutely written account of the impact of the eruption on the life and viability of this small Caribbean island, with a quizzical eye for the undertones of the experience – the way, for instance, the awakened mountain becomes a favoured place for car-borne lovers' trysts – as well as for the more public manifestations of the way her people responded to the disaster. As Director of Culture who organised a theatrical review that was taken round the refugees in the temporary shelters, she was well-placed to observe and listen; one of the qualities of the book is the way it brings the voices of Montserratians so vividly to life. She captures a world split between the new scientific vocabulary of seismography and pyroclastic flows and the Old Testament talk of Sodom and Gomorrah and sins punished. But *Volcano* is above all a personal and intimate account of the processes of stress, loss, grieving emptiness and the rebuilding of a heart and sense of self; of confronting the "nothingness that hollows me" when everything by which she has known herself – home, family, friends, landscape -- is taken from her, when faith is tested to the core.

But it is the quality of Yvonne Weekes' writing that makes *Volcano* a work of art as well as record. Her prose is always alive, conversational and clear, rising to memorable heights when she describes the terrible moments of blackness against which all life demands to be reviewed.